Best Regards

Brett Post

The Real War
Against America

Brett Kingstone

Specialty Publishing Company

Library of Congress Cataloging-in-Publication Number 2005920461
ISBN 0-9755199-2-1
First Edition

Printed in the United States of America
10 9 8 7 6 5 4 3 2 1

The Real War Against America
Printed and designed by Specialty Publishing Company.

Specialty Publishing Company, Inc.
135 E. St. Charles Rd., Carol Stream, Il 60188
www.specialtypub.com
Publishers of Start Magazine, www.startmag.com
630-933-0844

Cover art and design by Jung Choi and Richard Heiner.
Super Vision International
8210 Presidents Drive, Orlando, Fla. 32819
www.svision.com
407-857-9900

Edited by Chauncey Parker III, gpg3@juno.com; Ted Kovowras,
Panoramic Consulting, info@panoramicconsulting.com; Joe
Tamborello, jtamborello@fisherlaw.com; and Peggy Smedley,
psmedley@specialtypub.com.

Specialty Publishing books are available at special quantity discounts
to use as premiums or for corporate educational training programs.
For more information, please contact Special Books Manager at
630-933-0844.

FOREWORD

The story that my friend Brett Kingstone tells in *The Real War Against America* is as good as any spy novel you can pick up. There's mystery. There's danger. And there's a plot that a good author can take from the edge of implausible and turn it in to a heart-stopping story.

There's just one difference between *The Real War Against America* and any other spy or crime novel: Brett Kingstone's story is true. Every word of it is true.

So disturbing is the story of what happened to Brett's company, Super Vision—his life's work—that I'd urge readers to take a step back and resist the temptation to just read the book as an espionage thriller.

What's all the more worrisome is that stories just like Brett's are growing more common each and every year.

During a hearing of the House Judiciary Committee in 2003 I had the occasion to press Attorney General John Ashcroft about the need for prosecutions in the area of intellectual property theft. The effect the piracy of technology, music, and movies has on our nation is not isolated to industry giants such as Disney and Universal. Operations such as Brett Kingstone's Super Vision—a company that provides excellent incomes and real benefits to employees—are hit the hardest by this growing trend.

Today, intellectual property theft costs American industry an estimated $250 billion a year. And the price tag is rising.

In the U.S. House of Representatives, we've taken several

steps to curb piracy. Most notably, I joined with some of my colleagues in co-authoring a bill called The Intellectual Property Protection Act. Congress can take all the action it wants but it will ultimately be up to those that enforce the laws to take a strong stand against this problem.

We've long instilled in our children that here in America you can go as far in life as your dreams and ambitions take you. Brett Kingstone's imagination and can-do entrepreneurial spirit has taken him around the globe as he's developed exciting new technologies, along the way picking up dozens of U.S. and foreign patents. He's consistently given back to his community and made Super Vision one of the companies that make Orlando, Florida the greatest place in the world to live, work, dream, and play.

But there's a threat against the Brett Kingstones of America, a threat that continues to undermine the entrepreneurs in a country built on ideas. It's the real war against America. The dreams and imaginations of Americans is something worth fighting for. Let's hope we win this battle.

Ric Keller
United States Congressman
8th District, Florida

*To the thousands of American companies
whose cries for justice went unanswered.*

ONE

A voice blared over the speakerphone. It was
our factory manager who told me that the cabling machine
had "blown up again." I headed down the concrete stairwell
that led from my office to the manufacturing floor. With
each step down I imagined the voice of the cabling-machine
operator, like Scotty in the engineering room of the Enterprise, saying, "Aye Captain, the di-lithium crystals have failed
and the matter-antimatter fuel cells have shut down, I can't
get us to warp drive and the impulse engines just can't take
much more." I wryly smiled at the thought as I entered the
manufacturing floor. Although it was a warm and sunny day
in May 1998 in Orlando, Fla., the vast two-story 80,000
square foot factory of Super Vision International, Inc. was
cool due to air conditioning and brightly illuminated due to
rows of suspended metal-halide lights.

The light reflected off the hulking machinery that every
day wound the miles of our main product. Super Vision
manufactured the glowing fiber-optic cable used in commercial signage and lighting for amusement parks, hotels, restaurants, shopping centers, and residences. Our fiber-optic
cable provides an energy-efficient and maintenance-free
alternative to neon and incandescent lighting.

Our products provide the color and light for the AT&T
sign and Coca-Cola bottle in New York's Times Square, the
parades and displays at the Disney and Universal theme parks,
the 1,000 foot tall Victoria Arts Center Spire in Melbourne,

Australia, the pool and patio at the Westin Resort in St. John, British Virgin Islands, the giant Ferris Wheel at the Tokyo Dome in Japan, signs at the domestic airport in Moscow, and the giant Pepsi globe in Caracas, Venezuela. Our products literally light up the skies around the world.

But today our machinery was stopped. As I walked across the polished concrete, my factory manager, Roy Archer, wriggled out from inside the guts of our giant cabling machine. Next to Roy was his young and energetic assistant responsible for running cable production, John Gonzales. He was holding a wrench, both his arms covered in grease up to his elbows.

I could see my reflection in the window of the cabling machine. I was 39-years-old, with thick, wavy light brown hair, and hazel eyes. Normally I could pass for much younger, but lately more lines had been creasing my forehead, accenting the scars across my right eyebrow. Perhaps the additional lines were due to the stress brought on by the thefts of our equipment, or the numerous breakdowns we were now experiencing with our machinery. I was wearing my usual workday attire: blue jeans, tan work boots, and a blue polo shirt embroidered with our Super Vision logo.

My jeans were loose around my waist. My shirt fit tightly across my chest. I'd been running and lifting weights a lot lately to relieve some of the ever-mounting stress that had been building over the past several months. Working out helped me blow off some of the stress. Twice a week I stepped into a makeshift boxing ring we set up next to the weight room with Obadiah (O.B.) Hunter, a light heavyweight who tried to keep me in shape. Still, I wasn't quite the same young guy who had founded this company 10 years earlier. My reflection no longer matched the person that I'd like to imagine. My reflection quickly vanished as I walked past the cabling machine.

"Brett, I don't know whether to fix this damn thing or

shoot it and put it out of its misery," Roy said as he stood up to greet me.

In his late twenties, Roy was tall and broad shouldered, with arms thick as most men's legs. Roy could bench the rack in our gym and then some. After so many early mornings and late nights at work, he'd given up on shaving and started growing a beard. It hadn't filled in yet, but already it was giving him an aura of maturity to match his position of authority as our factory manager. He'd been with me since day one, and was one of my most trusted confidants.

Roy reached inside the machine and pulled out the broken belt from its place around the spindle that wound the individual fibers into cable.

"First the extruder starts gumming up with our PVC (polyvinyl chloride) and seizes up on me, and now this! I just put this belt on along with a new set of bearings," he complained, shaking his head in disgust. "And the damn thing snaps and shuts down on me again. We seem to be blowing belts all the time."

"Well, what do you recommend?" I asked. "We've got to keep making cable and shipping orders."

Roy scowled and shook his head, brushing away the brown bangs across his forehead.

"Don't worry, Brett. You know we'll patch her up, just like we always do."

He winked at me, a smile reappearing on his grease-smudged face as his typical good humor returned. "I guess it'd get boring around here if everything ran smoothly."

"I couldn't say," I chuckled as I headed back to my office. "Nothing ever runs smoothly."

"Well, if it did, you wouldn't need me anymore," Roy said, turning back to the busted machine.

"Don't worry, Patron!"

I glanced back. It was John Gonzales calling out to me. I'd forgotten he was there, now on his back under the machine. All I could see of him was the top of his head; his bushy black hair was matted with dust and grease.

"We'll get this hombre back on line for you even if it takes all night," John said.

"We will make it happen. We will not keep our customers waiting, Patron."

That's what I loved about our company. Just about everyone at Super Vision, all 80 of us, worked tirelessly, putting our hearts into everything we did.

Every Super Vision employee was a shareholder. We were like *one* big happy family, I thought as I headed up the stairs towards my office. Our team spirit showed in everything we did, including all the furnishings.

The staff and I had salvaged old, rusted, steel beams from a scrap yard, torched them to size, and then sanded them to support the polished granite slabs that formed our receptionist's desk and our boardroom table. This was the same for our showroom, nicknamed "The Pulse."

We'd constructed it on weekends, 5,000 square feet of fiber-optic cable and LED lighting displays in venues that included an outdoor landscaping scene, a hot tub area, a home theater set-up, a living room/bar area, a retail store façade, and a Disney World-type Time Tunnel attraction that showcased the magical and special effect of our products. Adjacent was a 75-seat auditorium/class room where we trained architects, pool builders, electrical contractors, sign manufacturers, and lighting designers for the use of our fiber-optic lighting products.

Not bad for a company that just eight years ago was operating out of a small garage. Two years ago we'd moved into this custom-built facility constructed of steel beams and tilt wall concrete. I had personally overseen its construction, far exceeding the Orlando building code's requirements for hurricane resistance.

So when the last hurricanes had stormed in, many of us

chose to sleep here rather than in our own homes. We'd order pizza for a crowd exceeding more than 100, including family and friends.

Now, after a decade of grueling effort and a successful IPO (initial public offering), our company generated $10 million in annual sales. We'd been honored as one of the Top 50 Fastest Growing Companies in Florida, and one of the Top 500 Fastest Growing Technology Companies in America.

And after all those years and all those miles of fiber-optic cable spun, you'd think it would get easier, I thought to myself, pondering the debacle I'd just come from on the manufacturing floor.

Of course, at that point, I had no idea what real trouble was brewing.

TWO

After returning to my office, I settled in my chair. In a daze, I aimlessly scanned the walls surrounding me. They were covered with framed newspaper articles and awards Super Vision has received. Shelves held pictures of my family and gifts from my distributors around the world: a Russian Army hip flask for vodka from Vladimir, my Russian distributor, a scale model of a wooden fishing boat from United Neon in the Philippines, another model of an Arab dhow from Maher Abdelkarim in Kuwait, a Malaysian dagger from Tajuddin in Kuala Lumpur, and pieces of the Berlin Wall from Ernst, our distributor in Germany.

My desk fronted a window facing a man-made lake, fringed with palms. I swiveled around, taking in the scene and thinking maybe life was not so bad after all.

Then the phone rang.

"Brett Kingstone, this is Garry Armitage."

"Hi, your Lordship, what's doing?" I glanced at my watch. "You're working late. It must be close to 10 p.m. in Merrie Olde England."

Garry was my British distributor, a rotund little guy capped by a large matt of shaggy, sandy blond hair. He looked as if he could play alongside Benny Hill on a late night British comedy TV show. Somewhere in his late forties, his chubby, boyish face made him look years younger. I liked to tease him by calling him the Earl of Lancashire, of Robin Hood fame. Garry lived near the fabled Sherwood

Forrest. His company, Newlink U.K. Ltd., had been doing business with us for about two years.

"Well we are not very merry here in England right now and I didn't call to make small talk," Garry said in his clipped British accent. "I just want to know what the bloody hell you think you're doing." His angry tone came through loud and clear over the hiss and crackle of the trans-Atlantic connection. "Why in the world would you want to screw me? What have I done to..."

"Garry, slow down," I interrupted, confused, and concerned. "Start at the beginning. I don't know what you're talking about."

"I'm talking about you doing business with another distributor here behind my back."

"No way!"

"Don't hand me that, Brett. I just came from a trade show, and I saw your products at another distributor's booth."

"That's not possible." He had to be mistaken.

"I know what I saw, Brett." He sounded more weary than angry now. "I saw those products with my own eyes."

"Well, they didn't get that stuff from us."

"Well, if they didn't get your products from you," Garry challenged, "Where did they get them?"

"That's a damn good question, Garry."

This led to silence on both ends of the line as the impact of our exchange hit home. I could feel my temperature start to rise and droplets of sweat began to build on my forehead.

If Super Vision products were showing up at a trade show in the U.K. and they weren't coming from us or our distributors, that meant somebody was illegally creating copies of our products.

"Garry," I said, taking a deep breath. "Exactly what products did you see?"

"The SV150 FiberPro, for one" he said.

"Unbelievable, that's barely off the drawing boards!"

The SV150 fixture used a 150-watt metal halide lamp to illuminate the fibers. That much wattage throws off a lot of heat. Our system used our patented, innovative two-fan system. It featured a blower fan to force air between the lamp and the optical fibers and a ventilation fan to move air through the unit so a tremendous amount of light could be generated without the heat from the lamp melting the plastic fibers. The SV150 had a number of other innovations that were fresh out of our research and development (R&D) department, like a patented locking head to hold the fibers in place when they were twisted and dragged, something that happens at a rock concert, for example.

"Did you see anything else?" I felt afraid to ask, but I had to know.

"I saw a lot of Sideglow and Endglow stuff with standard-sized fiber and also some cables with larger diameter fibers."

"Oh, man…"

Garry not only described copies of our light source and cable products we were now selling, but also products that we still had in our R&D department and had yet to release. For our first seven years, we'd used the .75 mm diameter fibers that were the standard in our industry. But I wanted to deliver more light from our cable, and so we came up with the idea of using larger diameter 1 mm fiber. The first few prototypes were miserable failures, but after more than a year of trial and error we honed in on the correct procedures to make a dramatically improved cable using larger diameter fibers. We trademarked these in various thicknesses as "Sideglow" and "Endglow." The super bright cable using larger diameter fibers was called "Ultra."

Sideglow meant the cables were twisted inside a clear plastic PVC jacket so the cable would illuminate evenly along its length.

Endglow referred to cable of fibers run in parallel in opaque black or white PVC jackets that illuminated only at the end. The larger diameter fiber cables he was describing were the products being pioneered for our new and yet-to-be released Ultra line.

We used plastic fiber, rather than glass, because it was less expensive and would not break. Our Sideglow was intended to replace neon tubes that highlight gasoline stations, restaurants, and retail stores. Our Endglow was meant to replace the conventional track lighting and flood-lighting systems of display cases, swimming pools and hard-to-reach areas where light bulbs are difficult to replace. The fact that our fiber-optic systems used only a fraction of the energy of incandescent systems, required less maintenance, and did not transmit electricity along the cable, only light, made them very popular with architects and lighting designers.

"Brett, do you suppose someone is knocking off your products?" Every trace of Garry's anger was gone now, replaced by concern. "If that's the case, you'd better get on it, because I haven't told you the worst, yet."

"What's that?"

"They're undercutting you on price," Garry said. "These products are identical to yours, but they cost a hell of a lot less."

I felt like someone had punched me in the stomach. "Let me call you back when I know something," I barely managed to croak. I hung up and slumped back into my seat.

THREE

A **high-pitched** explosion echoed throughout the factory and warehouse. That noise was followed by a low, shrill whine. I recognized it as the sound of the planetary cabling machine shutting down. A chill raced down my spine and I could feel the acid start to build up in my stomach. I had heard this sound before. The whirl of 14 spindles that rotated around each other, like planets in the solar system, had started to shake and vibrate the machine as they screeched to an abrupt halt while the fiber continued unwinding off the spools.

I ran towards the cabling machine.

Seconds later a fluttering sound, like hundreds of decks of cards being flipped onto the floor, started to mount. With it I saw the delivery dates for hundreds of our customer's cable orders start to evaporate right before my eyes.

"Damn it to hell, not again!" yelled a now infuriated John Gonzales as his hand pounded against the service door of the fiber-optic cabling machine.

"That's it Roy, now I am going to my truck and getting my gun, I am going to shoot this damn machine and put it out of its misery once and for all."

On the floor in front of him were hundreds, perhaps thousands, of feet of unspooled optical fibers that continued to fall to the ground long after the drive belts had snapped.

"Basura, nothing but garbage," sighed John Gonzales as

he shook his head sadly.

Roy Archer just shrugged his broad shoulders and let out a groan. The two stood silent, taking in the situation that they had seen far too many times this month. They both knew what this meant—cleaning up and starting the production run all over again. But the repeated failures of the extruder that placed a PVC jacket on the cables, as well as the snapping of the drive belts on the cabling machine, were wearing them down.

"All right, Amigo" barked Roy, simultaneously urging himself and John back into action. "We know what to do. Let's pick up this mess, toss it in the garbage, and start over." Roy began to replace the belts that had snapped while John cut and wound up the spent fiber on the floor. Then Roy decided to check the other belts on the machine.

Two more belts also seemed to be in the process of splitting. One appeared to have been cut half-way through, the other was not only slit halfway, but was also starting to stretch and tear. The clean cuts on the belt were clearly not caused by the machinery. Had Roy not noticed them, these belts would have remained like ticking bombs, exploding only days or weeks later.

"Brett, this is NOT a failure of the machine and I am now thinking the same of the earlier failures as well. This looks like somebody has been deliberately sabotaging our machinery."

"Well who the hell could be doing this to us Roy?"

"Well, it can't be Simon or Cruz," Roy said referring to the two previous employees that were arrested several months ago for theft. "They have been out of the building for months and I replaced some of these belts only a few weeks earlier. Besides, those two knuckleheads are not even smart enough to figure out how to operate this machine, much less harm it."

John agreed. "Whoever did this Patron knew how to

operate our machinery; you can't reach all these belts without being able to turn on the machine and rotate all the cradles and shafts on the cabler."

The cabling machine weighed several tons. Each steel cradle that held a fiber-optic spool weighing more than a few hundred pounds when the spool was full of fiber. The entire drive mechanism was controlled by a solid steel shaft, itself weighing at least half a ton. No one could have simply rotated all the spools on the cabling machine without typing in the operating codes and activating the electronic drive mechanism. It simply could not be done by hand.

"So who the hell could have done this to us?"

"I have no idea Brett, but I sure as hell would like to find out," bellowed Roy while a very angry John continued to pace and stamp his foot on the floor. John slammed his fist down on one of the wooden pallets piled beside the cabling machine splintering one of the 2 by 4s. The gravity of the situation was now starting to weigh upon John heavily. We had another traitor in our midst and this time it could likely be one of his staff, someone from his own department. John was taking this very personally.

I leaned over and whispered to Roy "this time, if John gets a hold of them before I do, I don't think they'll be lucky enough to make it to prison."

Roy nodded his head in agreement; however, he was now lost in his own thoughts about who could be responsible and why. As head of production Roy was also concerned about delivery deadlines. It was now early June of 1998, we were already in the peak of our swimming pool season.

"Brett, we have a huge backlog of cable orders from our swimming pool customers. These breakdowns are occurring at precisely the wrong time. The pool builder's won't hold up construction just to wait on our cable, they will cancel their orders. This can kill us if it doesn't stop soon."

After the thefts, the phone call from Garry in the U.K.,

and the sabotage, I walked back up to my office thinking that *things couldn't possibly get worse.* I was wrong.

FOUR

My telephone rang only moments after I returned to my desk.

"Brett-o-san, this is Keiji."

Keiji Yamada did not have to tell me who he was; he'd been my friend and my distributor for more than seven years, and his father was a customer for several years before that. His voice was immediately recognizable, but out of courtesy he would always announce himself.

Keiji did not fit the part of a traditional Japanese businessman and son of a successful industrialist. He hadn't chosen the safe route by taking over the multimillion-dollar family business, Togo Industries, Japan's largest manufacturer of amusement park and roller coaster rides. Instead, he undertook the challenge of going out on his own. Keiji's adventuresome spirit was not limited to business. He was a daring and talented surfer, ultimately winning the Tokyo championship. When I visited him for sales meetings in Japan, he always looked out of place in a suit and tie. With his long slicked-back black hair, lean torso, chiseled features, and perpetual tan, he looked as if he belonged on a beach rather than in a boardroom.

Keiji and I would travel to meetings near the coast with our wetsuits and boards stowed in the back of his van. To get as much time in the water before sunset as possible, Keiji and I would strip off our business suits and change into our wetsuits right in the open beachside parking lot. We sometimes caused quite a stir with a few elderly Japanese ladies out for their afternoon constitutionals.

Keiji had even flown halfway around the world to serve as one of the best men at my wedding. He was normally jovial and upbeat, which is why I became worried when I recognized the grave concern in his voice.

"Brett-o-san, I think we have a problem."

Keiji was a master of understatement. Four years earlier, he and I had taken a vacation on my boat the "No-Problem." Less than two hours off the coast of Miami, heading towards Bimini, we heard the engine shudder and seize up. My 30-foot Bayliner had only one engine. We knew we were in trouble. But at least we had a Loran and a radio, so we could record our position and transmit for help. I picked up the handheld radio receiver and turned it on. Nothing. I then looked at the instrument panel. All the gauges were dead, as was the LCD display on the Loran. So there we were, rudderless and without power, floating around somewhere in the Gulf Stream between Florida and the Bahamas. Land was nowhere in sight and we had no way to communicate our position even if we were able to determine it.

For hours we floated helplessly, hoping for someone, anyone, to pass by. As the sun started to set, we started to lose hope that we would be found before nightfall. The waves were starting to rise. Our floating now became a process of rising and falling. Heavy chops began to pound against the hull. We continued to scan the horizon as the waves continued to build and the skies began to darken. Keiji and I looked at each other; we each knew what the other was thinking. We could probably survive the night, but not several days at sea without food and water. That was the first time he said to me, "Brett-o-san, I think we have a problem."

Keiji's voice on the phone now carried that same gravity. I listened as he told me how he had been contacted by a company in China and he received a brochure. He was not sure if it was the manufacturer, the agent, or distributor. The caller indicated that he knew Keiji's company had been a distributor of Super Vision's products in Japan for the past 7 years. The caller went on to inform Keiji that he could buy "everything" in the Super Vision line from him at less than half Super Vision's distributor price.

A chill raced down my spine. That was actually less than our own production cost.

I asked Keiji what he meant by "everything." Keiji then stated that he could simply refer to the catalog and cite the page or model number and they would deliver it within a week and invoice him at less than half of what he had been paying to Super Vision.

"Brett-o-san, I would never buy from these people, but my competition may, and if they do, it will be difficult for me to maintain my sales. We may lose the entire market in Japan."

"Who are these people?" I asked. Keiji gave me a Website from their brochure, but it was linked to a P.O. box in Hong Kong and further searches on the Internet led nowhere as to the identity of the owners of the company.

Most likely a shell company, I thought, reflecting that the situation seemed as dire as on the boat that night in the Gulf Stream. Back then, we had started to batten down all the hatches and tie off flashlights to the bow and stern to avoid being run over by a freighter during the night's sleep. Just as Keiji headed down to the cabin to turn in, off in the distance I saw what looked like a pair of bow lights heading in our direction. I called to Keiji, who quickly came on deck. We both ripped off our shirts and began frantically waving. As the lights appeared brighter and closer we began to become hopeful. Within minutes the boat pulled alongside. On board the 50-foot, twin-deck fishing boat was a father, son, and cousin returning from a fishing trip off

Bimini. The three men had heavy Spanish accents. I asked where they were from.

"Argentinos" the son responded. "We will be happy to rescue you. Now take the line and we will tow you back to Miami."

The father and son were Gustavo and Martin Caraballo. Gustavo was a senior partner in one of the most prestigious law firms in Argentina, Bunge Born. His son, Martin, had just finished law school and was a renowned polo and rugby player who hoped to join his father's firm. Gustavo, in his late 50s, was large and powerfully built. His son did not stray far from the family tree. The cousin did not appear similar to either of them in either stature or mannerisms. Whereas Gustavo and Martin seemed confident and almost amused by the challenge that now lay before them, the frail and shy cousin did not seem too pleased about embarking in this endeavor.

The ocean was growing rougher and all of us started to get a little seasick at the slow pace it took to tow us back in. Several times the rope snapped and I would jump into the ocean to retrieve it. Each time I retied the rope we were closer behind the stern of Gustavo's boat. Just after I retied the rope for the third time, I could clearly hear the cousin complaining bitterly. I knew enough Spanish to know he was now pleading with his ship mates to just cut the lines and let us float out to sea so they could go full speed back to Miami. He could not bear the slow pace or his seasickness any longer. He said they could radio our position to the Coast Guard when they returned to Miami. "Brett-o-san, Brett-o-san, are you still there? Do you hear me?" Keiji was now raising his voice to pull me from my memories of the last time our lives seemed in jeopardy.

"What do you plan to do Brett-o-san?" said Keiji. "We could lose everything."

"I don't know Keiji, but I will think of something," I said, trying to muster enough confidence to sound convincing. I was now as worried as the night we spent at sea as our saviors were reconsidering their rescue mission.

"Leave these people where they are, this is not our problem" the cousin had said.

But Gustavo had remained steady behind the wheel and Martin vigilant at the rope, which he would grab with his bare hands and guide our boat back into position after a wave knocked us off course. Eventually we saw the lights of Haulover Marina in Miami.

As soon as we were safely tied up, Keiji leapt off the boat and ran down the dock towards Gustavo and his son. Keiji was overwhelmed with gratitude. With all the discipline and formality he could muster, he repeatedly bowed before Gustavo and Martin. In all his excitement and relief he did not realize that he was thanking them in Japanese. Although Gustavo and Martin did not understand a word, it was clear they understood his meaning.

Today's crisis seemed even more alarming. There was no one to rescue us, not even our own government or the laws of our land that were supposed to protect all Americans. Super Vision had attracted a predator. This predator had copied our product line and was bent on destroying us.

I said goodbye to Keiji, offering some words of hope as I hung up. Deep inside, however, I felt frustrated and furious. I had no idea on how I would fight this faceless enemy, but I was well aware of how devastating these acts would be to our business. I had faced this type of theft before in a previous company. The results proved disastrous.

I had already known that we were experiencing a steep sales decline overseas, particular in Asia, but until then I had attributed this to just a decline in economic conditions. I looked across my office at the many gifts from our foreign distributors. I wondered how many of them had been approached as Keiji and Garry had. I looked out my window and watched a snow-white Egret plummet through the blue Florida sky and skim the silvery surface of the pond. His talons plunged swiftly beneath the water line and he emerged with his lunch.

Predator and prey, I thought. Someone was now eating our lunch.

FIVE

I went down the hall from my office into the rest room and rinsed my face with cool water. *It can't be happening again to my company. Not again,* I thought, pondering my pale expression in the mirror above the sink.

But what if it is?

What if this is like the last time?

In the early '80s my Stanford buddies and I had been fooling around with a new type of fiber optics in our dormitory. Instead of the traditional glass form used to transmit data in telecommunications, we were experimenting with the new plastic optical fibers that had recently been developed by Du Pont to transmit light. We found that if the fibers were arranged properly, we could create dazzling animation effects. Our discovery earned us a few small orders from local sign companies, enabling us to relocate to a garage in Palo Alto. In time we added a few people to our staff, but we never much grew out of that garage. My fellow Stanford grads, pursuing more lucrative careers on Wall Street, joked about how I was still toiling away in my tee shirt and jeans while they were becoming masters of the universe in pinstripe suits.

My big break came when I met Dr. William Glenn, a tall, lean and impressive looking scientist in his late sixties who still sported a full head of thick sandy grey hair. He looked like a modern day version of Thomas Edison, and next to Edison he held the second highest number of patents ever issued to a single U.S. inventor. A former director of research and development at General Electric and CBS, he would often gaze off into space while pondering a question and then beam broad smiles while giving his response. He inspired me with his wisdom and brilliance.

He showed me how to take the same fibers I was working with and use them to create large-scale, full-motion television displays. Using Dr. Glenn's process I was able to automate the placement of thousands of fibers in neat horizontal rows in a thin display screen where each fiber would act like a pixel on a television screen and each line function as a line of resolution. The resulting product yielded a flat-panel television screen that was durable, light and more cost effective than currently available cathode ray tube, gas plasma or liquid crystal displays. Dr. Glenn and I partnered up, I licensed his patents on the process, and we established a company in Boulder, Co., that we christened FiberView.

Our team at FiberView was young and idealistic. We had a mission—to challenge the world's largest Japanese TV manufacturers and beat them in the industry they had come to dominate. A few decades earlier the U.S. had had dozens of manufacturers, who produced more than 90% of the world's television sets, but at that time only one remaining U.S. manufacturer remained, Zenith, whose market share slipped to less than 2%.

It was 1987. I was 27 and naïve enough to believe that with our new technology we could beat the world's largest TV manufacturers such as Sony and Mitsubishi.

A few investors bought into our dream and we raised $1 million in venture capital. Our staff grew to 20, and soon our prototype, a fiber-optic television screen, was produced. We were invited to partner with Unisys on several defense contracts for rugged, high-impact display screens. Word of our thin, plastic, flat-panel displays spread fast. Our first such television screen was 6 feet high by 9 feet wide and only

4 inches thick, not earth shattering by today's standards, but absolutely leading edge two decades ago. Less than a year later we were invited to present our first completed prototype to a joint session of Congress. It was a great day for me as I sat at that presentation table before a joint House and Senate Committee on Science, Space and Technology, next to the presidents of AT&T and Zenith, testifying about the future of high-definition television (HDTV) in the United States.

Actually, that great day was soon followed by the worst day in my life, so I thought.

At that very moment, across the Pacific, the Japanese manufacturers who had invested billions in their liquid crystal display (LCD) flat-panel screens realized that their investment was imperiled by our technology.

When they figured out that they couldn't license Dr. Glenn's patents (he was dead set against the U.S. losing out on HDTV to Japan) they tried to have his patents invalidated in Japan.

And when that didn't work, they simply stole them.

How could they get away with that? Easy. Mitsubishi decided to "license" a process from an alleged American inventor, Steven Sedlmayr, a nobody whom they paid $5 million to claim that he had invented a process similar to ours, but "unique." In reality, his process was the same as ours. Several years earlier, Sedlmayr had learned the process during a two-week visit to Dr. Glenn's laboratory under the guise of obtaining a license. Soon afterwards, Sedlmayr established a company that later traded on the Denver Penny Stock exchange called ADTI.

I notified Mitsubishi and ADTI that they were infringing on our patents and manufacturing processes and demanded that they stop. Case closed, or so I thought.

Then, just days after my presentation to Congress, federal marshals burst into our building. Armed with a court order, they carted away our prototypes, products, and, most important, our filing cabinets filled with blueprints, including those of products and machinery I had designed at Stanford almost a decade earlier. I was informed that our materials were trade secrets that I had stolen from ADTI and Mitsubishi. The marshals also picked up and carted away a fiber-optic winding wheel I had designed and built several years earlier, prior to the founding of ADTI. That too was allegedly a trade secret I hold stolen from Sedlmayr.

Sedlmayr, together with support from his new company president and major shareholder, Mukesh Assumoll, had told a Colorado Federal Judge, Lewis T. Babcock, that I had stolen their technology only a few months after I placed them and his Japanese partners on notice for patent infringement. My competitors had managed to convince this judge to issue both injunction and seizure orders in a closed "ex-parte" hearing without giving me an opportunity to present my side. In a meeting I'd never knew about, a group of sharp-eyed and well-financed lawyers convinced a gullible judge that all my years of hard work and sacrifice had never happened.

The plan executed against me was a stroke of evil genius. Instead of their waiting to be hit with a patent suit from my company, my opponents launched a preemptive strike. The sweeping court orders they obtained guaranteed that my company would be rushed into an early hearing for which I would have almost no time to prepare. (The alternative was to shut down our business.) In the preliminary injunction hearing, my fury probably did not help matters. Worse yet, our evidence was all labeled "secret" and locked up in a federal warehouse, so it had become inaccessible for our defense. Predictably Judge Babcock upheld his initial ex-parte ruling against me in the hearing and further found me to be "100% incredible."

I had been blindsided. It was the first time I had ever

been involved in a lawsuit. This awful experience taught me a lesson about our legal system that I would never forget. My competitors had me outgunned. Where I could spend a dollar on legal defense, they could spend a thousand. There was no way I could go on. My adversaries at ADTI and Mitsubishi, knowing I didn't have the money to survive a protracted legal battle, pounced on what I had left, mainly our exclusive licenses to the Glenn patents. After brief settlement negotiations, they got the keys to our facility, and ultimately, the Glenn patents. The foreign predators were able to use our American legal system to destroy FiberView. They did us more harm in the courtroom than they could ever have achieved by competing against us in the marketplace.

I wound up shell-shocked and bitter, recalling these events as I stared at my reflection in the washroom mirror. In 1989, after I'd lost everything to these thieves, I lost both my faith in the justice system and my hopes for the future. At a loss, I retreated to my boat in Miami and sailed aimlessly around the Caribbean, licking my wounds, letting my hair and beard grow, wearing ragged, sun-faded shorts, and wondering what I could possibly do with the rest of my life.

I had been advised by friends and colleagues to stay out of the fiber-optic business, that the court decision stripping me of my patents would "cripple me for life" in what had been my field of expertise. So I thought of trying to make a living by becoming a charter boat captain. But that idea quickly faded. My only real nautical talent was my ability to find every sandbar on the way into port.

My talents lay in manufacturing. All I had ever wanted to do was invent and build things. At night, as my boat rocked gently in some quiet Bahamian harbor, my dreams were illuminated with twinkling lights emanating from long, thin plastic fibers. I dreamed of ways that I could one day light up the world.

Calls were starting to pile up on my answering machine and I had been told the stack of mail at my post office box was becoming formidable. Some calls were from friends wondering if I was still alive; others were from former employees keeping me up to date on the activities at my former company. A few calls I retrieved from ports where I could use my calling card told me of the declining fortunes of the merged company. Management was looting it, while the employees were being laid off without severance. One message talked of a "federal investigation" of President Mukesh Assumoll. Another talked of some stock scheme whereby Assumoll had looted a savings and loan of tens of millions of dollars using his worthless ADTI stock and other fraudulent assets as collateral. He plea-bargained for a reduced sentence of five years and three months in prison, without the possibility of parole, in exchange for testimony against his accomplices.

The last call I played back before I headed out from port informed me that the company had been all but shut down. Only one part-time employee and an answering machine remained. The Japanese appeared content simply to have run off with the patents and the notes to all the processes. Sedlmayr, the famed "inventor," disappeared completely. The caller inquired if I was going to start another company. I did not know, but I felt a ray of hope. For a moment I actually stopped feeling sorry for myself. Perhaps I was no longer a cripple.

And then a message reached me from a contractor in Orlando. He was working at the soon-to-be-opened Universal Studios theme park. He'd heard about my fiber-optic lighting work from former Disney World employees, and wanted me to help him light up a display for the new park. I didn't know this man, nor what job he had in mind, but I did know one thing: I wanted to work again. It was time for me to sail home and get myself a shave and a haircut.

I docked at the Bayside Marina just before nightfall. As the reflection of the Miami skyline faded from the water, I headed up the dock back towards civilization. I didn't realize it then, but my second company, Super Vision International, was about to be born.

Now, I thought bitterly, the same sorts who had screwed me over with my first company were back to plunder again.

I'd lost everything and these predators had also destroyed the livelihoods of my 20 dedicated employees...

Could it happen again? Would I now be able to protect my 80 employees from a similar fate?

I went back down to the manufacturing floor, where I took some small satisfaction in the fact that Roy had managed to get the cabling machines back on line.

"Roy," I called over the din. "I'm getting calls from our distributors saying exact copies of our products are turning up all over the world."

"Well, that's probably why we've noticed a downturn in orders here," Roy said.

"It gets worse," I replied. "They're not only copying our existing stuff, they're knocking-off new products like the SV150. Who the hell could be doing this to us?"

"I don't know, Brett." Roy looked down at the floor. "What are you fixing to do?"

I shrugged, feeling helpless. All I knew was that if I was not able to identify and stop these counterfeiters their actions would consume us like a cancer. Our company would be dead in less than a year.

But I did not want to leave Roy feeling scared. If he were to lose hope it would devastate the morale of the company. So I made light of the matter. I glanced at my watch. It was almost 9 p.m.

"Well, Roy, I can tell you now that I have a much more serious problem on my hands."

"What's that Brett? What could be more serious than this?"

"For the third time in a row this week I've missed dinner and putting the kids to bed. If I don't go back right now and beg my wife for forgiveness, she's going to kill me."

Roy chuckled. He knew about my wife's hot temper and realized I was not straying far from the truth.

He slapped me on the back and told me he would take care of the problem. Roy smiled briefly; however, the concern was still evident in his eyes. He stood silent as he watched me walk across the factory floor.

SIX

It was a cold sweat. The kind of sweat that is often accompanied by chills racing down your spine. I gripped the steering wheel a little tighter and clenched my teeth as I shuddered and tried to shake off the chills. I reached over to turn off the air conditioning in my car on this hot summer night, but the chills kept coming and beads of sweat dripped down my face. I wiped my brow with my shirtsleeve and struggled to focus on the road ahead. It was difficult to concentrate. If everything I had been told today was correct, I knew my company and my employee's livelihoods would soon be destroyed.

The 10-minute drive from my office to my home seemed to take forever. I was unlucky enough to get stopped by almost every light along Sand Lake Road in my olive green Land Rover. For a brief moment, I smiled at the thought of my first corporate vehicle. It was a '69 Plymouth Valiant that I had bought from a Stanford professor's wife for $400. I'd used its cavernous trunk to cart samples around to customers.

I'd come a long way from Super Vision's birth in a studio apartment in Orlando, to our present 80,000 square foot facility and our stock traded on the NASDAQ.

But now that was all about to change. Our company had attracted a predator. A foreign enemy that was attacking our company's markets overseas with the technology it had plundered from within our laboratories and manufacturing facilities. They were bent on our destruction. Ten years of hard work and millions of dollars of shareholder investments were being ripped right out from under us.

Now some of our past problems that we had thought unrelated were fitting together. Products and components were regularly being reported missing. Valuable customized test equipment were stolen from our locked R&D laboratories. New machines were mysteriously failing. In addition to the sabotaged belts on the cabling machine, the PVC formulas for our fiber-optic cable's plastic jacketing had been corrupted. This ruined plastic would gum up the extrusion head so that the production line would have to be shut down for hours while the errant PVC was removed and the extruder was thoroughly cleaned.

We were under siege, being attacked from the shadows by some unknown foe, who was now closing in for the kill. *Who was counterfeiting our products overseas?*

I then realized that there had to be a mole inside our organization. The sabotage was wreaking havoc on our production in much the same way their counterfeiting was slashing away at our overseas sales. Our company was beginning to hemorrhage with red ink.

I guided the Land Rover down the palm tree-lined streets of the Dr. Philips neighborhood bordering Universal Studios Fla., finally pulling into the driveway of my home, a two-story, Spanish-style villa with white stucco walls, a red terra cotta roof, and tall windows trimmed with wrought iron. That last bit was a nice touch added by my wife, Maisa, who wanted the house to evoke warm memories of her native Argentina. The house was most breathtaking at night, when the landscaped tropical grounds were lit up by state-of-the-art Super Vision products.

Our Sideglow fiber outlined the pool perimeter in a soft halo of light and our Endglow cable flood lighted the pool and the surrounding waterfalls and palm trees in cascades of colored light.

No sooner had I opened the door from the garage to the laundry room than Luis pounced on me. Someone had forgotten to tell this 5-year-old, 90-pound yellow Labrador that he was no longer a puppy. He wouldn't stop jumping on me, alternately landing his paws on my chest and licking my face. Luis never had a care in the world; all he wanted was love and attention. As he showered me with affection, my worries started to fade.

In the distance from the kitchen I could hear the click clack of steps on the Spanish tile floor coming my way. A smiling little face framed with long curly locks of light-brown hair appeared. It was my one-and-a-half-year-old Victoria, shuffling behind Luis in a pair of Mommy's high-heeled shoes, along with a hat and a scarf she had borrowed from my wife's closet.

"Daddy, Daddy, I love you!" said Victoria. Her arms reaching up to me.

I reached around Luis and picked her up, "I love you too, my little tootsie fruitsie."

I carried Victoria into the kitchen with Luis right behind, jumping on my back or pawing at my legs as I made my way toward the stove to see what was for dinner. In the distance I heard a voice from upstairs. My wife was telling me she was changing our son Max's diaper and she would be down soon to serve dinner.

I looked in the pots on the stove to see that Maisa had whipped up a batch of her creamy potato soup. On the counter that surrounded the cooking island was my place-mat with a salad waiting. Warming in the oven were a few empanadas that Maisa must have bought at a local Latin bodega. I stole one and nibbled on it as I held Victoria, while Luis bounded up and down hoping that something would ultimately be destined for him.

After a few small bites, I threw the rest to him. After today's events, food tasted like ashes in my mouth.

Minutes later, my wife Maisa descended to meet me holding our son.

She still looked as young and radiant as the day we met on a blind date in Buenos Aires five years earlier. She had the same deep brown eyes and petite features as my daughter; however, her face was framed by silken and shiny dark-brown hair that fell well beyond her shoulders.

She greeted me with a broad smile and a warm hug.

A chubby little Max, with a tuft of light-brown hair, continued to coo away on her shoulder. She asked how everything had gone that day; I tried to avoid showing her my concern and just said everything had gone all right. But I wasn't able to return an equally confident and beaming smile. I could sense that she already knew something was wrong, but she did not press me.

"Let's eat, darling. I made you your favorites, we can talk later," Maisa said as she turned down the heat on the stove and shut off the oven.

After dinner, we walked through the brick archway to the adjacent living room. I remembered her directing the masons two years earlier to lay the concrete between the brick in a thick and uneven fashion in order to create an old world appearance.

As we sat down to play Maisa's favorite game, Boggle, I glanced around, remembering what this room had looked like before we could afford to furnish it, nothing but a few boxes and end tables from our previous two-bedroom town home. Our only other furnishings then were the oil paintings we had received from Maisa's stepmother, who owned art galleries in Argentina, and Maisa's ever growing collection of tennis trophies.

Although English was not her native language, Maisa always beat me at Boggle. But tonight I was playing particularly poorly. As Max crawled around on the rug and Victoria colored at the coffee table, Maisa put the game away and asked me to lie down on the couch and tell me what was wrong.

I rested my head in her lap and stretched my legs across the couch. Maisa stroked my hair while I stared at the ceiling and contemplated our fate. I glanced over at our children. I wondered what it would be like to lose everything we had worked and saved for.

I thought back to what had happened at FiberView. I was single and much younger then. It wasn't such a sacrifice to start over again. But now I had a wife and two young children. This time it would really matter. The mortgage, our children's education, and our employees' families weighed on my mind. I tried to tell myself that it couldn't happen again…that these predators wouldn't win this time, but I knew I was kidding myself. Our company was about to be stolen out from under us all over again.

Meanwhile, one question kept repeating itself over and over again in my mind…

Who was attacking us?

My worry must have been evident. I looked up at Maisa and she nervously tried to muster a comforting smile as she continued to stroke my hair.

"Brett, what is going on? Tell me, please."

So I did. I told her about the calls I'd received from my distributors, the prior thefts, and the problems with the equipment, filling in for her the significance of it all.

Maisa was quiet for a while after I finished. "So, you think it is happening again to you the way it did with FiberView?" she asked finally.

"Yeah, I feel like I have so much on my shoulders. Eighty employees' families are counting on me for their livelihoods."

"You could go to the authorities for help."

"The law is helpless against this kind of international piracy," I told her, drawing on my personal experience

Maisa had been patient with me in the early years of our

marriage as I concentrated on building Super Vision, but I knew she'd had to endure too many dinners alone, and too many weeks with me gone traveling to trade shows overseas. How would she feel about my resuming that work schedule again if I had to start over?

Ironically, it had been Super Vision, responsible for keeping me away from Maisa, that had also led to my meeting her in the first place. I smiled at the recollection of our courtship. As I waited for her response, my thoughts faded back five years to the day we met in Buenos Aires.

SEVEN

Maisa Lorena Dragubitzky was just

19 when I met her. In 1993, on my first sales trip to
Argentina, my customer was surprised to discover that we
shared a religious affiliation. With my fair complexion and
my name, Brett Kingstone, it was not at all clear that I was
Jewish. With his name, Diego Lowenstein, little was left to
the imagination. Diego was dark and handsome. His olive
skin and slicked back jet-black hair accentuated his broad
smile. He was the scion of a powerful Argentine family that
had owned the largest chain of hamburger restaurants in
the country. The family also owned the largest cattle
ranches and slaughterhouses, which serviced the restaurants. The family's holdings extended to Miami Beach,
where it owned the Di Lido, Seville and Ritz Carlton hotels.
Diego's company wanted Super Vision to install fiber-optic
signage in its restaurants and shopping centers in
Argentina. His company had invited me and a few of our
staff to join them in Buenos Aires to accomplish this.

About the third day of my visit, Diego decided that it was
his mission to find me a proper date, "a nice girl," he said.
Diego's definition of a "nice girl" was: "rich father." After a
few disastrous dates, I had developed what I called Kingstone's theory of relativity: "the weight and width of the
daughter are in direct proportion to the wealth of the father."
I begged Diego not to set me up on any future blind dates.

There came, however, one further recommendation

that this time came from Diego's fiancée, Gisella Attas. Gisella was popular and well known in society circles in Buenos Aires. If she arranged a date, her plans were not to be toyed with or disrespected. As much as I liked Gisella, and I told Diego I would be happy to meet someone as beautiful as she, the memory of my three past engagements was too bitter to risk a replay. The more I protested to Diego that I didn't want to go through with this, the angrier he became. He finally thundered, "OK. Señor Kingstone, let's just put it this way. You don't show up, Gisella gets angry. My Gisella gets angry, I tear up your contract!"

My response was, "About what time do you want me to show up, Diego?"

While I was furiously protesting the date with Diego, the other party to the date was even more vociferous with Gisella about her refusal to attend. "You want me to do what?! You want me to go out with some treinta y tres-ano gringo Norte Americano! He is probably fat, ugly, bald, sloppy, and stupid." Maisa later grew fond of telling her friends that she "was right on at least three of the five counts; they would just have to guess which." But, Gisella was not going to knuckle under any more than her equally strong-willed future husband. Maisa finally agreed to attend.

Diego's car pulled up to the hotel entryway. I opened the passenger side door to get in. Sitting at the other end of the back seat was a stunning beauty with long, dark hair wearing a short red dress. I paid particular attention to the long sleek and shapely legs that were politely crossed at the knee. I followed them up to a slender waist and athletic figure beyond. We both had broad smiles of relief on our faces, seeing that our worst fears at least, were not justified for the moment.

Diego introduced me and I responded with something along the lines of "I see that your father is not rich." Maisa's smile quickly turned to a disapproving frown and Gisella glared at me as if she was going to cook me for dinner.

Thankfully, Diego let out a tremendous roar of a laugh. He knew my hidden meaning and although the other passengers did not, they at least realized that I had not meant any offense. We pulled away from the curb and sped off to a night of club hopping around the famous nightspots of Buenos Aires.

Sometime after the typical late-night Argentine dinner, probably past midnight, I told Maisa I was going to marry her. She responded that I was either much too bold or full of crap to say such a thing on the first date, but she did not totally brush me off. As I again insisted that we were to be married, Maisa laughed, "You are just saying that to get me in bed." Our date ended about 5 a.m. and, despite her obvious apprehension at my impetuous approach, she agreed to see me the next night.

We met every night for the next two weeks. Sometimes she would just come over to my hotel room and curl up with her schoolbooks while I was on the phone with clients. Other times we would talk about each other's lives. We seemed to fill voids in each other. We were both strong-willed, and shared many of the same ideals and values, but we came from entirely different backgrounds. When I first met Maisa, she had more servants in her summer houses in Mira Flores and Punta del Este than I had employees. I had grown up being entirely self-reliant, while she grew up not knowing how to boil water or use a washing machine.

Maisa's family's main residence in Buenos Aires was an entire floor in a building on Avenida Libertador, the Argentine equivalent of Park Avenue. Several government ministers as well as captains of industry lived nearby. It was clear that Maisa would have to step down in her living standards to marry me, and it was by no means clear that her family, particularly her five over-protective brothers, would approve. I was, however, determined to fight for the right to marry her.

EIGHT

"Brett, Brett!" Maisa yelled as she began to tug at my hair and shake my head to get my attention. "I am talking to you! Are you even listening to me?"

But what she said next took me by surprise.

"Brett, get off your behind and save Super Vision. Fight for it like you fought for me!" She tugged playfully at my hair. "Don't imagine that the same thing will happen as it did with FiberView. Instead, learn from that experience. Remember how your enemies outfoxed you that time and take the offensive now. Go out and make something happen. Vamos Papito!"

I thought about what she was saying. I was used to fighting for what I believed in. But in the past I had always been able to see my adversaries, and with the one exception of FiberView, I'd always been able to vanquish them.

I suppose my hatred of thieves stemmed from my childhood. My father and grandfather ran a small mattress factory in New York. They had me sweeping the factory floor at age five and on the delivery truck by the time I was 12, going around with the driver making deliveries to small furniture retailers and warehouses in Harlem and the South Bronx.

Sometimes young thugs would try to steal our receipts. Other times they went after the mattresses in the back of the truck. If a mattress was stolen the amount was deducted from my pay.

Since I was saving my money for college, I made damn sure that the mattresses stayed on the truck.

Today's crooks were a lot more sophisticated, I thought. But what it boiled down to was that somebody was still trying to steal the mattresses off my truck.

They'd gotten away with it once. Would I let them do it again?

"Maisa?"

"Yes?"

"I'm going to find out who's attacking us, and I'm going to fight back."

"Tell me something I didn't already know," she laughed. "Okay, I will," I said. "This time we're going to win."

NINE

〰

Super Vision was the rekindling of my dream. It rose from the ashes of FiberView like a Phoenix. After arriving in Orlando towards the end of 1989, I teamed up with a young television technician, Roy Archer, whom I had met while visiting contractors and designers at Universal Studios. Roy wasn't much of a talker, he was a doer. He could drive a truck, lift any load and fix almost anything so I presumed he would make a good partner, particularly if my first prototype again blew up on me and needed repairs.

Our first project was to produce two fiber optic trade show signs for Universal. We didn't exactly have an order, but some people in the promotion department at Universal said if we could build a few attractive signs for their trade show booth, they might decide to buy them. Although we did not have an office yet, we were operating out of my studio apartment, we thought it would be important to have at least a name for our company. "Super Vision" grew out of a combination of ideas we kicked around.

We borrowed a desk, a few drills, and a soldering iron from our friends at Century III Communications who had a facility next door to Universal. One of Universal's kind-hearted legal staff, Larry Haber, also allowed us the use of his dining room table on more than one occasion. Over a period of several nights, and a few early mornings, we crafted two fiber-optic trade show displays. The fiber-optic end points that created the Universal Studios logo in a black plastic-panel raced in waves of continuous chasing colors followed by showers of sparkles and twinkling animation. Universal not only liked them but also gave us a few small orders to build illuminated fiber-optic displays for its new park under construction. Soon a few Disney engineers heard about our "toy lights" and decided to give us a few contracts as well.

By January 1990, we had quit our part-time work at the borrowed facility and started full time in my studio apartment in Orlando. One contract led to another and by year-end we made the "big move" into our first office at the Orange Bank Building on Kirkman Road, just across the road from Universal. The building manager overlooked the fact that we were inappropriately operating a factory in an office building because her son, Roy Archer, was my co-worker and her daughter, Pam Archer, was my accountant. Roy and I worked well as a team. I would put on a tie and go out and sell something, then later I would take off the tie and Roy and I would build what I had sold. I look back in amazement at how we were able to produce anything in that two-room office facility, let alone our first few hundred thousand dollars of sales. One of our greatest challenges was finding a way to get what we had built in the office out the door and down the elevator to deliver it to our customers.

One day, while Roy and I were panting and sweating, trying to maneuver a giant Disney display piece into the elevator, it occurred to us that maybe the time had come to lease a garage. Roy noted that at this point it looked as if our backs were going to give out before our bank account. So in 1991, we took a big entrepreneurial leap and rented a "warehouse." Roy told me he would take over production so I could spend my time selling to pay for the new lease.

Our warehouse, on L.B. McLeod Road in Florida, was two miles away from our first office and just wide enough to

fit one and a half cars. We had a one-room office in the front and a small showroom in the back. Years later, Roy and I would chuckle when we heard stories of other entre-preneurs who began their struggles in a garage, since we had to graduate from a borrowed facility and studio apart-ment before we were able afford the luxury of a garage.

As our company started to grow, Roy took over manag-ing the manufacturing facility while I would go out and man our booth at lighting and signage trade shows, first domes-tically and then overseas. We started signing up reps and distributors for our fiber-optic lighting and sign products. We also hired more staff and expanded our sales to other industries. One such hire was David Vaughn, who wandered into our facility one day. He had heard from a friend that worked with us on the production line that we were building some fun products and he told us he had just decided to join our team. We were short-handed and pressed for time then, so a referral from a current staff member was as good as a resume and interview. We hired David on the spot and he started assembly work that afternoon.

Another key early hire was a young man named Paul Koren. He was 19 when he joined us; he was full of energy and creativity. Paul played water polo on nationally ranked teams and spent most of his life in and around pools, he immediately saw the potential of our fiber-optic lighting products for the swimming pool industry. Paul single-hand-edly developed all our fiber-optic swimming pool products and established our sales and distribution network in that industry. He became a key man on our team from the early stages of our company. While David had found us, how we found Paul was an entirely different story.

TEN

Paul Koren came to me, and ultimately the employment of Super Vision, by chance. He was a hungry young immigrant who came to the U.S. from Russia via Israel on a tourist visa. He stayed and worked diligently at thankless and difficult jobs which he would gladly take since he did not have a green card. Paul worked hard and never complained. He knew what life was like for him and his family in Russia. He was never able to finish college, but he was bright and learned quickly, due to his intelligence coupled with his real-world experience.

One night, I went to a Jewish "singles event." I did not like going to these events, but at age 30 and single, I was being labeled as "hopeless for not even trying" by family members. I was somewhat lacking in social skills, which no doubt made me unappealing to most women. I didn't fit or look the part of the typical "nice Jewish boy," but in spite of all my rough edges, my adventuresome and somewhat crazy personality did appeal to a certain segment of the Jewish female population who were tired of dating what their mothers had insisted upon in the past.

As soon as I sat down at the table, I noticed an exotic blonde beauty, with unusually high cheekbones and almond-shaped eyes. She later turned out to be a few years out of Moldavia, via a short stopover in Israel. Rita's accent as well as her looks became quite captivating. It was nice to learn that she took a similar interest in me, or at least she

did at the time. I was also thankful to learn that the equally blond young man sitting on her right was not her date, but in fact her brother. As time passed, Rita would tell her family the joke about how I later became more interested in her brother than her. As a result, she married a Jewish doctor, and I hired Paul.

ELEVEN

❧

One of the most exhilarating moments of my life was the walk I took with Paul Koren across the "Freedom Bridge" that links the Canadian side of Niagara Falls to the American side. For us, that walk came to symbolized that with hard work, determination, and a little creativity, even the "impossible" can happen. It was also an experience that would bind us for life.

In October 1991, Super Vision was awarded the biggest contract in its early history, what later became its most famous accomplishment, a several hundred thousand dollar contract to produce the world's largest fiber-optic sign and the first fiber optically lit display to grace the lights of Broadway in New York's Times Square: the Coca-Cola Bottle.

We were all thrilled by the opportunity, but became less than thrilled when we learned we had to install the fiber optics in the 40 foot tall fiberglass Coca Cola bottle at the fiberglass plant of MFG in Union City, Pa. For those who are not familiar with Union City, you haven't missed much. The farm animal population exceeds the human, and most of the human population works at the MFG plant-spraying fiberglass into molds for car bumpers and truck hoods. The hot spots in town were the one local bar and luncheonette that quickly overflowed when our staff walked in for a break. We settled in the only hotel that could accommodate a "crowd" of our size, 12 people, which was Michael Angelo's

Hotel and Restaurant.

Michael Angelo, yes, that was really the owner's name, gave me a list of rooms in which my staff were located and listed the names of the two boys and two girls that were in each room. Every week when I returned to check on the progress of the project, I noticed that the names had changed on the rooms, going from all-girl and all-boy rooms to girl-boy and boy-girl. As time passed, people played changing roommates like musical chairs. Michael Angelo gave up trying to keep track and I stopped bothering to even ask. After all, there was not much to do in Union City and if this kept them happy, who was I to argue?

After six weeks of "banishment" in Union City, the staff visibly became tired and frustrated by their surroundings. It was clear that a "road trip" was in order. Since the team had worked ahead of schedule, the three-day wait for the fiber-glass work to catch up with our fiber-optic drilling and placement gave us a great chance to take a much needed break. I decided to take the entire staff to see Niagara Falls and spend a few nights enjoying the beauty of this natural wonder from both sides of the border.

After the three-hour drive, we walked toward the border station at the famed "Freedom Bridge" that crosses the falls. All of us were excited, except Paul Koren. Paul froze in terror 10 steps from the door of the border station. He insisted he was not crossing the bridge. All of us, particularly me, pleaded with Paul to join us on our adventure. After all, Paul did have a driver's license as identification and "everything would be OK." I considered myself one of the most persuasive persons in the group, and sure enough, it was I who finally persuaded Paul to cross. Big mistake.

TWELVE

Paul got across the bridge just fine; returning was another matter. A lean, mean border guard and former Marine drilled into Paul's eyes and then cast a stone-cold gaze on the driver's license he was holding alongside Paul's head. He asked Paul a few questions, apparently just to hear him speak. He studied Paul's heavy accent and asked him where he was from. As soon as the word "Russia" came out of his mouth, Paul was yanked into a small room, his shoes were removed, and he was handcuffed to a chair. Paul would later say that he was treated rather sternly in that holding room by the border guard, but added that the guard was at all times civil and fair. We waited in the lobby of the border station for an hour before being told we could go, but Paul would have to remain behind.

Panic broke out among the staff. Some cried, some talked of going home, and a few were ready to run back to Florida that instant. I calmed them as best I could and told them to get back to work, that I would stay behind with Paul and somehow, I had no idea how, would bring him back. One staff member, Laurie Bernota, was particularly distraught. With tears in her eyes, she made me pledge before God that I would not come back without Paul. I gave her my promise, because I knew she would not return to work without it. Six years later she became Paul's wife and the mother of his child.

Paul was eventually released, but told he had to stay in

Canada. Apparently he had been in the U.S. illegally and would not be allowed to return to the United States. We walked across the bridge together, it was now late at night in the dead of winter, and it was bitter cold. We checked into the Holiday Inn hotel on the Canadian side of the falls. It was not a palace, but it had a heated indoor swimming pool that proved to be a good diversion while we were awaiting our fate.

We used the hotel coin phones in the lobby to make our calls every day. Paul would call his family, who informed him in great distress that all the lawyers they had talked with said he would never be allowed back in the United States. I was hearing the same from every immigration lawyer listed in the Buffalo, N.Y., yellow pages. Words like "living in violation for several years" and "fruitless to even try" kept ringing in my ears. Paul's family was terrified, fearing he would be sent back to Israel, or worse, Russia, where he would be forced into military service for several years before he could even hope to apply to return to his family. I finally found a lawyer across the border in Buffalo who would take our case, or at least he took his hefty fee to represent us. He told us not to worry because he was a personal friend of the immigration director and if we only waited a few days in Canada, he would get back to us after he spoke to him.

Waiting was not in our genetic makeup, so we decided to visit Canadian sign and lighting companies within driving distance of our hotel and try at least to make some sales in the meantime. We were able to get appointments immediately after our cold calls to these companies because we told the receptionists our story of peril and said we could not afford to make appointments much beyond the moment of our call. We drove up to Toronto and met with the presidents of Canada's leading sign companies, such as Steel Art Signs and Claude Neon. They exhibited great humor and interest in our tale of how we got stuck in Canada and admired us for making the best of our time as fugitives. At night, Paul taught me how to do the butterfly stroke in the swimming pool.

As the days passed, we kept calling the lawyer in Buffalo, over and over again, to check on his progress. The response was always the same: "I am working on it." Finally, out of desperation, I called the office of the director of immigration and naturalization in Buffalo, N.Y., only to learn that the director's secretary had never heard of our lawyer and neither had the director.

Just as things seemed at their worst, while Paul and I walked up and down the Canadian side of the icy river to choose the location of that night's planned crossing, I was inspired with an idea. For several hours thereafter, we worked the payphones calling congressmen and senators. We started with those in our home state of Florida and worked our way up to Senator Alfonse D'Amato's office in New York. Senator D'Amato had previously been the Nassau County Supervisor where I grew up and he never forgot a constituent. Neither did our United States Senator from Florida, Bob Graham. Both Senators' offices started ringing the immigration director's phone. That was immediately followed by phone calls from the Chief Employment Legal Counsel, William Bernstein, of Coca-Cola, and Bob Jackowitz, the vice president of America's oldest and most esteemed sign manufacturer, Artkraft Strauss. Bob also just happened to be the project manager on the Coca-Cola sign and we made it clear, "No Paul, No Coke bottle."

We even enlisted the aid of our recently made friends in the Canadian Sign industry, all of whom implored the immigration director to let the now "famous Russian fiber-optic sign engineer, Paul Koren," to go back to his work. They all made it sound, with a little coaching from me, that the fate of the country's most important future landmark now rested in Paul's hands and that an exception should be made for someone of his talents who would no doubt be thrown into a gulag in Siberia if forced to return to Russia. One public servant, Lydia Mount, of Senator Bob Graham's office, deserves special credit. She personally called the immigration director's office with such force and frequency that it began to have an effect on him. Less than a week after my first call, where I was told "impossible" by the immigration director's secretary, my next call was met with an entirely different response. I certainly was not loved by the office staff, but I at least had their attention. When I called and asked if I could meet with the director, I was angrily told that I had better report to him in person "immediately."

I felt uncomfortable walking into the office of the Director of Immigration, having only worn blue jeans, construction boots, and a company work shirt that I had been living in for the past week and a half. But I knew this was my one chance to save Paul; I had to take it. The secretary glanced at me and said something to the effect "so you are the one causing all this trouble around here," as she guided me into the director's office. The director didn't even give me time to take a seat. He threw a paper across the desk and snapped, "Now take it and get the hell out of here!" I picked up the paper, it was an order signed by him allowing Paul to return to the United States for "humanitarian reasons." I asked what "humanitarian" meant and the director responded that "it doesn't matter but if so much as one more congressman, senator, sign maker or indian chief calls me one more time, I am liable to revoke this and hunt you both down and throw both your asses out of the country."

Paul and I approached the bridge still reading and re-reading the "Humanitarian Reprieve," grins beaming across our faces. We were a rugged and worn looking lot, still wearing the same crumpled clothes that we had when we first crossed the bridge almost two weeks earlier. It was foggy and there was no one on the bridge that morning; the walk to freedom across the "Freedom Bridge" looked almost sur-real. We felt as if we were playing a role in our own movie. As we approached the border station, we overheard one of the border guards calling to the other, "Hey, you are not going to believe who is here." The stern looking guard, now clad in his old Marine Corps leather jacket, almost ripped the paper out of Paul's hand.

"Unbelievable," he shook his head as he read our letter, "absolutely unbelievable. Never seen one of these, a 'humanitarian reprieve.' So, which one of you two knuckle-heads is married to some Senator's daughter?" barked the former leatherneck.

"Neither" we replied and then briefly told him our story but he cut us off midway and said the director has already called ahead and told him so he would not think the document we were carrying was fake, the same as Paul's driver's license.

The ex-Marine then turned to me and asked, "Why did you stay?"

I replied I was from a military family, that Paul was my responsibility and that I had been told never to leave a man behind.

The guard's eyes narrowed and again drilled into mine as they once had into Paul's when he got caught. Then he just handed back our paper and said, "Go!" pointing the way to the door.

Just after we exited the border station door and crossed over onto American soil and to freedom, the guard jogged out after us. We turned and froze in our tracks. Paul and I looked at each other in horror. After all we had been through; this guy now was going to find a way to take us back. "Shit!" we said, "Now what?" Paul and I continued looking at each other, wondering if we should make a run for it. The guard stopped a few feet from us. He still had on his Marine leather jacket and now leather gloves as well.

He took off his right glove and presented his hand to Paul saying, "No hard feelings." Paul, quite relieved, quickly shook his hand and agreed, "No hard feelings." The border guard then turned to me and shook my hand as well and said, "Never leave a man behind. I respect what you did kid. Semper Fi."

At that point, I really wanted to respond with a salute, but, not being a veteran myself, I didn't think I had the right to salute him. I just looked him back in the eye and nodded in acknowledgement.

On New Year's Eve, 1993, at two minutes before midnight, the Coca-Cola sign's inaugural illumination ceremony was broadcast on Dick Clark's "Rock 'n' New Years Eve" to an audience of millions worldwide. As Paul and I looked up at the world's first fiber-optic sign to grace the lights of Broadway in Times Square, we beamed with pride and enthusiasm. *After all we had been through,* I thought, *"Anything now was possible. There must be great things to be achieved in the future."*

THIRTEEN

〔✦〕

The Coke project helped us land several other landmark projects including the AT&T sign in Times Square, the Pepsi-Cola globe in Caracas, Venezuela, and the Euro Disney Electric Light Parade in Paris and the Disney SpectroMagic Parade in Orlando. We also started getting calls from customers and distributors all over the world who were interested in our products and capabilities. The first international distributor that we signed up was from Reykjavik, Iceland. He owned the largest sign manufacturer and billboard advertising company in Iceland and had seen our sign in New York and decided to "drop in" on us during the International Sign Show that was held in Orlando that year.

Johannes Tryggvason was a tall, wiry man with a broad smile and a perpetual twinkle in his eye. He was also, as he would call it: "well marked." Johannes lost his right arm as a child in an accident in a fish processing and cannery plant. He did not let that setback stop him; he focused on his soccer game and became his country's leading player on the national soccer team, traveling worldwide to bring home championships to the tiny but proud country. Johannes also had a creative way of even focusing on his shortcomings and turning them to his advantage. At several price negotiating sessions that I would attend with him with his customers in Iceland, Johannes would turn to me in the middle of a heated price debate and say: "You see Brett, I give this man a finger and he takes off my whole arm!" The mortified client would eventually back down and they would come to an agreement.

Iceland, with a population of 250,000, has less than a quarter of the inhabitants of Orlando, however, the country is almost entirely self-sufficient. The Icelanders provided their own food from the sea and generate their own heating from steam pipes that are sunk into the ground underneath every home. The natural volcanic steam that is in abundance in Iceland heats all the homes, schools, offices and communal pools at no charge to the inhabitants. Icelanders are innovative by both culture and necessity. Johannes came up with many innovative ways to apply our fiber optics to billboards, advertising signs, and displays that we never dreamed of. His orders flowed in on a regular basis with each new innovative use that our "Crazy Iceman" would come up with for our products. Soon Reykjavik was covered with fiber-optic Christmas trees and the public and private office buildings were lined with Christmas garlands permeated with green and red sparkling points of fiber-optic light. During my last visit to Reykjavik during the month of December, the entire city looked more like a Super Vision showroom than the nation's capital.

Other distributors gradually signed on and soon more than a third of our gross sales were overseas. We welcomed the opportunity to export our products and applied for CE approval marks in addition to our UL (underwriters laboratories) certifications to further our international sales. However, some international sales projects were more welcome than others. We learned that with the growth of our international markets came new problems requiring new "cultural understandings" and adaptations.

FOURTEEN

We were contacted by a Mexican company that had a big project in Cancun, Mexico. They asked us to fly down to meet the owner. Figuring there were worse places in the world to go on a sales call than Cancun, I agreed hop on a plane and meet the owner at the construction site the next week. Two tall neatly dressed men, one holding a sign "Mr. Kingstone" were waiting at the airport to greet me. They turned out to be employees of the owner. One was the limo driver. I wasn't sure what the other did, but he always seemed to follow the owner around but never seemed to do any work other than stand by his side.

I was driven about 20 minutes to the Zona Hotelerena on the coast of Cancun. Resorts and hotels lined the street bordered by pristine beaches and turquoise ocean for as far as the eye could see. When I arrived at the old concrete former folklore theater/arena that was being converted to a Planet Hollywood restaurant I was immediately presented to "the boss," a thin man with black bushy hair wearing a gold chain with a solid gold camel dangling around his neck, his name was Adiv Macisse.

Depending on who you talked to in Cancun, you would get different descriptions as to exactly what businesses Mr. Adiv Macisse was involved in. One thing was for sure, he was the owner of several restaurant chains in Mexico including Bice, and whether or not the restaurants themselves were the source of his wealth or not, everyone agreed that Mr.

Macisse was a very rich man, and not a man to be taken lightly. Apparently, as I learned later, there were a few contractors who made that mistake, and as the Mexicans would say: "estan con Dios" (they are with God).

Adiv told me that he heard about our company from Planet Hollywood's President, Robert Earl. Robert was also the former founder and president of the famous Hard Rock Café restaurant chain and we had done work for him on several of his restaurants in the past. Adiv told me he had a very short deadline to the grand opening of the Cancun Planet Hollywood. Already he was making plans for the arrival of all the press and movie stars including Sylvester Stallone. He wanted to make sure we added some spectacular applications of our products throughout the interior and exterior of the restaurant so the grand opening would be memorable. He told us we had six weeks and we must work around the clock and "spare no expense." As we found out later, getting paid for the expenses was quite another subject.

Adiv walked me through the hollow shell of the building where numerous groups of contractors were working simultaneously to complete the project on time. There were dozens of Mayan Indians sitting barefoot, cutting and setting tile on the floor, while a group of four welders flown in from Texas clad in protective welding hoods and uniforms, were welding the hand railings into place along the stairs and balconies. I thought that the Texans must have looked like Martians to the Mayans. Carpenters were also busy cutting wood on sawhorses throughout the building and framing up walls and bar countertops. Painters were hanging off scaffolding at different levels, painting the walls and ceilings as soon as the drywall hangers had placed the panels into position. It was quite an impressive site.

Adiv would point to one bare space near the bar and describe his vision of a solid wave structure caste in fiberglass that he would have flowing over the heads of the bar patrons. He informed me that he wanted the wave to look like it was actually moving. I suggested we drill through the structure and place our fiber optics throughout the crest of the wave and then create motion effects with chasing waves of blue and white color. Adiv liked that idea and immediately placed an order with me on the spot.

We then moved on to discuss his desire to see a giant constellation of sparkling stars in the ceiling. There was only one problem; the ceiling was solid concrete, two-foot thick, and almost impenetrable to any drill bit. I suggested to Adiv that he hang a giant fish net underneath the dome of the ceiling. Our workers could then cable-tie the fiber-optic strands throughout the fish net. Adiv liked that idea too and immediately summoned his staff to place an order with a local company that made fishnets.

We then walked outside and Adiv proclaimed that he wanted the largest and most spectacular sign in Mexico to be displayed above the front entryway. He also wanted it to be changing colors using fiber optics. Again I described how we would achieve this and again we were handed another immediate order. The only rules were that we complete everything in six weeks. I was to fly every member of my staff to Cancun the next day to start work immediately.

As a small company I did not want to commit to shipping such a tremendous amount of product to another country and without getting at least a down payment. Adiv protested that I did not trust him when I demanded a 50% deposit to be paid up front. I tried not to offend Adiv but remained firm and explained that we are just a small company and could not otherwise afford such a large undertaking. Ultimately, he paid us our 50% in cash before I left. I later learned that we were one of few contractors to get such a payment. Several contractors never got paid at all, including a few local companies even smaller than ours, like the artistic company that did the interior faux palm trees owned by the artist Patricia Zuñiga. Some of these companies folded after this project for lack of payment.

The Super Vision staff diligently worked day and night to complete the project. We not only stayed on schedule, we stayed ahead of it. The staff entertained themselves during the few hours they slept at night by playing more rounds of musical rooms in much the same manner that they did during the construction of the Coca-Cola bottle in Union City, Pa. I was also getting tired of the 18-20 hour days. One night, just after I was able to put my head on my pillow for what I hoped would be a few hours of sleep, my phone rang. It was Adiv screaming at me on the other end that the world was coming to an end and that I had to come over to his villa on the beach immediately.

"Adiv for God sake its 3 a.m., are you sure this can't wait?"

"No, no, no, no...you Americans don't understand anything? I said I need you now, that means now my friend, this can not wait?"

"What's going on Adiv, what could be so important at this hour that it is such an emergency?"

"Again you insult me with such questions! My driver is waiting for you right now in the hotel lobby, go with him and he will take you to me and you will see."

I was groggy and too tired to fight with Adiv anymore. *This better be good*, I thought as I put on my shirt and pants and headed towards the lobby.

I arrived at Adiv's villa on the beach about 15 minutes after I left my hotel room. Adiv was standing in the entryway of his home wearing nothing but a pair of red speedo style underwear and a gold chain with a solid gold camel dangling around his neck. Although the air conditioning in the home had been turned on full tilt to the point you could probably refrigerate meat in his living room, Adiv was sweating profusely. It looked like he had not slept in days and was being kept up in a frenzy of energy by some unknown substance. *Probably white powder*, I thought.

"There dying, there dying, they are all dying….you must help me my friend! You must!"

"What the hell are you talking about Adiv, who is dying?"

"You must help me Brett, they are dying, they are dying I tell you!"

"Who Adiv?" I was shouting at him by now.

"My turtles, they are dying, you must help them."

"What! I am an engineer not a doctor Adiv. What can I do?"

"No, no, no, no, you Americans are so stupid you don't know what I mean, come with me and I will show you loco gringo."

Adiv took me by the hand and walked me over to his palatial bathroom which had a large tub filled with water and sea turtles. Evidently Adiv, in one of his sleep deprivated hallucinations, had a vision that it was his mission in life to save the sea turtles. He instructed about a dozen of his staff to wait around the many sea turtle mounds on the beach for the hatchlings to crawl out and then gather them up and bring them to his bathtub for safekeeping.

Adiv was correct in his assumption that the vast majority of the hatchlings never survive even their first week at sea. Perhaps less than one in a hundred survives and grows to adulthood. The baby sea turtles small size makes them easy prey to almost any predator in the ocean. Fish and pelicans can easily swallow the small creatures within weeks after birth with just one gulp. Adiv's plan was to preserve and grow the sea turtles in his bathtub until they grew to a size that would significantly improve their survival rate when released into the ocean.

Adiv had buckets of salt water poured into his giant hot tub and he even consulted local professors about diet.

There was only one problem. Replenishing the oxygen in the hot tub. Salt water in the sea moved and aerated, salt water in Adiv's tub did not. So Adiv sent his private jet to Miami to pick up a few aeration kits. There was a shrink-wrapped pallet load of them waiting for me in the hallway outside the bathroom to assemble.

I looked at the pallet, I looked at the hot tub filled with the cute little creatures and then I looked at Adiv who by then had tears welling up in his eyes.

"OK. Adiv, I will help you do this good deed, perhaps both of us now will have a better chance of going to heaven."

As tired as I was, I just did not have the heart to say no to Adiv. Here was a man, who regardless of his past, was genuinely committed to what he felt was a good deed. Regardless of how strange his plan seemed that early morning, I admired him for it and was a very willing partner in this endeavor.

Adiv kept me going by feeding me sandwiches made by his personal chef that was on call 24 hours a day. Adiv had been reading Fit For Life and ordered his chef to prepare all his meals in accordance with the principles in that book. I dined on lettuce and cucumber sandwiches between my assemblies of aerators, pumps and filters. After completion of my work, I shook Adiv's hand and went back to my hotel room. On the ride back I said to myself over and over again: *I have to find a better way to make a living.*

After the trip to Mexico I decided that our company needed to find more stable and perhaps saner work. The custom design special effect business was exciting but it was anything but reliable. The life of going from one giant project to another in an either feast or famine mode was becoming too unpredictable and uncertain. I knew if the company was ever going to become stable or have a hope to grow beyond a few million a year in sales, we needed to develop a few standardized products that we could mass produce and sell on a regular basis through our growing domestic and overseas distribution channels.

If we could get sign manufacturers worldwide to buy our fiber-optic cable by the foot like a commodity item, and do all the custom installation on their side of the fence, we could mass produce and grow rapidly. The same could be said for pool contractors purchasing our fiber-optic cable and light sources for commercial swimming pools and electrical contractors for installation of our products on retail, commercial and residential buildings. The key was to develop an innovative new product that would not only yield a high level of light output to satisfy these customers but could also be mass produced at a low cost. For the next 12 months we dedicated ourselves to this effort.

FIFTEEN

Roy Archer flipped on the switch as David, Paul, and I watched in amazement. It worked. Our fiber-optic cable with a reflective center core, which we had hand crafted into a prototype the night before, lit up spectacularly. Even at 3 a.m. the blurry-eyed staff members watched with tremendous enthusiasm. Cheers rang out. We now knew we were on to something. Our little company that started out making "toy lights" for Disney and Universal, was finally was going to go somewhere. What we saw demonstrated that we could now pursue a multibillion-dollar market for the replacement of neon.

The landmark Coca-Cola project garnered us a lot of publicity and recognition from the industry. Orders started coming in fairly frequently and our sales started increasing exponentially. We even started making the list of the fastest growing companies in the city and state. We were proud of our achievements even though we were still a small company with little more than 20 employees towards the end of 1993. Up to now, we were still making everything by hand. Now with this great breakthrough, we believed we were finally going to grow beyond a custom manufacturer of "toy lights." Now, we just had to find a way to automate the fabrication of our new fiber-optic cable. This would not only allow us to grow, but it would allow us to lower our prices so we could meaningfully compete with a large commodity product in a much larger market.

We manufactured our first few fiber-optic cables using a rather primitive method which consisted of two garbage cans, two broom handles with fiber-optic spools attached, and two neighborhood kids running around those garbage cans unspooling the fiber into cable. If we needed longer cables, we just spaced the garbage cans farther apart. As long as those kids didn't run out of energy, or the desire to make $5 per hour, we were in business. If we got large orders with quick delivery requirements, we were in deep trouble. We knew we would eventually need to contract out our cable manufacturing to a cable company, which had the machinery to automate the tasks.

Our initial attempts to teach a few copper wire cable manufacturers to wind and jacket our cables ended mostly in failure. The tensions and abrasiveness that were tolerable for copper wire cabling operations were totally intolerable for plastic optical fiber. Most of our cable came back scratched, stressed, and strained beyond its capability to transmit light. Some percentage of each cable run came out perfectly. The cable would light up evenly and consistently, with only a few scratches along the way, for more than one hundred feet. We had to find a way to duplicate the perfect cable and eliminate the scrap. We also had a concern that our cable design was flawed in that the fibers in the center of the cable were wasted because the light from these fibers was not being "seen" outside the cable and therefore was a waste of money buried inside our product.

Roy Archer, Paul Koren, and I pondered this problem for evenings on end. We often found our best ideas after consuming two magic potions: beer and pizza. The more we consumed, the closer we got to a promising solution. Soon, these late night brainstorming sessions had grown to more than half a dozen staff members. We studied the problem over and over again but we could not find a solution.

Finally, in desperation, I went back to the broom handle

that we had used to hold our spools for winding cable. I wound the fibers around the broomstick by hand and discovered that the tighter I wound the fibers, the more light would glow off the fibers. I taped and wound fibers at various intervals around the broomstick and noticed how long the light traveled along its length and also the variations of light intensity. We knew we were on to something when we compared the old cable we had made with many more fibers to the new cable we were making by winding fewer fibers over the broom handle. If this prototype could be duplicated and mass produced, we could make a fiber-optic Sideglow cable at less than half the price of our competitors and, more importantly, within a few percentage points of the price of neon. This would allow us to "hit the big time."

There was only one problem: we had no money to buy the machines that would allow us to do this.

But we did have enough money to file a patent. The money we saved by working through the night and weekends gave us a little nest egg, which we were able to use for R&D and new product ideas. To cut costs, I typed up the initial disclosures and list of patent claims myself. A rather jovial patent attorney who was then operating out of a two-man patent office, Jim Beusse, of Hobby and Beusse, took pity on our small operation and agreed to charge us only for the hours he spent making our application presentable. The fundamental breakthrough in our technology was the concept of a reflective center core that would replace the costly fibers in the center of the cable, while directing more light outside, making the cable brighter. This later gave rise to the idea of using a hollow tube for the reflective center core that was able to dramatically improve the flexibility of our fiber-optic Sideglow cable and its ability to compete with neon in both cost and performance.

Much to our surprise, the patent office notified us of its early approval. There were few comments or objections to our claims. Apparently, we had truly broken new ground and all our patent claims were allowed by the patent office. This is extremely rare, since many new inventions that are submitted for patent have at least one or two claims objected to resulting from previous inventions known as "prior art." However, even with patent in hand, we were nowhere closer to our goal of automating the manufacturing process. We needed several million dollars to construct our own cabling and extrusion operations and, as we would later learn, hundreds of hours of testing to perfect the process we invented. The one thing the patent did do for us was give us something of value to show to Wall Street. As Roy Archer said, it was time for me to put "my tie back on and go try to sell something."

SIXTEEN

Roy grew fond of kicking me out of the factory and telling me to go out and not come back until I brought home another order. This is the way we would all make sure food was on the table the next day. It had also got us our two largest and most famous sales to date: the huge fiber-optic parade floats in the Walt Disney World SpectroMagic Parade, and the Coca-Cola sign in Times Square.

One of the great advantages of youth is naiveté; we were just too young and stupid to believe that anything was impossible. So occasionally, when naiveté is supported by persistence and hard work, the impossible does happen. In November of 1993, I put on my tie and went to Wall Street, patent and business plan in hand. Day after day I waited in offices of investment banking houses, only to be rewarded with a 10 minute meeting after a several hour wait, followed by a door being slammed behind me. There were of course a few firms, which promised us millions of dollars in investments if we could just front them a few hundred thousand dollars first for their "fees", but even I was not so naïve that I did not see through that ploy.

After fearing that my hotel bill was going to max out the limit of my credit card, I finally decided to contact the one investment banker that I knew from my past, J. Morton Davis of D.H. Blair & Co. J. Morton Davis, or "Morty," as he was called by his good friends, was a Wall-Street titan, a centamillionaire who had been featured several times in *Forbes*

Magazine. Morty started out selling vacuum cleaners door to door, finally graduating to selling securities and eventually his success at selling allowed him to buy the firm he was working for. In less than a decade, he built D.H. Blair & Co., Inc. into one of the most prolific new issue power-houses on Wall Street, taking dozens of biotech and technology companies public each year. I wasn't sure if Morty would actually see me. My previous meeting with him, while I was working at another company during my years as a student at Stanford, was brief and uneventful. Morty had taken many companies public that made headlines and millions of dollars. Our company was only a few steps out of the garage and had just earned its first million dollars in annual revenue. We were not even big enough to be a rounding error on his personal financial statement.

Much to my surprise, Morty agreed to meet with me. As I entered his multi-chandeliered and mahogany paneled office that consumed several floors at 44 Wall Street, I couldn't help but feel overwhelmed and intimidated by my surroundings. I was politely ushered from the lobby down the hallway leading to Morty's office by a delightful woman named Debbie Cook. Her glow and good humor calmed the fluttering butterflies that were now racing around in my stomach. In Morty's office, I saw pictures of him with past and present presidents, boxing champions, and famous actors. As I reached over to shake his hand, I almost tripped over one of the many sculptures and awards that adorned his office. Fortunately for me, Morty found my clumsiness amusing, he smiled and asked me to take a seat.

I immediately launched into an impassioned speech about our company, our products, and our patents. I explained that the market for neon, although perhaps not as glamorous as the software or personal computer business, was a real, existing, $3 billion market, which was ripe for a new technology that would offer a more energy efficient, safe, and maintenance free alternative. I pointed to our patent as the method by which we could make this technology cost effective and competitive, and outlined why we needed the money and how we would invest it.

By the time the meeting was over, I had a commitment for a $5 million public offering and an initial private placement of half a million dollars that would be raised in advance so I could pay the legal, accounting, and SEC filing fees necessary to launch the public offering. This would all be realized while leaving myself and our staff still in control of the majority of our stock and voting rights. "You seem like a good jockey to me, kid. I don't bet on horses; I bet on jockeys," Morty said, as he walked me out of his office adding, "just try not to fall on your ass with my money in your pocket." It became clear to me at that point that I had not won over Morty with my sales pitch. We were a small deal for him that normally would not justify his time. He just decided he liked me and he was both wealthy and generous enough to be able to give me a shot at making my dream come true. After the money was raised, the "not fall on your ass" part would become the greatest challenge. We had to find a way to deliver on our promise to Morty and to our new shareholders.

One of the greatest thrills of my business career was the walk I took from D.H. Blair's office in March of 1994, with a $5 million check in my pocket to deposit at the offices of Republic National Bank. I thought that the smile on my face must have betrayed me to everyone in New York City that I was carrying a check for $5 million. As I walked, I kept holding the check in my pocket, desperately trying to subdue my urge to take it out and read it again. I just couldn't believe it was real. I deposited the check at Republic Bank, owned then by Edmund Safra who was related to Maisa's stepmother. Republic agreed to wire the funds to our local bank account for a small fee. There were no lavish parties or memorable celebrations after the successful completion of our public offering. Morty's "not fall on your ass" warning was now ringing even louder in my head.

I flew back on my usual supersaver coach seat that night and the next morning the staff at Super Vision were back at work sifting through cabling and extrusion machine manufacturers' catalogs as well as reading the back sections of industry trade journals for used equipment and bankruptcy auction sales. We wanted to make sure we were able to make every cent of that $5 million count and last as long as possible. Until we planned for the delivery of our new machine, we stayed in our existing premises. There would be no plush carpeted floors or executive suites. Our capital investment at the time consisted of the removal of a wall partition. We kept the money in the bank or invested in our equipment. The discipline of being poor and self-funded in prior years maintained our humility and frugality, which later insured our survival in the years to come. Most dot.com venture funded companies that went public often drowned in their own excesses, making money vanish faster than Houdini. We did not want to join them.

SEVENTEEN

In 1994, our first year as a publicly held company, we had two landmark events. First, I was listed in the business journals as the lowest paid CEO of a publicly held company in the State of Florida, an honor I went on to hold for several years. Second, we were able to purchase and install our entire fiber-optic cabling and extrusion system well below the budget that we had projected in our initial offering's use of funds proposal. Production and delivery initially seemed to be on schedule, but not without several mishaps that led to a major panic and another round of all night trouble shooting.

Although the cabling machine would not scratch or scar the fiber-optic cable, somehow it would not allow the finished cable to generate the brightness that we experienced in our hand made prototypes. Customers were noticing this and rejecting cable by the pallet load. At one point, David Vaughn and I took up residence on the second floor loft we had built above the cabling line. David would hold the fiber-optic cable that we had just produced at one end and place it inside the light source to light it up, while I would crawl down the other end with a light meter to measure the intensity and the noticeable drop off.

David and I would take turns crawling up and down the cable so our knees would not give out. We would often work for hours without leaving that loft. Quite often the alarm would be set by staff members who didn't realize that we were still in the building. Several times our movements would later set off the alarm, drawing visits from the local sheriff. On a few occasions, David, a tall, muscular, black man with an immaculately shaved head and a big diamond studded earring, would be staring down the barrel of a sheriff's gun while I tried to offer an explanation for our nocturnal activities. The reports that were gleefully shared by the staff became known as "Brett and David's Excellent Adventures."

For a time it seemed as if we were heading for disaster. Although our new machine was able to avoid the old copper wire machinery's problems of scarring and scratching, it was not able to duplicate the light output achieved with the small percentage of "good cable" we were able to make with the old machinery. We had spent in excess of $1.2 million with one of the world's largest glass fiber-optic cabling manufacturers to build the world's first automated plastic fiber-optic cabling process. Our results were succeeding in making nothing more than the cleanest low performance cable in the industry. We had already lost our largest customer for our cable to date, Philips Lighting in France, and we were about to lose several dozen other major customers and distributors. We had to do something, and quickly.

Roy, Paul, David, and I decided to retrace every step in the initial handmade and contract manufacturing process and identify and isolate each individual procedure. After we identified each individual variable and tested its effect, we hoped we would be able to identify what we were doing wrong or perhaps not doing at all. It turned out that the latter was the problem more than the former. We learned that by buying the most sophisticated cabling machine that was geared to handling the most delicate of glass optical fibers used for telecommunications, we were not generating the torque and back twist that we actually needed. This did not allow us to put the proper amount of strain or stress on the plastic fibers to cause them to micro bend or leak out light along the length of the cable. Without the proper tension and twisting, the result gave us a dull glow along the length of the cables. We learned that with the sophisticated cabling machine we were actually overcompensating in solving one problem at the expense of creating another. We were now going in the opposite direction of where we should have been going with our product. We had to rebuild and redesign our machine.

We finally learned the right number of grams of tension when Roy brought a fish scale with him when he flew up to visit our old subcontractors to test the tension generated on the copper wire cabling machines. The key was not to go over these tension levels even by a few grams, for the result would render more of the useless cable we experienced earlier. The good news was that our electronically controlled machines were able to record and maintain the consistency and accuracy that the older mechanically controlled machines could not. This allowed us to be able to routinely duplicate "good cable." We devised a plan to customize the new machines we bought with a complete set of weights, tensioning devices, dies, and pulleys that we crafted together to allow us to achieve the proper tensions and twisting angles known as "micro bend" or "back twist" that we needed. Before implementation on our new machines, we built a small mock up and again tested the tension and pull weight on Roy's trusty fish scales. We tested, measured, and re-tested over and over again. We knew we had to rebuild the machines immediately. Customers were getting impatient waiting for their orders to be filled and the costs of generating scrap cable were impacting our financial statements.

We had a plan to accomplish the goal of rebuilding our machines in only a few weeks. It involved moving up several workers from other departments to help the cable department in that effort. One of those workers was a recent hire named Jack Caruso.

EIGHTEEN

෧෨

Jack Caruso was introduced to me by my wife, Maisa. Maisa has a heart large enough to share with everyone and everything in need of help. She would often bring home stray dogs, stray cats, and turtles that she found imperiling themselves in the middle of roadway. She also one day brought home Caruso. Caruso was out of work, and did not have money to keep a roof over his head nor food on the table for himself and his daughter. His wife by now had already left him. Life had treated him very unfairly. The neighbor at the adjacent town home had told Maisa of his plight and asked if she could find work for him. Before I knew it, we had "loads of repairs" that needed attention. And so, Caruso came over almost every other morning for several weeks cleaning leaves out of the rain gutters, and patching and painting scratches on the wall from other furry friends Maisa would rescue. After several weeks, I started noticing the same jobs would be done over again, at which point Maisa raised the question with me: "Brett, why don't you find Jack a job at your office?" At the time our business was still small, we had only 12 employees and did not really need someone extra, but the same pleading eyes that had convinced me to invite every lost creature into our home now implored me to bring this lost soul into our company. As usual, Maisa won.

Caruso turned out to be a very hard worker and a quick

study. He had a photographic memory. After reading a manual, he could repeat information both by page number and by paragraph. He quickly rose from his initial $5 an hour shop laborer position to an $8 an hour post on the light source assembly line and later to a $12 an hour day shift operator in our cable department. Caruso proved very mechanically adept at his assembly line roles and always was vocal about wanting more challenges and opportunities to move up at the company. The disaster we were having with our cabling machine provided yet another opportunity for quick promotion and a large salary increase as cable department manager. He finally had an opportunity and was determined to prove to himself that at Super Vision he could rise from the repeated setbacks he had experienced with other companies in the past. From that point on, Caruso would refer to the cabling machine as "his baby."

Caruso often worked into the early hours of the morning implementing changes on the cabling machinery, expressing excitement about getting "his baby" finally running again. He was extremely capable, if not brilliant, with fixing and operating the cabling machinery. But his excitement began to boil over in unexpected ways. With his increasing power and responsibility in the company Caruso became increasingly tyrannical to the staff that worked under him. It was "his way" or "no way." His subordinates started complaining that Caruso was starting to play the role of "dictator rather than co-worker."

But Caruso had an equal interest in playing more roles than the one he had been assigned. He never obtained an engineering degree, a shortfall he regretted deeply, but he would read engineering books and claim his knowledge allowed him to operate on a "Ph.D. level" in engineering. He sometimes read law books in his spare time and became the self-appointed in-house lawyer, often trying to advocate changes in our worker's compensation policies, OSHA

(Occupational Safety and Health Administration) regulation adherence, and shareholder publications. He would cite from memory chapter and verse from the law books he had read just as deftly as he would cite maintenance procedures from the machinery repair manuals. As Caruso's income and importance to the company grew, so did his ego and so did the number of additional roles he assigned himself. Then came the stories. Stories of his former service in the military where he was assigned to Special Forces or assassination squads, stories of the secret work that he had done in the past on the Lantern and Patriot missiles with Lockheed Martin before being laid off. Caruso started to reinvent himself as well as reinvent his past. There were other outlandish stories he told too, but we just didn't pay attention to them, we simply wrote them off as another part of his creative eccentricity.

We were not entirely surprised when he showed up at the company Christmas party with a woman that we had never met, whom he announced was his new wife. The woman was a relative of another factory employee. Caruso had been introduced to her only a few weeks earlier. The two decided to marry. She immediately moved in with Caruso and his daughter from his previous marriage. He later hired his daughter to work at Super Vision as well as his daughter's fiancée.

The staff thought that this new addition to Caruso's life would calm him down and bring him back to earth. We had hopes that married life would be an improvement for Caruso. We later learned that our hopes were not well founded.

NINETEEN

True to form, Super Vision solved the cabling
machine problem in a timely manner. Weeks of hard work
and dumpster loads of pizza boxes later we completed our
task and started shipping the best quality cable we had ever
made in a consistent and productive manner. What we
learned was the key processes necessary to implementing
what we patented. None of this information had been disclosed in our initial published patent, we simply focused on
the design of the cable itself, which would be obvious to anyone who looked at our cable. As for the process, if it was difficult for us to finally discover how to make consistently
bright and flawless cable, then it would be next to impossible for our future competitors to do so as well. We kept this
information as a trade secret, known to only four or five key
staff members. A trade secret is a proprietary process that is
not published or shared outside the company in order to
prevent that process from being used or duplicated by the
competition. Patents, on the other hand, are either proprietary products or processes that are published. A patent
only gives you protection if you are able to file a suit and win
a judgment against an infringer. It does not stop someone
from copying your idea. There was a joke back at the engineering department at Stanford that the definition of "Chinese blueprint" was a "U.S. Patent." We were therefore
encouraged to patent new products but keep the processes
used to make these products secret.

Once we caught up with our order backlog, Roy, Jack, Paul, David, and I rewarded ourselves with one weekend day off. I slept the entire day.

After the repair of the cabling machine, sales started to skyrocket. The first full year following our public offering, we grew from $1.4 million to $2.5 million. The next year, 1996, our sales grew to $6.8 million and we generated in excess of $356,000 in operating profit. In 1997, our sales grew to $9 million with $402,000 in operating profit. We had distributors from Reykjavik to Kuala Lumpur and our products were being sold on every continent. Our stock climbed from its initial $3 dollars per share to more than $10.

One Fortune 500 company, Cooper Industries, purchased 10% of our outstanding shares for an additional investment of $2 million and started to market our products through its lighting division. Another company, Hayward Industries, the world's largest pool product manufacturer, purchased another 10% of our newly issued stock for $2 million and marketed our fiber-optic cable products to pool builders for swimming pool lighting. I had also decided to set aside 10% of the company's stock for our employees' stock option program. To this day every single employee is either a shareholder or optionholder in the company. As our sales and earning grew, our parking lot started to fill and even a few of the employees were able to purchase new cars with the profits from their stock options.

Roy moved from a trailer to a new house, Paul bought a new house and moved in with his fiancée, I moved from my apartment to a town home and later purchased my own house. David rolled up in a pre-owned Mercedes that he had detailed in gold trim. Caruso bought a new van with a company loan against his stock options. We were now nearing almost 90 employees and things were looking very positive for us. We were starting to succeed; we were not "falling on our ass."

In 1996, Super Vision began planning the construction of its new manufacturing facility. By then we had so badly outgrown our current facility that we had to work from two buildings. The three-mile drive back and forth to both facilities became unnerving for many of our management team. We longed to be together again under the same roof. We also were tired of moving, having had more than five moves and expansions in just the last five years. We hoped to build a place where we could stay awhile and grow, but most importantly, where we could all be together.

In 1997, we moved into our new 80,000 square foot facility. This was the first new factory of our own. The entire staff entered the new building in absolute awe as they carted in their cardboard boxes with their personal effects. You could see the pride evident on their faces. The day we moved in was a little like Christmas and New Year's day all rolled into one for us. Roy wandered around the warehouse for hours, not knowing where to set up machinery first, he seemed both lost and amazed. "Sure looks big Brett, you better go out and get a ton of more orders to fill this place up," reissuing his constant warning for me to sell so we could pay for each new expansion.

As our monthly sales grew by leaps and bounds, it became obvious that we would soon reach the $10 million annualized sales level. However, several of our directors determined that the company might have outgrown my initial entrepreneurial management skills and I agreed. Not wanting to be one of those entrepreneurs who held back the future of his own company, I decided along with our Board of Directors to hire professional managers. The company by now was several times removed from a garage. Our shares were traded publicly, we had 10K's and 10Q's to file with the SEC (Securities and Exchange Commission) and we had a large staff now requiring the post of a human resources manager and many other managerial requirements that were beyond my level of sophistication. We brought several new professional managers, MBAs, CPAs, and PhDs, and they in turn brought in more.

In January 1998, I stepped aside as president in favor of one of these managers. I changed my title from president and CEO to chairman of the board and "Minister of Fun." After the dramatic changes that these managers made in our company, my title became as appropriate as the name I had previously given my boat. Things at Super Vision took a turn for the worse, it became anything else but "Fun."

TWENTY

By mid 1998, our sales, our company, and our profitability hit a brick wall. After almost 10 years of consistent annual sales increases, Super Vision had its first sales decline in history. The effect of the sales decline was like a car wreck: first the big crash and then the dazed stumble out of the car wondering what happened and where to start picking up the pieces. Almost overnight our sales in Asia evaporated. Projects that we had bid and believed we were destined to sell disappeared. We had to drop prices just to stay in the bidding process on jobs. Often the pricing pressures would erode our gross profit margin to near zero. The company starting to hemorrhage cash and red ink.

The professional managers that we had hired just a year earlier to run the company started to call for "reorganization" of the company based on our falling fortunes. They got their wish; they completely changed the corporate culture of our entrepreneurial company. We had our first layoffs in company history. This was perhaps the most demoralizing thing that happened to us. We had always prided ourselves on being a growth company and job creator. The fact that we had to now collapse our staff back to 60 was a terrible blow to our morale and self-image.

By June 1998, many of our top engineers and key employees started to leave. They realized the cuts were necessary, but they were demoralized by the new management. The "entrepreneurial spark" at Super Vision was dimming along with our falling fortunes. Steve Faber, one of the first degreed engineers that we had hired right out of college left in frustration, and Richard Heiner, our marketing director, gave notice. Jack Caruso, the man who helped us install and retrofit our cabling machine, walked out the door soon after. He told me before his departure that the reason for his leaving was to avoid paying alimony to his second wife due to their bitterly contested divorce, but somehow this explanation did not seem right to me. I tried to keep Caruso from leaving, for he was key to our manufacturing process. "Why jettison your career and your salary, just to spite your wife and harm your family," I told Caruso. "Stay on, you'll continue to earn more and you will be able to provide for all your obligations." I even referred to the time that my family had helped Caruso in his time of need, and questioned him for now abandoning us during ours, but to no avail. Caruso had already made up his mind. While I did not fully believe his reason for leaving, I thought he too had just become disenchanted and somehow in his mind this explanation was an easier way out for him.

The greatest blow to hit me personally was when Paul Koren walked into my office with tears in his eyes and told me that it was time for him to leave. Paul's departure actually came a few months prior to Jack Caruso. Paul had been one of the initial five founding employees of the company. I had a lot of personal, as well as business history with him. For me, Paul's departure was like a sign that the end was near. As Paul came in to hand me his key, he told me that it was not the drop in our financial fortunes, but the lack of passion and direct involvement he saw in the new management that made him come to this decision many months earlier. I understood what Paul meant: the new management may have been successful in their previous positions in larger companies, but they completely lacked the entrepreneurial spirit. They only knew how to manage by the book.

"We are not a family anymore, Brett, we are just a business," Paul announced somberly. "All these MBAs have succeeded in doing was to take us from a chaotic success to a well-organized failure."

Paul just didn't see a place for him at Super Vision any more. As I listened to him tell me of his new plans to start his own business, a waterfall company he would name Oasis, I had visions of our early days together in our garage and the excitement we had developing our first new fiber-optic pool lighting products together. Paul was our most entrepreneurial employee with a knack for taking an idea scribbled on a napkin one day and turning it into a product by the next afternoon. To me, Paul was part of the very heart and soul of our company. My heart sank as he said his final goodbyes. I wished him well in his new venture. Part of me wanted to follow him out the door.

TWENTY-ONE

Amid all the anguish we felt over the departures of key staff members, we also started to experience a wave of repeated breakdowns in our machinery and mysterious disappearances of both inventory and equipment. After several repeated explosions in the cabling machine, Roy Archer showed me conclusive evidence that the problems we were experiencing with both our cabler and extruder were not just bad luck. It was deliberate sabotage. The accounting department by now confirmed that shortages in our inventory exceeded $90,000. To make matters even worse, the calls I was getting from several of our overseas distributors who were being solicited by some mysterious competitor started to accelerate. Our distributors were now being methodically called with great frequency to switch over their purchases of Super Vision products to some new company we never heard of based in China. All our attempts to determine who was behind this company ended in failure. With each new entity we discovered representing our products we felt we would discover a new path to the perpetrators. With each new investigation we discovered yet another trail that led to nowhere. Whoever was behind this was very adept at setting up corporate shells.

There was a period of several days where the machinery failures and the phone calls from distributors came in like an avalanche. I felt almost crushed by the weight of what was happening to us. At times I felt as if it were even difficult to breath. I could not openly show my concerns to my already nervous staff for fear that panic would set in and our slide downward would go into a freefall.

However the effects of the counterfeiting and sabotage were beginning to take their toll on me. After one particularly bad day, during my drive home on one sultry June night in 1998, I broke into a cold sweat. I was angry and frustrated. *Who was doing this to our company? Who was sabotaging our machinery, stealing our technology, and counterfeiting our products?*

As angry, frustrated, and victimized as I felt then during that drive home, I didn't realize that there was someone else that in fact was actually paying a much higher price for the acts of these criminals and thieves. Had I known earlier what was happening to my employee, Mike Jacobs, I might not have wasted so much time feeling sorry for myself.

TWENTY-TWO

Two thugs smashed Mike Jacob's head against the bathroom stall. It impacted with a loud crash that echoed down the adjacent hallway.

As Mike tried to rise to his feet, the thugs grabbed his hair and again smashed his head against the metal door of the stall. They demanded that Mike never talk. Mike tried to respond, while trying to maintain consciousness, that he would not talk to anyone. The two thugs told Mike what would happen to him if he ever said a word about what he had seen. Mike looked back at his attackers as best he could through his swollen eyes and promised not to divulge their secret. He could only see their blurred silhouettes now, one was tall and thin, the other short and stocky. The thugs grinned at him mockingly, but they weren't finished, they punched and kicked him a few more times as he laid sprawled across the floor. Mike tried to roll over on his side so his back would shield his chest and stomach from the blows. As he faced the wall he struggled to get up.

Mike stumbled to his knees, as his head continued to swell with pain and his eyes watered to a blur. Mike was now growing numb with pain. He started to feel his fear fade away as a compelling curiosity poured over him. *All this for only a few stolen light sources and a couple of coils of cable,* he asked himself. This was petty theft at best compared to what they were subjecting him to now. Mike sensed that there might be someone or something that these two thugs feared more than the fact that he witnessed their theft at work. Mike began to become emboldened by this thought; perhaps he had discovered their weakness. The two thugs noticed the change in Mike as if he were now telegraphing his thoughts to his attackers. As Mike pulled himself up to his knees and began to stand, Mike leered back at his attackers with a defiant smirk. It was as if the two thugs were no longer important now. Mike's new demeanor now made the attackers uneasy. They started backing away from him.

"Don't you get any ideas now Mikey," said one of the thugs with a heavily accented voice. "Keep your damn mouth shut....you're not the only one who can get hurt."

Mike now understood what they meant. His self-confident smirk and defiant stare quickly faded. The two thugs, sensing that their point had been made, slowly backed away while casting their sinister smiles in Mike's direction. Mike sat down next to the commode, shaken and pale.

Mike had been enduring these beatings for the past three months. Several times a week, whenever they felt Mike needed a "reminder," the two thugs would follow him into the bathroom or outside the building when he took a smoking break. Sometimes it was only a few harsh words and a push or a shove, other times far worse. The message was always the same. Mike Jacobs would not talk. Their secret was safe. That is, until they crossed that certain line which even Mike could not bear.

Mike was 19. He was a production worker on an assembly line for Super Vision. He was a white kid with short, blond hair and medium build who grew up on the rough side of town. He had to rely on himself for support from an early age. He dressed the part of a kid from the hood, wearing baggy jeans, sometimes with exposed boxers, and several layers of baggy shirts. However the tough outer appearance was nothing more than a layer of protection to hide the soul of an honest, kind, and sensitive young man. Mike had very few material possessions at this point in his life, but he worked hard and, together with his fiancée, was saving to get a place of their own. Mike Jacobs did have one great treasure in his life, his love for Teresa. Mike and Teresa were living together and planned to marry as soon as they could save enough to buy their own home. Mike held down two jobs, as did Teresa. He worked assembly during two shifts at two companies; Teresa worked at the mall during the day and as a telephone operator at night. The two did not go out much; choosing instead to save every penny for their dream.

Teresa was a stunning brunette with long, flowing, silken hair and deep, dark eyes. While Mike worshipped the ground she walked on, Teresa loved Mike for his selfless devotion. Mike would endure anything for Teresa; he had already endured three months of relentless beatings to keep her safe. The thugs made it clear to him earlier that she might be next if he informed company management of their misdeeds.

One day the two thugs made a big mistake, they crossed a line with Mike, they went past a point where he no longer cared or feared for his own safety. Rumor had it that Mike was planning to tell the company president the whole story. The thugs concluded more pressure was necessary. They followed Teresa home that night.

Teresa noticed the bright high beams from the car trailing behind her. The black Mustang had been following her at a slow crawl as she walked across the parking lot to the front door of her apartment. Worried before, her fear now grew to terror as the lights flashed. As she walked towards the door of her apartment, she nervously fumbled for her keys as she heard the car door open and two pair of footsteps approach.

Teresa's hands started to shake as she sensed the two men were just behind her. They shoved her against the doorframe. Her breathing became paralyzed by her fear.

Their ominous message was delivered. There was no mistaking what would happen to her. They told her in detail.

After they left, Teresa finally found her key in the bottom of her purse. She had difficulty putting the key in the lock, her hands still shaking badly and her eyes almost blinded by tears. Mike found her still shaking and crying when he arrived home.

Mike and Teresa moved out that night, staying instead at the home of a friend. The next morning, Mike bought a gun.

Mike told only one person that he had bought a gun, a staff member he liked and respected named Michelle. Michelle was a devout Christian and member of the Army National Guard. As a member of the National Guard, Michelle knew guns and knew what they could do in untrained hands. As a born-again Christian, Michelle felt she knew the Lord and she had to help her friend and co-worker. She decided to tell the company founder and chairman.

TWENTY-THREE

Michelle strode into my office: "Mike Jacobs has bought a gun."

I didn't take the news very seriously at first: "So is he going to ask for a raise or something?"

Michelle expressed her concern that Mike was being threatened and he was more likely to blow his own brains out in the process of protecting himself. To prevent that, she asked me to teach him how to use it.

"Brett, could you please take him to your rifle range and give him some training?"

I told Michelle that I thought we had a bigger issue here than training. "Michelle, I think we need to find out why he had to buy the gun in the first place."

Michelle did not know who was threatening Mike, but she insisted that I not take the gun away from him. "Mike's scared and he trusted me, if you take his gun away he will feel like I betrayed him."

"Michelle, I would never disarm a man who was trying to protect his family. What I want to know is who is threatening Mike?"

Michelle could not tell me, she had not gotten that far with Mike. She'd heard only about the threats and the gun. For her that was enough at the time. She again urged me to take Mike to my rifle range and talk to him.

"Brett, if you can gain his trust, he will eventually feel secure enough to tell you what you want to know."

"OK. Michelle, have Mike meet me during lunch."

Mike entered my office just around noon. He did not say a word. I grabbed my keys and Mike followed me down-stairs towards the car.

As we left the building and entered the parking lot, I asked Mike if he had his gun with him. He hesitated in his response at first, he looked at me as if to read whether or not I would just try to take it away for him. He finally nod-ded and told me it was in his car. We hopped in my car and I swerved around the parking lot, stopping so that my trunk was just behind the trunk of Mike's car. Mike got out of the car and popped open his trunk. Under a blanket beside the spare tire was a sawed off, pump barrel shotgun.

As I looked at the shotgun and the boxes of shells he had bought, I understood how real the threat to Mike must have been. In a nervous attempt at humor, I asked him whether he planned to, "take out a whole flock of geese or something?" It was the only time I saw Mike smile, but his smile faded fast and then he just shrugged and put the gun in the back of my car.

We pulled into Chick-Fil-A and grabbed two sandwiches and fries for the road, figuring it would be quicker to eat in the car on the way to the shooting range. Mike said he needed to be back before his shift started again.

At the range, it was clear that Mike did not know one end a shotgun from the other. I demonstrated how to load, pump, aim, and fire. I then told Mike that a standing target at the end of the range bore no resemblance whatsoever to the stressful situation created by a real-live person coming at him intending to harm either him or his family. Mike prac-ticed firing, pumping another round in the chamber, and firing again. As the target moved on the track from down-range towards him, his confidence began to build. I short-ened the distance of the target from him and hence the time it would take for the target to reach him. Mike leveled his shotgun at the target and without being flustered, continued to pump and fire until the target reached within a few feet of him.

At that point, I was confident that Mike was more likely to shoot an attacker than himself. I asked him to tell me who was bothering him.

Again there was silence.

I felt that Mike was not ready to open up while standing in this unfamiliar range. I patted Mike on the back and told him it was time to go. We could talk more in the car on the way back to work.

We placed our guns into the back of my car. As the door closed and the car started, Mike turned toward me and began to open up:

"Brett, two guys from the company have been threatening me"

"Who Mike?"

Silence. This time he couldn't even look at me. I sensed I was losing him.

"OK, Mike, let's not worry about who, let's just talk why. What do these guys want from you?"

"They just want me to keep my mouth shut."

"About what?"

More silence, as Mike stared straight ahead through the windshield.

"They followed my girl home."

"Teresa?"

"Yeah, Teresa." Mike looked down as he said her name, his face flushing with anger. "These guys are bad, Brett, they are gang bangers. If they don't hurt her themselves I'm worried that they know people who would do it for them. They said they know crack heads that will kill anyone for 300 bucks."

Mike told me that he saw two guys from work tossing perfectly good products, still in fresh boxes, out the shipping door and into the dumpster. He also saw one of them throw out what looked like new file boxes filled with files as well. Mike's only offense was that he was unlucky enough to happen to walk by them as these two thugs were engaging in their illegal activities. Both offenders initially panicked, they later started their practice of following Mike into the bathroom and intimidating him to keep him quiet.

"Mike why didn't you tell me about this earlier?"

"I was worried about what they might do to Teresa."

Mike didn't mind what they did to him as long as they stayed away from Teresa, but when they went after Teresa, he decided he would have to take matters into his own hands. I implored Mike to tell me who these people were, assuring him that I would see to it that he and his fiancée would be safe. I offered to put them up at the hotel down the street until I could have these people arrested and put in prison.

Mike continued his silent stare out the windshield. After a long pause, Mike finally blurted out:

"Ron Simon and Jose Cruz."

"From shipping?"

"Yeah."

I drove Mike Jacobs directly to the Adams Mark Hotel, at the Florida Mall, a few blocks from our office. I checked him in and told him to call Teresa and let her know they would be spending their nights there until I dealt with Simon and Cruz. Mike's biggest worry was who was going to tell his shift supervisor so he would not lose his job. I told him I would take care of it.

When I left Mike at the hotel, I did not want to show the extent of my anger. Mike had been through enough, I did not want to rattle him any further with my own fury.

These bastards, I thought, *preying on a young guy trying to start a family and life for himself.* I identified with Mike. Two decades earlier I could have been Mike while I was working my way through college and holding down two jobs to pay tuition. *This was not going to happen in my factory, not on my watch,* I thought while parking my car in the lot of our facility. As I walked toward the warehouse, I started having visions of bullies from my past and what I had to do to defend my family.

TWENTY-FOUR
༆༅

I had a particular dislike for bullies and thieves. I did not grow up in a wealthy, gated community where I could safely engage in liberal philosophical debates on crime and punishment. After my father died we moved to a two-room apartment. My mother, Renee Kingstone, provided for three boys as a nurse, lifting patients and changing bedpans, at a nursing home in New York. Criminals preyed on the working class, as a result we did not share in the idea that these criminals should be "understood;" we believed they should be punished.

My father and grandfather also had me adhere to a strict family code of honor. I was expected to stand in for my younger brothers if an older or stronger bully tried to prey on them. Several times my father sent me to school to defend my brothers and several times my father was called to the office by the school principal to pick me up after my expulsion. My brothers knew that if they were ever threatened, they were to either stand up for each other or report the bully to our father. As the oldest brother, I was the one most often called upon to settle the score.

On the first night that I came home on summer break from my first year away at college, I saw a large, white Lincoln Continental following me home. As I left the sidewalk and began to walk across the street, only two blocks from my home, the car gunned its engine and sped up to cut me off midway across the street. The side door handle grazed against my waist as the car passed by me. I regained my composure enough to pound on the back of the trunk as the car swerved past me. The car stopped just a few feet in front of me. The driver side window rolled down and a large, young man in a crew cut and tank top emerged from the passenger side door.

The driver and passenger both grinned at me in a strange, but menacing way. It was as if they knew who I was and now were going to finish their business with me. As the large passenger with the crew cut approached me, I decided I would try to talk my way out of a fight. Although I was confident in my ability to defend myself, this guy was still much larger than me and I had no idea if the driver had a knife or gun in the car. It was dark and it would be difficult to see if they reached for a weapon. I felt that if these guys were determined to hurt me, even if the fist-fight went my way, things could eventually escalate beyond my control.

When the passenger grabbed me by the arm I told him that I didn't want any trouble. Again he smiled as if he had dealt with me before and now was just going to dish out some more pain to me. I again told him that all I wanted to do was to walk home. He turned away and smiled at the driver, still maintaining his grip on my arm, and then swung his arm around and tried to sucker punch me in the face. I was able to deflect the first blow so it only grazed the side of my cheek. As he released his grip on my other arm and pulled his fist back to strike me again, I realized I had no options with this guy. I started to feel my body boil with anger with the thought that this guy was simply planning to use me as a punching bag to show off to his friend. I did not like being his captive and I did not like being used as a toy.

I moved in closer to cut off the distance between us. I struck at his throat with the ridge of my hand before he was able to deliver his blow. As he crumpled forward, I grabbed both his arms for balance and delivered several kicks to his face and midsection. His head snapped back. The look on his face was puzzling, the guy seemed more surprised by my reaction rather than fearful of my attack. As I released my grip on his arms and stepped forward to strike again, he caught his balance and ran around the back of the car to escape.

The burly passenger tried to pull the handle of the passenger side door, but the door would not open. The terrified driver had rolled up the window and had locked all the doors during the fight. There was a brief comical moment as the passenger started screaming at the driver to open the door. He now seemed angrier at his partner than he was with me. I gave chase hoping to scare him away while he ran around the front of the car screaming at the driver to open the door. The driver finally complied and as the passenger door was swung open the passenger yelled for the driver to hand him "the knife." At that point I decided to run away in the opposite direction of my house, not wanting to confront two-armed men and also not wanting to lead them to my home which would endanger my family.

I told the story to my father the next day. I was curious who these guys were and what they wanted from me. I was haunted by the fact that they seemed somehow to know me yet, I had no idea what they wanted. Days later, after a few discussions with neighborhood kids, I heard that someone had seen a guy with his face covered with bruises. He had gone around asking who did this to him. He was sure it could not be my brother Monte, for he had threatened and bullied him several times before without a challenge. The young man's name was Ricky and his accomplice who was driving that night was a neighborhood punk known as "Piglet." Ricky learned that Monte's older brother had returned from college and that's who he had tangled with, mistaking him in the darkness of night for Monte.

My brother told me that Ricky routinely picked on him

while I was away at college. The bullying intensified during the summer. Monte did not dare tell our father what was happening for fear that he would send me against Ricky, who my brother thought was bigger and stronger than me. Although I would have wanted to know in advance, I respected my brother for trying to protect me. He knew my father's code of honor; it was a certainty I would be sent up against Ricky. Monte feared for the outcome, just as I had feared Ricky's initial approach. What Ricky did not count on was that ultimately my hatred of bullies exceeded my fear. What Ron Simon was about to discover was that my father's code lived on long after my father's death.

As I walked towards the shipping department I saw Michelle and Ron Simon working at the shipping desk. For some reason, Jose Cruz was not at work that day. Ron smiled and nodded his head to me in acknowledgment as I approached. My icy stare quickly made the smile fade to a frown.

I grabbed Ron by the throat and dragged him across the factory floor. He continually tried to deny harming or threatening anyone. My disgust with him only grew as he proved to be as accomplished a liar as he was as a thief. As I pulled him by the arm and throat up the stairs, Simon did not even try to defend himself. *How very true of bullies*, I thought; *they are not as capable on the receiving end as they are in delivering*. I threw him in my office and slammed the door shut. There I could get more information from him against Cruz and whoever else was helping them. The police could deal with both of them later, after I was finished. At the time, I had no idea what the confession I was about to extract would lead to. I was angry and all I wanted was justice.

Two hours and several pages of written confession later, I escorted Ron Simon to my car for the drive to the Orange County Jail on 33rd Street. In the car, I called ahead to the sheriff's office to say I was bringing someone in. Two deputies, Detectives Kelly Boaz and Dave Bareno, were going to meet me by the side door of the administration building next to the jail. As I drove Ron to the prison, I could not help but think that I still did not have the full story. Simon implicated his accomplice, Jose Cruz, but there still were unanswered questions as to what they did with the stolen products and who sold it for them.

I pulled into the driveway of the Orange County Corrections Center and looked over at Simon. This guy is certainly smart enough to steal the products, I thought, but not smart enough to sell them. After all, you just don't sell fiber-optic cable and light sources on a street corner like hot watches. There had to be someone much higher up who was moving the product. Perhaps someone from inside our company, I thought. Ron Simon claimed not to know; I didn't know whether or not to believe him.

TWENTY-FIVE

With five of my top seven initial founding employees gone for more than a year I started feeling very lonely at Super Vision. Our new president did not inspire me either and I felt as if I didn't belong in the company anymore. The new president sensed this as well and at one time during August of 1999, he came to my office to discuss other "options I should consider for my future." It was clear at that point that either I had to leave the company or take back control in what would be a very bloody coup. The new president had installed new directors in almost every department that were loyal to him and in order to remove him, I had to remove them.

As the weeks passed and the company's red ink intensified, I started getting calls at my home by some of our long time employees in middle management complaining of screw ups at almost every level that I had not been previously aware of. Angel Newsome in customer service called me at home and threatened to leave if I did not fire that "idiot" in charge of engineering.

When I finally had lunch alone with the engineers, some confessed that they were scared to tell me their true opinion for fear they would get fired, others just gave up and were sending their resumes out. Three out of the three new product developments that the engineering director had initiated were becoming black holes for cash with no hope in sight for production and sale.

As each delivery deadline passed, we seemed to build up more component inventory but did not have a salable product. Our inventory swelled from $1.5 million to almost $3 million. Much of it was garbage because it was dedicated to new products that we had yet to perfect and sell. At the same time, factory staff started grumbling about management and a few loyal people in administration began calling me at home, they questioned the direction we were heading. It was clear I had to come back and take over the company again, but I knew I needed help to do this. I could not possibly fire all those people that were hired by the new president and fill all those responsibilities myself. The combination of falling sales worldwide, coupled with our internal problems from within, made my head spin.

As I was pondering my decision to take over again as president and CEO, I started having visions again of working 24/7 and being away from my family. I worried about the toll it would take on my marriage. I told Maisa what I had to do and knew what sacrifices I would have to make.

"We are going to see a lot less of each other, Maisa," I warned.

I had enjoyed the extra time I got to spend with them since I stepped down from the president's position. I told Maisa it was my obligation to save the company but again warned her that I would now always be late for dinner and working late into the evening for the next few years. Now, just as our lives together seemed to be on track, I dreaded having to ask Maisa for permission to start all over again to try to solve this problem. However, I realized we had problems that these professional managers would not be able to handle, let alone comprehend.

Maisa and I had survived through many challenges in the past together. Our chance meeting in Argentina and whirlwind courtship, followed by my efforts to get permission to marry her, seemed like challenge enough. But now we had other family demands, including those of our children. While waiting for her response, I wondered what she might say...

TWENTY-SIX

The two guards eyed me cautiously as I approached the front entry of Maisa's apartment building on Avenida Libertador in Buenos Aires. They held open the door for Maisa who was greeted with sweet smiles. I was greeted with stern and ominous looks as I made my way to the elevator with Maisa in tow. The elevator opened into the living room of the family's suite. Sitting across the far end of the living room was Maisa's father, Luis Dragubitzky, and her stepmother, Norma Duek. Norma Duek was a striking woman. She was tall and graceful. Norma's shoulder length jet-black hair, olive skin, and piercing dark eyes further accentuated her visage in her elegant white evening gown. Norma Duek was a well-known society lady and the president of the Teatro Cervantes, one of Argentina's oldest and most famous theater companies which featured famous plays, ballets, and opera presentations. Luis looked very regal sitting ramrod straight on a Luis XVI chair in his black tuxedo. Luis was a tall, lean, and dapper looking man with slick black hair, perfectly drawn and combed over his head. His silver cufflinks glistened as he continuously checked his watch. As the owner of a metal-fabrication firm started by his father, Victor, Luis was known throughout his industry of being meticulously on time for every engagement.

I was told early on by Señor Luis that I would be granted only a half hour for this initial meeting. Norma and Luis were scheduled for a charity benefit with the President of

Argentina, Carlos Menem, thus justifying their formal attire that evening. Luis looked me up and down during his initial meeting, I must have presented an equally imposing site to him clad in my blue jeans, cowboy boots, and ripped Stanford University T-shirt. Maisa's brother, together with her four stepbrothers, lined up alongside Señor Luis. They were all typical Argentine young men, tall, dark, and handsome, ranging in ages from 19 to 25. It was not clear at the time whether or not their role was to listen in or perhaps escort me out.

Not much was said at this initial meeting. Just the normal perfunctory chit-chat. Señor Luis seemed more concerned with quickly sizing me up and then moving off to his next engagement. Norma did not say a word after her initial greeting; she just watched the limited conversation and smiled during her observation of the reactions of Luis and her sons. Something told me that in the back of her mind Norma was thinking *this is not going to be easy.*

A few weeks after our first date and meeting with Maisa's family, I decided to propose to Maisa, but not before having the all important and traditional meeting with her father to ask for his approval. Maisa's father was wary of our relationship and where it could go. He did not see much of a future in long-distance relationships and neither did Maisa for that matter. However, Luis Dragubitzky did not have much faith in love at first sight or "infatuation," as he called it. Luis did agree earlier, however, to allow his daughter to visit me in the United States with a chaperon, her stepbrother Nicolas. I knew it was crucial to win over Nicolas if I was to get Maisa's hand in marriage.

In the first meeting with the family, Maisa's five brothers eyed me suspiciously; they were very protective of their only sister. Fortunately Nicolas and I grew to be great friends. At a certain point, convinced that our union was meant for life, Nicolas pretty much decided to leave Maisa and me alone.

He used his one week in Florida to visit the other important sights such as Walt Disney World near I-4 and the "Doll House" on South Orange Blossom Trail. When Nicolas returned, he told his father, "If Maisa doesn't marry him, I will."

The next week, convinced of a good report back to the family, I decided to fly to Argentina to ask Maisa's father for her hand in marriage. In retrospect, it seems pretty ridiculous to ask the father of someone you knew only a few weeks for permission to marry, but Maisa and I were so consumed by our love that even the impossible seemed normal to us at the time. However, at the meeting with Maisa's father in Buenos Aires, almost nothing seemed "normal."

Nicolas served as my translator at the lunch I arranged at the Recoleta, the Argentine version of the Champs d'Elisee with a long strip of elegant outdoor cafés and trendy bars. Nicolas was very nervous at that meeting; he started tugging at his collar and tie while sweating profusely. Not a good sign. When I finally prodded him to ask the question of Mr. Dragubitzky, Nicolas faced his stepfather and tried to open his mouth but nothing would come out. He then turned to me and said something to the effect that "tomorrow is a good day and why don't we just do this tomorrow?" On the third or forth time I prodded him, Nicolas regained his speech. The impatient but pleasant face of Luis Dragubitzky drained to a pale white. His eyes widened as if in horror and minutes ticked by before he even uttered a word in response. Mr. Dragubitzky finally regained his composure and uttered the now famous words that will forever be repeated at family gatherings: "Are you sure?"

"Are you sure?" This was the question I had to ask myself before I asked Maisa for permission to start over again one night in August of 1999.

Maisa and I had been married for more than five years by

now. After I stepped down as president almost a year earlier, I was finally able to enjoy some time with my family them. I started showing up on time at the dinner table and I did not miss many important events as I had in the past. I wasn't quite sure I was ready to return to my old work schedule.

After a long evening of explaining all the problems at the company, I asked Maisa what she thought about taking over the company again and rescuing it from its present predicament.

Maisa, paused for a long time, and tried to gather her thoughts. Her stern face then melted away into a broad smile: "Go rescue the company. Vamos Papito!"

I was not only relieved, but also I knew now why I loved my wife so much. She not only knew me, she believed in me. I would now move heaven and earth to prove her right.

TWENTY-SEVEN

The next morning seemed like a page out of Joseph Stalin's playbook. We had what can only be called a Stalinistic purge. One by one, I walked into the offices of our president, vice president of sales, and vice president of engineering with our human resources director and told them that this was their last day at the company. It seemed as if all the other staff knew this was going to happen that day but them. Most of our staff was elated; however, a few junior staff members who had been hired by the outgoing management were less confident in my returning to the office of president. They had been told all too often that I was as obsolete as a dinosaur and an entrepreneur in a now mature company. I realized it would take time to win them over and ultimately the results we achieved would be the only proof that the decisions we were making were right for our future.

I knew I would inherit quite a mess when I retook the helm as president and CEO. Our sales had fallen in the past year for the first time in the company's history. Most of the damage was due to the savage competitive attack that our products had come under in Asia and elsewhere overseas, but we also saw some of our sales growth starting to erode domestically as well. In addition to our sales falling from $9.6 million to $8.5 million, we saw our previous year's $450,000 operating profit dive to a current annual operating loss of more than $1.4 million. The loss was a combination of the unforeseen loss in sales overseas and some pretty bad planning at home. It was the worst year in history, cash was down, inventory skyrocketed, sales had plummeted, employee morale had cratered, and engineering and new product development was a complete disaster.

Before I decided to retake the helm of the company, I had to decide who I would bring back to get the company back on its feet. I not only had my list of people that I had to fire, I also had to have my list of the people I had to hire. This first step I took as president was to contact four of the five key people I needed to rehire to re-energize the company. I thought long and hard over the talent I would need to turn our fortunes around. I had a list of five people that had left the company that I wanted to hire back immediately. Initially I hired back four of the key founding team members who had left. They all agreed to rejoin the company within weeks of my reassuming the role as president.

With most of the founding members back in control of the company, it was suddenly like the "old days" again. Everything was possible again regardless of how dire the circumstances. It was in that spirit of possibility that I continued to think about Paul Koren. Paul was someone who I believed would play a crucial role in bringing the creative entrepreneurial "spark" back to Super Vision. I actually contacted him prior to undertaking my plan to overthrow the current management team. I needed to know if Paul would agree to come back and at least get his input if Richard Heiner, our former marketing director, Steve Faber, our former chief engineer, and a few key production staff would consider rejoining as well. As I was pondering my plan to reassume my role as president I knew I had to limit the number of people who knew of my plan before I won over our Board of Directors for approval. It was very lonely for me at Super Vision during the past year, I longed for the same spirit of camaraderie and euphoria that I had when I walked back across the freedom bridge with Paul. I longed for his return to the company and had missed both his enthusiasm and his friendship.

I remember Paul telling me before he left that he would have stayed at Super Vision if we maintained the founding management and the entrepreneurial atmosphere. He made it clear he was leaving because he felt he could no longer be an entrepreneur at Super Vision. This was precisely the reason why I wanted him back. We needed to re-energize the company with people who could also hit the ground running due to their pre-existing knowledge of the products and the markets. We had no time in this turn around plan to learn as we go. Paul and I had not talked in more than a year. I had no idea how he was doing in his new company or if he would even consider re-joining Super Vision. I had also realized I was taking a big risk calling him out of the blue and confiding in him of my new plans, especially since the previous management team thought he was competing with us in his new business and was violating his non-compete agreement. I did not have time to worry about protocol. I knew I needed him back on the team. I needed to take action. I decided to give him a call.

TWENTY-EIGHT

I called Paul the night before I was going to fire the existing management team. It seemed funny to call a former employee to confide in him the day before you orchestrate an upheaval. But somehow it all made sense to me since Paul's agreement to rejoin us was crucial, filling a key position that I soon would make available. I also wanted his advice, since Paul had the most prior knowledge of the company as well as the products and the marketplace. Since Paul had not talked to me for almost a year, he was initially surprised to hear my voice on the phone. Paul was very stiff and reserved in his response. Our current president had previously sued Paul personally and his company, Oasis Falls, for violating his non-compete agreement. The suit was still pending and Paul viewed me as a potential adversary.

Paul held out on me with his true feelings until I told him I planned to remove the top management of the company. The minute I confided this to him, it was as if a dam broke and a torrent of interest and emotion that had welled up inside Paul flowed freely.

"So when are you coming over!"

"I don't know, Paul."

"How about NOW!" insisted Paul.

I traveled to Paul's small warehouse in Sanford at 8:30 p.m. that night. I confided in Paul about my plans to reorganize and reenergize Super Vision. Paul confided in me that he had a falling out with his partners and that he too had become disillusioned with what he was doing. Paul wanted to come back, but he did not want to throw away the hard work that he invested in his company. He wanted Super Vision to buy out his partners so he could fold his waterfall company into Super Vision. I had concerns that the board, which just bent over backwards to agree to my rather wild plans to stage a coup, would at the same time agree to an acquisition of a product line that seemed unrelated to our core products. But I told Paul I would try. Paul later agreed to come over to Super Vision even if we did not buy Oasis Waterfalls, but he hoped that somehow we would strike a deal with his investment partners. With Paul's confirmation that he would return, along with his belief and assurances that the other key team members would follow, I was ready to put my plan into action.

The first four founding team members actually rejoined the staff before Paul. Paul's return was delayed by the almost unending negotiations with his former investment partner in Oasis, Rami Yosefian. Rami agreed to fund Paul and he was not too keen on parting with his investment even though the two had fought bitterly during the past year.

The announcement of Paul coming back was also not uniformly welcomed by the team. After all, some employees believed that Paul was selling fiber-optic lighting along with his waterfalls in an attempt to compete with us and in violation of his non-compete agreement. They pointed to the lawsuit Super Vision's former senior management had filed against him. Most people wrote off this litigation as just a case of bad blood between our former president and Paul Koren, but a few were still angry that he had abandoned us just when we needed him most. Several months after we changed management, during one of our weekly Monday morning meetings, I basically told the remaining doubters on the staff that they were going to have to learn to live with the idea of Paul coming back because he was starting "next Monday."

Something must have bothered Paul on his first day back; the normally jovial and effervescent Paul hardly said a word. The next day Paul and I hopped on a plane to see our largest pool-products customer, Hayward Industries, in Elizabeth, N.J. Hayward was one of our largest shareholders; they owned 10% of our outstanding stock. Hayward was also our largest customer in the pool industry. If anyone ever hopes to revive its company's fortunes, then the largest customer was the best place to start.

On the drive to the airport, Paul Koren did not say a word. As soon as the airplane left the runway Paul said a lot. He cried for the entire two and a half hours of the flight. What he told me sent my world into a tailspin. The mastermind behind the theft and counterfeiting of our products was one of our former Chinese distributors who had almost unlimited resources, a man named Samson Wu.

TWENTY-NINE

꧁꧂

Samson Mong Wu was the scion of a wealthy Chinese watch-making family. Samson Wu's lineage was traced from a wealthy father who left Taiwan to make millions of watches similar in design to name brands in Hong Kong and Shanghai and an equally wealthy mother whose father profited in his position as a general in charge of all rice distribution in Shanghai during World War II. After his mother and father joined forces, the mother, Debbie Wu, quickly took over the family watch businesses and brilliantly expanded the manufacturing and distribution. They also diversified their business by copying the Kodak 1 Hour photo labs and setting up a separate factory in Shanghai to copy these systems that they would sell at less than half the price throughout China. As the family's wealth grew, so would their interest in expanding into other businesses. Their two sons, including Samson Wu, also hungered to prove themselves outside the family's very successful watch business. They yearned for projects "of their own" to prove that their capabilities would rise far beyond their birthrights.

Wu's hunger was not limited to his ambition. He would eat insatiably like a pig at a trough. As a result, his silhouette was an almost perfect sphere; he was as wide as he was tall. Samson Wu was the older of Debbie's two sons. The other brother, Thomas, had a resume that would later feature a much storied career in real estate, but he actually only served as the manager for the family's existing properties. Wu was not just the oldest; he was the "smart one" in the family. Thomas Wu's greatest gifts in life were being born into a wealthy family and being able to hang on to his big brother's considerably large coat tails.

Wu's prowess in math won him admission to the University of California at Berkeley, and ultimately, a Master's degree in mathematics. At Berkeley, Wu met a Japanese American, Susan Sumida, an undergraduate who he had tutored in mathematics. Tutoring turned to dating and dating turned to marriage. They later had two daughters together; one would later win admission to Massachusetts Institute of Technology for her prowess in math and sciences the other would graduate from Boston Law School.

Upon graduation, Wu initially joined the family's watch business, Marsam Trading Company in the United States. What he lacked in street smarts and the instincts of his mother and father he made up for in his schooling and knowledge of the ways of America. Wu later learned Spanish and Portuguese and assisted in the growth of the family's operations in Panama, Mexico, Argentina, and Brazil. He also made a key strategic move to grow the family watch business. He hired a former Bulova watch executive, David Winkler, and brought him in as chief operating officer of the company, Marsam Trading. Marsam Trading's business started to grow significantly in now legitimate watch manufacture and sales. Wu created a division of the company that now was a legitimate licensor of a name brand watch.

With Winkler's help, Wu eventually received the exclusive distributorship from Bulova Watch for South America. Soon container loads of watches were shipped from Wu's Hong Kong and Shanghai factories to Marsam Trading's sales offices and retail stores in South America via Marsam Trading Company's bonded custom's warehouse in Miami, Florida. In the first year since Wu brought David Winkler on board, the Bulova Watch business grew from $4 million to almost $17 million in sales. Wu bought himself a 12,000 square foot mansion on the 14th Green at the Doral Country Club in Miami, one mile away from his warehouse near the Miami airport.

But the watch business was not really his; he could not claim the victories entirely for himself. He had his eye open for other opportunities that would make him even richer than his mother and father. He set out on his quest to find the perfect new business for him to expand the family empire. He would later call his new venture Optic-Tech Corporation.

One day, on a flight from China to the U.S., Wu read an article in *Forbes* Magazine about a fast growing fiber-optic lighting company. He marveled at the bright lights and spectacular displays created by this technology. *This is something that would grow rapidly in China*, he thought. He ripped the article out of the magazine and decided to contact the company's founder when he returned to the United States.

In early 1995, Wu had contacted Super Vision to become the exclusive distributor of our products in China. We welcomed his visit; at this point we had generated no sales in China and looked forward to the opportunity to expand to overseas markets. We allowed him to tour our offices, taking great care not to show him the production areas of the facility. We were interested in creating a customer, not another competitor. After the tour and presentation of our products in our showroom, he very enthusiastically agreed to generate a minimum of $500,000 in his first year of sales with Super Vision. He only would agree; however, to buy samples and inventory that amounted to a few of each product in our catalog up front. We agreed, hoping that this initial purchase would ultimately lead to more sales.

Winkler, who accompanied Wu during his trip, was not impressed. Winkler was a tall thin bespectacled man with a large nose and receding hairline. Winkler's bookish appearance fit the role of his chosen profession, a detail-oriented operations officer and manufacturing manager, who would count every penny and meticulously plan every investment. As Wu's eyes would increasingly widen with every display our multi-colored twinkling lights, Winkler's eyes would just gloss over in boredom. The more Wu would express his interest, the more Winkler would just shake his head in disapproval.

"Samson, we are making millions with Bulova in the watch business, why the hell do you want to mess around with this nonsense?" pleaded Winkler in his never ending mantra to Samson to leave "these silly toys alone."

Winkler initially did not take our product or our business seriously. In fact, he did not take anything other than watches seriously. Winkler's father was in the watch business, his grandfather was a watchmaker, and his great-grandfather was a watchmaker. He bickered with Wu about placing an initial order and he would bicker and hold back payments for the future orders that followed. For Wu, this business was "the future," for Winkler it was "just a waste of time." As time progressed, seeing that Wu would not give up new venture, Winkler took over managing it. Winkler thought that if Wu had to be in this business, at least he would see to it that it ran efficiently.

A few orders ultimately did come through in the months to follow. But so did a number of unusual requests for shipments of components rather than finished products and requests for licensing of our cable and light source manufacturing processes. We agreed to license and teach Wu how to make our small point of sales signs, since the process was very low tech and labor intensive, but we absolutely refused to instruct him on our equipment or manufacturing processes for our cable and light sources. This frustrated Wu greatly and eventually his orders trailed off. By the end of 1996, we terminated his distributorship. It was the last I heard from him. However, Paul explained on that fateful flight to New Jersey, it was not the last time he had heard from Wu.

THIRTY

During Paul's tearful confession, it did not shock me to learn that Caruso stole from us. It did shock me to learn that Paul, previously my most trusted friend in the company, had as well. This was when I first learned of the entire scheme to steal our technology and the real culprits behind it. I learned how the products and processes were stolen and then duplicated and sold by Wu worldwide through dozens of shell corporations from Shanghai to Panama in order to hide his identity.

When I stepped down as president and installed the new management, Paul just did not see a future or place for himself in the company. Far from the almost complete freedom he had to create and invent, he was now bogged down with reports and paperwork. His style was completely opposite to that of the new management. They saw him as "disorganized" and a "discipline problem." He clashed often with them, until one day he finally decided to give up. He started filling out reports and stopped inventing. It was about that time that Wu, began calling Paul. Wu was angry at Super Vision for canceling his distributorship and Paul was mad at Super Vision for not allowing him to continue to create. At that point Paul started dreaming of starting his own company and had already enlisted some financing for his new venture from Rami Yosefian, a local investor. Wu played on Paul's emotions and told him he would also finance him in his new company or alternatively pay him a consulting fee. All Wu wanted in return was "a little help."

Wu had actually tried to reverse engineer Super Vision's products; the distributorship agreement was just a ruse to get easy access to our products. When Wu later learned that there was more to the process of manufacturing these products then was evident in simply copying the products, he started calling Paul at home to try to lure him into explaining the manufacturing methods we used to achieve the end results. Paul had initially resisted the first few calls, but later, after giving up on his future with Super Vision, he acceded to Wu's advances.

Wu was like a Svengali to Paul. He started making payments to Paul through an account in Switzerland that was routed through a bank in Panama, which ultimately was deposited in a shell company, K&H Consulting. Paul had set up K&H Consulting in Sanford, Florida according to Wu's instructions.

Paul further explained he got an agreement from Wu to be paid $20,000 per month. Paul thought that the money would be convenient to cover the overhead and costs, beyond the requirements of his initial investment capital provided by Rami, for his new company for a period of one year. Paul thought he was using Wu to fund his new business. He soon found he had made a pact with the Devil. With each monthly payment Wu demanded more information from Super Vision to be delivered or he would hold back on making the $20,000 bank transfer. Without the payment Paul couldn't meet payroll or cover the rent on his new enterprise. He and his four employees depended on these payments while they were establishing their initial sales of their waterfall business.

At one point, the current president of Super Vision thought something was wrong, he received reports that Oasis was working on fiber-optic projects and that former customers had seen fiber optics in the Oasis warehouse.

This was a clear violation of Paul's non-compete agreement and a lawsuit was soon filed against him and his company. What Super Vision management did not know at the time was that Oasis was a legitimate company involved in the sale of waterfalls, whereas the real violations and stealing were being carried out by several secret shell companies located in South American and Asia which were controlled by Wu. The vehicle they used to transfer Super Vision's stolen technology to these other shell companies was K&H Consulting. Paul's involvement was suspected, but the corporate entity Super Vision targeted in the legal proceedings was wrong. The cover-up worked. With aid of lawyers who engaged in semantics in the courtroom, Wu and his cohorts were able to continue their stealing and counterfeiting undetected for at least another year. It also eventually allowed them enough time to ultimately publish their patents in the U.S. and Chinese patent offices which were based on trade secret information stolen from Super Vision.

To the chagrin of our new management, they lost the initial hearing on the matter before Judge Komanski because, according to sworn statements and affidavits filed in court later by both Paul Koren and Jack Caruso, the lawyers funded by Wu counseled the Oasis management to lie under oath. Not only Paul deliberately misled Judge Komanski, but Paul's lawyer, Brian Gilchrist of the Orlando law firm of Allen Dyer Doppelt Mibrath and Gilchrist, told the judge that his clients did not "have anything to do with optics, because they don't." These statements were made in court even though the lawyers' own billing records later proved that they were billing for the creation and filing of fiber-optic patents, using information originally faxed from Super Vision's own offices, more than five months prior to the hearing. The lawyers agreed to file these patents even though the individual sending these faxes still worked at Super Vision and was subject to confidentiality and non-compete agreements at the time. As long as Wu continued to pay their fees, they conveniently overlooked that most of the information was being sent from Super Vision's own fax machine at 5 a.m. in the morning.

The man behind the 5 a.m. faxes was none other than Caruso. When Paul could not or would not give all the answers Wu needed on the cabling process, Wu convinced Paul to approach Caruso. While Paul was initially a reluctant conduit for information, Caruso was like a powder keg ready to explode. Caruso not only had concerns that he was not appreciated by current management, he was concerned that he wasn't appreciated by anyone. No one knew how smart he was and how much he contributed to Super Vision; in fact, Super Vision simply did not deserve him anymore. He welcomed Paul's approach and absolutely reveled in the wining and dining he received from Wu. Caruso had agreed to help Wu loot our company of our technology after Paul resigned by staying behind at Super Vision. While Caruso was simultaneously taking salaries and payments from both Super Vision and Wu, Paul explained how Caruso stole the optical bench, piece by piece, from the R&D lab and later reassembled the bench and shipped it to Wu's manufacturing facility in Shanghai. According to Paul, Caruso also bragged to Paul of his night time endeavors of scaling over the drop ceiling and entering my locked office to steal blue prints and plans of our manufacturing process from my files.

Money flowed rapidly into Caruso's hands and Super Vision's blueprints, chemical formulations, diagrams, and stolen laboratory equipment flowed into Wu's hands in return. Paul further detailed how Caruso would take a week to steal a large piece of equipment from the locked R &D lab. He would disassemble it in the early morning hours and then ferret it out of the building one part at a time during his lunch hour or evening departures. Two members of the shipping staff also assisted by throwing needed products and components into the dumpster so they could be picked up at night and forwarded to China for copying, however no one was sure if the shipping staff were cooperating with Caruso or directly through Wu or some other third party.

By the time Caruso left Super Vision, Wu had completely cloned the company in China, replete with all our new products as well as all the products being developed in the R&D department. Paul brought the customer lists when he left. Soon it became clear that Wu had all the information he needed from Paul. Paul was of little value to him now. The real star was Caruso, since he was not only adept at acquiring all the valuable blueprints and equipment but he could also operate all the machinery.

Caruso eventually left the employ of K&H Consulting and started working directly for Samson and Thomas Wu at Optic-Tech. Oddly enough, Caruso became infuriated with Paul and the lawyers while hearing both Paul and Brian Gilchrist of Allen Dyer lie in court that they were not doing fiber optics. By then Caruso had convinced himself that he was in fact the inventor of all the technology and wanted to proclaim this in court. Caruso could not fathom how the lawyers would provide him so much attention in assisting him in filing patents on his brilliant inventions during the previous months and now wanted him to be silent on his inventive prowess, or worse, lie that he was not involved in such endeavors under oath. This was something Caruso was not willing to do and he was very vocal about it both immediately before and after the court hearing before Judge Komanski. At that point Caruso decided to separate from Paul and started lobbying Wu to find new legal counsel for future patent filings.

During a meeting with Brian Gilchrist after the hearing before Judge Komanski, Caruso told his counsel that he "wanted nothing more to do with him or Paul Koren" and then dismissed Gilchrist as his counsel.

Wu told Caruso he can "invent" whatever he desired with no restrictions in China. He promptly moved Caruso to Optic-Tech's Shanghai facility and later hired another law firm to pursue his patents. Caruso was provided with an apartment, a driver, and a cook in China. More money started flowing in the direction of Caruso and less money started flowing in the direction of Paul.

During his last trip to Wu's facilities in Shanghai, China, it became clear that Paul's "cooperation" would no longer be required. According to Paul, Caruso beamed with joy at a meeting when Wu informed Paul that he would not return his passport and would not allow him to leave China unless he signed over all his interests in all the patents that he had initially filed with Caruso. Wu wanted Caruso to be noted as the sole inventor and they knew that since Paul did file his name on earlier patent filings they would never have clear access to these patents without Paul's assignment.

Caruso and Wu stood up and left Paul to ponder his predicament in a locked room in the Optic-Tech Shanghai facility. Caruso didn't even try to hide his glee as he left Paul to ponder his fate. Caruso was finally "#1 Son" to Wu. He achieved his goal of taking over their enterprise. By pushing out Paul, he would no longer have to share the credit or income with anyone else besides Wu. It was at that point that Paul discovered how far he had fallen and what deep trouble he was in. Wu and Caruso kept Paul locked up overnight, past the day he was to fly home. In that threadbare locked room, Paul was left to contemplate his future while Caruso basked in his new-found glory.

The next morning, Paul ultimately agreed to sign the assignment agreement, leaving him with basically nothing of the company they had set up overseas and no rights or interests to any of the patents that they had filed. Paul circled the date of the agreement to show it was dated one day after the date of his originally scheduled return flight home. He looked at the language and was convinced that the U.S. lawyers at Allen Dyer had drafted this document; the document's English was too formal and accurate for Wu or Caruso to have prepared it. Some day, he thought, this can be used as evidence that he was held hostage and forced to sign this agreement. The lawyers would burn later, along with Wu and Caruso.

After Paul signed the agreement he did not get his passport back, but he was allowed to leave the room. Paul later broke into Wu's office, stole back his passport and headed straight to the airport. On the flight home, he broke down in tears, but not for what he had lost, but for the realization of the betrayal he had allowed himself to participate in of his former friends and co-workers. The tears were still streaming down his face while he poured out all he knew to me during our flight to New Jersey.

Paul knew at the point of his confession that he was risking my firing him on the spot. The job meant a lot to him. He had lived on his savings for the past few months, which had dwindled to next to nothing and his wife was pregnant with their first child. Yet Paul's conscience would not let him work one day more at Super Vision without this confession.

After recovering from the initial shock, I pondered what to do. Here was someone who had just confessed to knifing me and of all our staff in the back. But also here was someone who risked his own self-interest to tell the truth. As angry as I was at the time I did not feel it was right to reward his newfound honesty with punishment. After a long pause I said: "Paul, I sentence you to ten years hard labor at Super Vision. If you want to redeem yourself, you will do this by helping us turn our company around and helping me bring these bastards to justice." Paul let out a great sigh of relief and agreed, telling me about the thousands of pages of documentation and bank statements he had been saving at home for just that purpose.

Paul had the documentary evidence and proof to show the elaborate series of bank transfers that the Wu family used to pay him and Caruso to steal products and information from Super Vision. Wu had taken great care to protect himself by using a series of shell companies from Panama, Hong Kong, and Switzerland to engage in these transfers that ultimately went to the accounts of K&H Consulting. Paul said we had to act soon for if Wu and Caruso were able to continue with their plans, they would be able to undercut the price of our entire product line as well as steal or undermine our entire distributor base. Paul estimated that Super Vision would be bankrupt in less than a year if Wu and Caruso were not stopped immediately.

Had it not been for Paul Koren's conscience, we would have never been able to discover the true culprit or implicate him in our case before the damage they were doing would have destroyed us. Paul knew this, and that he had to help us. If he were to remain silent, he would soon be out of a job as well. I was stunned by the scope and scale of the conspiracy. When we returned to Orlando, I immediately hired a lawyer to represent us in the impending battle to come. I also called the FBI.

THIRTY-ONE

I called the FBI office in Maitland, Fla., I reached a junior agent who did show concern for my predicament but seemed to be overwhelmed with the volume of information, and perhaps the credibility in which I had presented it. Halfway through my description of what I had just learned from Paul, I started listening to my own words and questioned if even I would have believed the story if it were told to me by someone else. The junior agent was polite enough, but gave me the usual bureaucratic answer, "we'll get back to you."

I was not confident that "we'll get back to you" would result in anything meaningful. I had to find a group with credibility that would get the FBI's attention. At the time, our company's law firm was Holland & Knight, the largest law firm in the State of Florida. I had gone to a few of their annual happy hours and open house functions for clients and met everyone from local to state officials from all levels of government. I called the senior partner in charge of our account, Lou Conti, and told him enough of my story to pique his interest and requested a meeting with "every senior partner he could fit into a conference room in the next 24 hours." Lou was a good guy, and he wanted to help. He arranged the meeting.

The next afternoon, I arrived at the Holland & Knight conference room on the 23rd Floor of the Sun Bank building in downtown Orlando. It was early September 1999.

Seated at the large round table were several of the silver haired senior partners. I was a bit distracted by the magnificent view of the city through the floor to ceiling windows of the conference room, but I quickly regained my focus as I laid out all the stolen documents and wire transfer confirmations that Paul Koren had provided earlier.

After my 30-minute presentation, one silver-haired senior partner rose from his chair and with great eloquence and conviction told me that "this was the most outrageously heinous story of corporate crime that I have heard in my 30 years of law practice." He further stated, "young man you are in desperate need of legal counsel" and went on to explain that a case like this might require hundreds of thousands if not millions of dollars in legal fees. I was somewhat taken aback by this statement. I had come for help, not to embark on yet another path of certain destruction. My company was already hemorrhaging from losses; I could not afford to engage in yet another drain on our cash. However, Holland & Knight does not take cases on contingency and therefore they could not assist me with the steps I would now need to take. With that said, the senior partners excused themselves from the meeting and I was left alone with Lou to contemplate my fate.

I asked Lou: "What should I do now?"

Lou thought it over carefully and finally came to the same conclusion that I originally hoped, that is, until my admission of our lack of funds unceremoniously cut the meeting short. Lou understood that I simply wanted a referral from someone credible that would gain me the attention I needed from the FBI. Lou said there was someone in the firm who could get the FBI's attention, but he was not located in Orlando. This new senior partner was located in the Miami office, about an hour's flight away. His name was John Hogan, he was just recently hired as a partner with the firm after leaving his post as second in command at the U.S.

Attorney's office under Attorney General Janet Reno. "If John called the FBI, they would listen," Lou Conti concluded. I agreed and arranged to fly out to see him the next day.

THIRTY-TWO

John Hogan met me in the conference room of Holland & Knight's Miami offices. The view of Miami from the conference room windows was equally impressive and spectacular as the one I witnessed the day before at their offices in Orlando. John Hogan rose to shake my hand; I noticed he was a tall, broad shouldered man with a firm grip. John was someone who inspired confidence; he also seemed less concerned with billing me than he was with helping me.

I again laid out on the conference room table the piles of evidentiary documents and repeated my 30-minute summary that was by now burned into my memory. John rocked quietly in his chair listening intently with two index fingers pressed against his lips. I expected a sales pitch on Holland & Knight's services; instead I got action. He just picked up the phone and called the local office of the FBI. Two agents arrived in the conference room twenty minutes later. This time John ran through the case I had presented, almost word for word from memory. John had not missed a single point and his sense of urgency was now equal to mine. The two FBI agents hung on his every word. They knew who John was and they knew of his reputation. I studied the faces of the FBI agents as John went through his presentation; there was no question in my mind that if justice was ever going to be had, this would be my best chance to see it delivered.

At the end of the presentation, the two agents thanked John for bringing this case to their attention and shook my hand with a sense of purpose that inspired confidence. When they left the conference room, John asked if there was anything else he could do for me. I couldn't think of anything more he could have done. I thanked him and allowed him to get back to his busy schedule, while I collected my documents from the table and hurried off to catch my flight home.

The next morning I received a call from two agents from the Orlando office of the FBI based in Maitland, Florida. The agents were Special Agent Kevin Hogan and Special Agent Bill Hajeski, Sr. They asked when they could come over to see me, I gladly responded; "whenever you want." Their response: "Now." Less than an hour later we were meeting in our conference room with the same set of documents set out on the table and I made the same presentation of facts. This time the agents took notes and at the end of the presentation they asked to interview everyone in the building who could be a material witness in the case.

Before they got started I suggested the first person they needed to interview was me. I wanted them to know my background and also the one skeleton I had in my closet that may affect their ability to prosecute the case. Clearly the defense attorneys would try to use it against me. I told them in detail about the decision handed down by Judge Babcock in a hearing 12 years earlier when I was at FiberView. I told the agents that I did not want this to come up later and for them to think I was not forthcoming about this. The agents read documents and articles I had assembled on the past case and then scooped them back up into the pile of documents: "Looks like you got a raw deal, now let's proceed with our interviews."

The first person they wanted to interview was Paul Koren. Paul would clearly be the star witness in the case, since he knew the inner workings of the Wu family. However, they also made it clear that since Paul had been an accomplice, by his testimony and admissions he would be incriminating himself on several felony counts. At this stage of the investigation they could not make any promises not to prosecute him in exchange for his testimony. Paul would have to be made aware of this risk and decide if he would speak to them now or choose to do so through a lawyer later. In any case they had enough information about Paul's prior actions to warrant an arrest. Paul would have to decide this for himself. His conscience would determine his best course of action.

I went to Paul's office upstairs and explained what the FBI had told me in the conference room downstairs. Paul was already aware of the fact that by even in his initial admission to me on the airplane that he was putting himself in jeopardy and resigned himself to going forward with full disclosure of all his past actions regardless of the outcome. He felt he owed it to me and to Super Vision to give his complete cooperation in order to stop Wu and Caruso from destroying us. He felt responsible for the role he played in assisting them and if he had to now risk his own future to save ours then that was a decision he could live with. Paul sat before the two FBI agents and poured out his heart and soul. The agents were taken aback with the deliberate disclosure of all facts, including those which Paul incriminated himself. Paul seemed very believable as to how and why he had initially been lured away by Wu. He also appeared very genuine in his desire to atone for his sins. They seemed inspired by Paul's honesty as well as confident in what a convincing witness he would be to a jury.

It was clear that the agents had heard all kinds of lies from unapologetic and hardened criminals before. Paul was not only believable, he was someone that seemed to merit forgiveness. At the end of Paul's several hour interview, the agents again warned him that he might be indicted in the future for his past acts and that there was still no guarantee or agreement that they would not prosecute. Paul replied that he would accept whatever fate becomes him, he just wants them to save the company and bring Wu and his henchman to justice. The two agents shook Paul's hand before they left the room.

I entered the conference room just after Paul left. The agents told me that Paul's story was very compelling but that his credibility would come under attack by the defendants if the case ever made it to trial. Without corroborating evidence from someone still on the other side in the Wu camp, Paul's claims might just be written off as that of a disgruntled former employee. They had to have an admission from someone else on the Wu family organization. That meant a confession from Wu, his brother, or Caruso. I told them this was impossible since in their confession they would be incriminating themselves and thus sealing their fate. If they continued to deny and lie, at least with crafty lawyers, they had a chance to beat the charges. For a moment I saw their interest fade. I thought I was losing them and that the case might not be pursued at all. Then I came up with an idea. I suggested that we have Paul call Caruso and offer him a job at Super Vision. Caruso's enormous ego would make it hard for him to resist gloating at Paul's offer. Perhaps it would entice him to launch into a big speech about how rich and important he had become at Optic-Tech and how he would never consider coming back unless he was showered with similar riches. In the process of Caruso's bragging, I believed he would sink himself. Agent Hogan liked the idea but he said this would only work if my characterization of Caruso was accurate. I told agent Hogan that I felt I knew Caruso well enough to know how he would respond.

Paul, was called back into the room and a date for a tape-recorded conversation was set for next week, after agents Hogan and Hajeski could get the necessary warrant for the wiretap. Paul agreed to meet them at the FBI offices to make the call from a number that Caruso would not recognize in his phone directory or caller ID. The search for justice was about to begin.

THIRTY-THREE

Paul Koren and Special Agent Kevin Hogan sat together at a small table in the FBI offices in Maitland, Florida. On the table was a tape-recording device hooked up to numerous phone lines and jacks. One of those lines led to a receiver that was to be held by Paul, while the other line led to a headset that was to be worn by agent Hogan.

Paul's initial calls went right to Caruso's voice mail. Agent Hogan banged his hand on the table, thinking this signaled that their session would result in nothing. Paul raised his hand to reassure agent Hogan that things were alright. He did not speak to Hogan but did leave a very friendly message on Caruso's voice mail urging him to call about a new "opportunity at Super Vision." When Paul hung up, he told agent Hogan that Caruso probably suspected that he was being investigated by Super Vision. Caruso knew Paul had been hired back, and of course, had no way of knowing if Paul had told everything that had happened. Paul was betting that Caruso was actually home by his phone and was monitoring his calls for unknown caller IDs before he would respond. Paul believed that his message would result in a reply by Caruso.

By leaving a friendly message, Paul hoped Caruso would think that he had not jeopardized Caruso or himself by telling Super Vision of the theft. By suggesting that Caruso could now be a valuable asset to Super Vision, he was appealing to his well-known sense of greed and self importance as well as confirming that he had not told their story.

Agent Hogan just shook his head, not sure what to make of Paul's confidence in Caruso's behavior, but only a few minutes later the phone rang. It was Caruso. Caruso was more curious than talkative. He first asked Paul a lot of questions, all centering on if Paul "had said anything to Super Vision." Paul assured Caruso he had not and Caruso responded that "it is a good thing, since I have enough information to burn both of us." Agent Hogan's eyes lit up and he motioned excitedly with his hand for Paul to continue and take the conversation to the next level.

As soon as he was convinced that Paul was just as concerned with saving his own skin as he was, Caruso then turned to the question of "opportunities at Super Vision." Caruso wanted to know what Super Vision had offered him to come back and was only too happy to laugh in Paul's face when he heard the amount and bragged about how he already was being paid many times that sum by Wu. Caruso further stated that he had "already been paid in excess of $1.4 million" for his knowledge and information and that he now had a Ph.D. from a Chinese University as well as Chinese citizenship. He was living in China with his new Chinese wife and had two servants, a driver, and a cook all provided to him by Wu. He said he did not have much use for his former life in America and did not have much use for Super Vision either.

Perhaps the most important thing that Caruso told Paul during his height of boastfulness was the fact that the new company, Optic-Tech International, Inc., planned to debut its first products in America at the Lighting Dimensions Show in Orlando. He was confident that the damage Optic-Tech had inflicted on Super Vision would be enough to destroy it and now the company could confidently come to America to sell their products and steal Super Vision's customers without fear of reprisal. He added that Super Vision would not be able to afford to battle the much wealthier Wu in court and would not live to see the first day at trial. The more he tried to rub his newfound success in Paul's face, the more he incriminated himself and his colleagues. This was evident by agent Hogan's now frantic note taking and hand waving.

Hogan had almost completely filled up his pad with notes that he was matching in sequence to the recorder's built in time clock. By now, Hogan was running out of paper, however, he continued to wave his free hand to urge Paul on. Paul wanted to leave the channels of communication open with Caruso, but Caruso just conceitedly left it up in the air if he would grant Paul more of his valuable time in the future and then said his goodbyes. Paul hung up the phone with Caruso. Agent Hogan, normally very dour and circumspect, yelled "we got 'em!" Paul turned to agent Hogan and said, "The hell we do; they got us. If they show up at that trade show and undersell us by 50% in the U.S. market, we are dead meat." Agent Hogan's expression returned to sober again. The two men sat in the room for a few minutes more, not saying a word as agent Hogan reviewed his notes, then they both rose to leave.

Paul drove home not really sure what was accomplished in that tape-recording session. For Paul, the only thing he learned was the plan of impending doom for Super Vision. While agent Hogan might have been convinced that he won damaging admissions in that audiotape, Paul wondered if it would be played at a trial years later, after Super Vision had long since filed for Chapter 7.

THIRTY-FOUR

❧

I received a call from Special Agent Bill Hajeski, Sr., about 5:15 p.m. one afternoon in late November of 1999. It was less than a month after agent Hogan had recorded Caruso's conversation. He said it might be a "good idea" for us to hang around the Optic-Tech booth at the Lighting Dimensions Show in Orlando the next morning. There could be some things of interest worth seeing. Agent Hajeski had never called me to make suggestions before, he only asked questions. It didn't take much to read through the code. The FBI was finally going to do something. He wouldn't say what, but I knew I would be glued to the Optic-Tech booth for the first few hours of the show.

Before, during, and after the raid and seizure at the trade show, the FBI agents made it clear to me: "This was not going to be Super Vision's case; this was going to be the government's case." The agents underscored the fact that they were only acting on behalf of the government at the direction of the U.S. Attorney. They might ultimately prosecute or they might not. The evidence and their caseload would later determine if this case ever made it to indictments, arrests or trial. If I was going to have "my case," then I would have to do so in the civil arena with my own civil lawyers.

The FBI agents seemed genuinely dedicated to bringing the U.S. technology thieves to justice, but their past experience and knowledge of bureaucratic and budgetary issues made them cautious about offering any guarantees of further action. We had to have a civil lawyer if we were expected to move our case forward on my own timetable and at my own expense. The government would ultimately do what it decided at a time and place of its choosing, if ever at all. I learned this lesson after the government finally achieved its criminal indictments of my former adversaries in Colorado, two years after my company was effectively shut down and destroyed.

Acting in part on the FBI's advice and my past experience, I hired a law firm to represent me in the weeks between the wire tapping of Caruso and the seizure that was about to unfold. I stood by with my video camera, glued to the booth at the opening hour of the show. Several additional maintenance workers were also milling about the Optic-Tech booth along with a dozen or so prospective clients. But I did not see even a hint of an FBI agent.

Then in a flash, the "maintenance workers" stripped off their jackets to reveal blue jackets with giant yellow FBI letters emblazoned on the back. Two of the "customers" in business suits later turned out to be other FBI agents who presented badges to the Wus to identify themselves. They were quickly joined by agents Hogan and Hajeski who appeared out of nowhere and corralled Thomas and Samson Wu for questioning as the rest of the team dismantled and seized the Optic-Tech booth and removed it from the trade show floor. Samson and Thomas Wu appeared to be in a state of shock. David Winkler hurriedly reached for his cell phone and began to call their lawyers. Caruso started to protest loudly, but then smiled nervously as the agents informed him as to the nature of their investigation and the charges that might be brought.

As the Optic-Tech booth and its contents were being removed to a waiting trailer outside, I had three other companions with me witnessing this spectacle that could have been an episode on prime time television. One was John

Hollander, a marketing and sales manager from Cooper Lighting who was assigned to manage our partnership. I had asked John to join us because I just didn't think Cooper Lighting's senior management would believe me if I later decided to tell them what happened. My other two companions were lawyers, one a recently hired junior associate with the law firm of Fisher, Rushmer, Werrenrath, Dixon, Talley, and Dunlap, named Joseph Tamborello.

Joe was a slightly chubby, cherub-faced young lawyer fresh out of law school. Only his traditional suit and tie gave him the appearance that he was no longer a college freshman. Joe Tamborello had been up late until the early hours of the morning several nights before researching case law on behalf of the senior partner in his firm so they could file preliminary injunction orders against the Wus in civil court. I was very impressed by how this young lawyer could not only research and find case law to support every one of our claims in such a short time, but also by how he was able to recite every case from memory. Joe Tamborello could even recite, word for word, the pertinent parts of the judicial decisions that were "on-point" with our case. As a result, I later nicknamed him "The Human Computer," after that, the name stuck with his firm. This was not only Joe's first time to witness an FBI raid, this was his very first legal case. Only Joe's mouth and eyes were wider than mine as he watched the gun-toting FBI men seize Optic-Tech's booth and cart it away.

The last man in our party was a tall, trim, tan, and distinguished looking gentleman in his mid-'50s. His swept back black hair revealed a deeply furrowed brow. A close-cropped beard surrounded a square jaw, which was clenched on a fresh unlit cigar. Everything else about this Yale Law School graduate was distinguished except for the ridiculous T-shirt he was wearing. It featured Dr. Evil from the Austin Powers movie in his trademark pose with his pinky in his mouth. He told me that he intended to wear a Fat Bastard and Mini-Me T-shirt, but he complained that he couldn't find one in his size. The man's name was John Edwin Fisher, the senior founding partner of Fisher, Rushmer, Werrenrath, Dixon, Talley and Dunlap. John Fisher calmly continued to chew on his cigar as his office called on his cell phone. They confirm that the process servers had just served Wu's staff at Optic-Tech's Miami office with the Super Vision's lawsuit, preliminary injunction, and notice of the Temporary Restraining Order (TRO). We had obtained the ex-parte order in the week prior to the FBI action thanks to John's brilliant presentation before a State Court Judge and Joe's capable research.

"Well, I think we may have caused the opposition a bit of trouble today," John said with an understated wry smile. "Nice touch to be hit with an FBI raid, a lawsuit, an injunction, and a restraining order all in the same day. I think at least we got their attention."

THIRTY-FIVE

❦

John, looking resplendent in his dark
blue suit and paisley tie, leaned back in his tall leather chair
in his corner 15th floor office. He silently listened to my story
with a piercing gaze while thoughtfully chewing his cigar.
During my presentation he would often furrow his brow and
raise his eyebrows to express whether he was either amused or
in disagreement with my statements. But I later learned John
had a wild side, one that eventually won this rather conservative looking lawyer the nickname "Austin Powers," after the
famous movie, a name John later grew proud of.

When it became clear I could not afford the services of
Holland & Knight, I decided to give another partner in
John's firm, Ren Werrenrath, a call. Ren had already suc-
cessfully handled a case for another one of my staff members. Ren was kind enough to drop by and view a presentation of the case documents on our conference room table.
He shook his head in a combination of amazement and disbelief and said, "There is only one guy I know who would be
able to take on this case and he is also the same guy who can
decide if we can take this on contingency." The next day he
introduced me to the senior partner and founder of his
firm, John Fisher.

John told me at our first meeting, "I am the best lawyer
you ever met or ever will meet." He was not jesting, he
meant it. Great men have great egos and in John's case
there was no exception. John, however, also possessed a

great sense of humor. It was often his saving grace. He used his wit to win over other lawyers, judges, and juries that normally would have been put off by a man with such great confidence and capabilities. John knew when to be self-deprecating when it mattered most. As accurate as a laser beam, he would engage in self-depreciating levity at the precise moment when necessary. He was a man that would tangle with the most aggressive lawyers in the courtroom and rip them to shreds, yet moments later he would wrestle with his 9-year-old outside his office and take turns doing Fat Bastard and Dr. Evil imitations.

John and his son's favorite imitation was Fat Bastard. In unison they would put their hands on their hips and stick their bellies out as far as they could and yell, "Get in my belly" and, "I just ate a baby." John was the one who gave Samson Wu and his brother their monikers, "Fat Bastard" and "Mini-Me," which we used to refer to them throughout the court proceedings. It allowed us at times to make light of a very serious and taxing situation. John's humor was matched equally by his sense of adventure. He would climb mountains in Nepal, canoe down whitewater rapids in Colorado and jump into and out of anything that moved. But his most daring feats he reserved for the courtroom. There, John was king of the jungle and he knew it. At times I almost felt sorry for his adversaries and their attorneys. They were so terribly outwitted and outclassed that they even seemed sympathetic at times, regardless of their crimes.

John had a presence in the courtroom that captivated juries and commanded the attention of judges. He would at times even directly challenge judges on their orders. His command, credibility, and stage presence were such that judges would not object or find him in contempt. Any other lawyer daring to challenge a judge or jury would be thrown out of the courtroom, but not John. The risks he took where tempered by his skill and his experience. His challenges were always based on law. They were well researched and well documented.

Another great attribute of John was his honesty and his sense of ethics. John would never cheat, nor ever cross the line of law or common courtesy. He would never resort to the type of underhanded tactics that our opponents' counsel would routinely engage in. At one time, I complained that he was having a jousting match with a bunch of dirty criminals and street fighters and he needed to be more aggressive.

John just turned to me and said, "I don't have to play the game at their level. I am far more intelligent than them and I will outthink them and I will outsmart them. I do not have to break the rules to win and I will not break the rules to do so."

John would not deviate from his ethical standards, regardless of the relentless lies and fabrications the other side would present to the court. He made it clear that as long as he was my lawyer, he was in charge of the case and he was in charge of how my case would be conducted. I would just have to have faith in his intellect and faith in the outcome. Although I often argued with John on strategy, I never doubted his word or his capabilities. The result he achieved at trial underscored his message that in the long run, "the righteous will prevail as long as they remain righteous."

John had four sons, two from a prior marriage, one, Bradford, who followed his professional footsteps into the field of law as a prosecutor for the Florida State Attorney's Office and another, Mark, who followed his spiritual footsteps as a Presbyterian Minister for a church in North Carolina. In his marriage to Leslie, he inherited a son, Brian, who later became a force of nature on the football field for Vanderbilt University. Brian was a young boy when John married Leslie. Their marriage produced another son, Johnny, who was a constant source of entertainment for John and all his clients who came to know him personally.

John talked of all his sons with a great deal of pride evident on his face, but his comments about Johnny were always accentuated with an additional little twinkle in his eye. Perhaps John just found amusement in watching Johnny explore his ever-changing new world. Or perhaps John just found in Johnny his own second childhood.

Before I agreed to sign John's contingency fee agreement, I felt it was important that I disclose to him that one bad experience from my past that I felt the defense may try to use against me. Just as I had told the FBI before they took the case, I disclosed the story about FiberView and the ruling Judge Lewis T. Babcock made against me in that trade secret hearing. I did not want any surprises to surface later that might affect the trust in our relationship or our ability to respond to the defense attorney's attack on my credibility. John reviewed the *Forbes* article on the subject and listened intently to my description of the legal strategy employed against me, and the outcome. John did not seem too phased by what was one judge's opinion 12 years ago, but he was fascinated by how the opposing legal team dismembered me even before my first day in court. He asked me questions about the ex-parte TRO, the seizures, and the restrictions. He wanted every detail. The more I told him how terribly I was hammered, the more he started to smile and narrow his eyes in amusement.

John removed his now well-chewed cigar from his mouth and pointed at me and said, "And that's exactly how WE are going to nail THEM to the wall."

THIRTY-SIX

John Fisher's plans were brilliantly executed. He made sure that the Wus were hit simultaneously
from both sides and timed the civil action to correspond
with the FBI raid. Our opponents were reeling.

John would later inform me that the results of his plan
were attributed as much to a capable judge as it had been to
his brilliant strategy. This, John said, involved both "a little
bit of good luck and bad." Before we submitted our request
for an ex-parte TRO, we had to be assigned a judge for a
hearing. This judge would most likely also be the judge that
would preside on our case through trial. Minutes before
John headed to the courthouse to request an immediate
hearing, he called to tell me he was heading over and felt
confident in a good result as long as we got "anyone else but
Judge Baker."

After his hearing, John called me to tell me that we initially had "bad luck" in the draw process. By luck of the
judicial draw the court had assigned us the rather cantan-
kerous, arrogant, and offbeat judge, Joe Baker. Judge
Baker was not pleased to grant requests for rulings, since
he was not fond of hearing anyone else's viewpoint, but his
own. Baker routinely relied on his own thoughts, rather
than the evidence. But we had been "lucky" that Baker
would not be in court that day. Our urgent request for an
ex-parte TRO was referred to a well-respected Judge,
Lawrence A. Kirkwood.

On Nov. 18, 1999, Judge Kirkwood listened intently as John described and reviewed the piles of documentary evidence we had obtained against Samson Wu, Optic-Tech International, Marsam Trading, Shanghai Quialong Optic-Tech, and his related companies and cohorts. With great drama and eloquence, John painted a picture of the "intellectual property crime of the century." Paul Koren's affidavit and information detailing how the thefts occurred and how the money was transferred laid out the trail of deceit in detail.

Judge Kirkwood questioned John to make sure he understood all that was placed before him. He did not grant John's injunction and restraining-order requests immediately, instead he reviewed all the evidence to confirm that John's case merited the extraordinary sanctions of an ex-parte TRO and all the related search, seizure, and freeze orders that would go with it. He knew that these orders would initially cripple our opponents. He wanted to make sure that the potential harm he was causing our opponents was more than offset by the harm that our opponent's continued actions would cause us. He also set out another test, before he would grant John's requests, he wanted to make sure that the other party would be viewed according to Florida law as a "criminal enterprise" under Florida RICO Statutes. Only then would such ex-parte actions be justified. Typically, in commercial disputes, there should not be fear of overseas counterfeiting, fraud, and destruction of evidence, which would require draconian methods to both protect and seize evidence.

John's evidence was as detailed and well documented as his presentation was gripping and dramatic. He was able to offer documented proof and testimony from former insiders about the Wus' operations and its clandestine theft and counterfeiting operations. Judge Kirkwood granted a sweeping TRO in his preliminary injunction that not only ordered Optic-Tech to cease all counterfeiting activities of Super Vision's products, but ordered all personal and corporate bank accounts of Mr. Wu to be frozen pending an upcoming hearing or trial. Judge Kirkwood's order further granted the rights of replevin to Super Vision.

A replevin order is the right of a company or individual who has made a convincing argument of theft by another party to have permission to break into and enter the home and/or business of the party accused of stealing. This action usually must take place in the presence of a police officer, who must supervise the breaking and entering by a professional locksmith and the search and seizure of the stolen property by the plaintiff. We were granted replevin rights to Wu's home and Miami offices and warehouses, Caruso's home in Orlando, and the personal residences of all the other officers and directors of the many corporations wholly or jointly owned by Wu. These were referred to in Judge Kirkwood's order as "The Wu Family Enterprise." From that point forward, "The Wu Family Enterprise," became the term used in court to refer to all the individuals and companies involved in this massive criminal web spun by Wu.

Within a few days of the raid, I called the Dade County Sheriff's Office in Miami to schedule the first possible date of the replevin action to the Marsam Trading and Optic-Tech warehouse in Miami, Florida. The Dade County Sheriff's calendar was quite busy, and it became clear we were not going to be able to replevin at the Marsam/Optic-Tech warehouse first. We were able to schedule the replevin of Caruso's home in Orlando in a matter of days, so we jumped at our first opportunity.

I arrived at Caruso's home with my video camera in hand. The Orange County Sheriff's deputy was waiting outside to greet me at 8 a.m. We knew he was inside, since his van was parked in front of his garage. We did not wait for the locksmith because we were fairly certain the sheriff would force Caruso to open the door. The door swung open and a bleary-eyed Caruso, wearing sweat pants and a T-shirt, opened the door. On the couch right by the door were piles of our fiber-optic cable, still tagged with our serial numbers. It seemed that he was preparing to clean house and leave town. His bags were packed and his car appeared loaded with papers and boxes, which we later searched. His son-in-law at first tried to make light of the situation, waving at my video camera chanting "hi mom" every time the lens passed in his direction. It was only when I moved to search his room that his demeanor changed. Travis Ponchintesta, Caruso's son-in-law, took over Caruso's house along with his daughter when Caruso moved to China. Travis was quite miffed that I was going to "disturb" all the boxes that he had so neatly piled in front of his closet. The boxes contained nothing but clothes, but behind them were shelves full of our cable and light source products. As my video camera recorded the evidence, the "hi moms" abruptly changed to "this is not mine."

The sheriff and I loaded all the stolen products into my SUV. Before I drove away, I warned Caruso that if he left the country, he had better not plan on ever returning if he failed to show up for his hearing and trial dates. Caruso was still defiant. He just stood at the edge of his driveway grinning as if this would only be round two and there would be many more rounds to come.

THIRTY-SEVEN

I flew to Miami to join the Dade County Sheriff and a local locksmith to enter the Optic-Tech and Marsam-Trading's warehouse in Miami Florida. We agreed to pay overtime to the sheriff's office to do the search and seizure at night, hoping to catch our opponents off guard when they were not present to slip evidence out the back door. We knew that Wu must have already been wary of a potential replevin action. No doubt by now, word of the search and seizure at Caruso's home must have reached him. The locksmith picked the lock to the front door in minutes. As soon as the door swung open, the alarm went off. I ran in with my video camera sensing I only had a few minutes of unfettered access to the facility before Wu and his henchmen arrived.

For a moment, I froze in the lobby, not knowing whether I should run into the warehouse or offices first. My heart was pounding and the adrenaline rush from the break in was making me dizzy and indecisive. The scene was almost overwhelming. From the lobby I was able to see piles of documents stacked up on the floors of the open offices. Someone was just about ready to do a huge amount of "house cleaning." I decided to video as much documentation that I could first to confirm its existence should it later "disappear." My concerns were further confirmed by the already overflowing bin of the shredding machine beside Wu's secretary's desk and the huge stack of documents already placed in a cardboard box marked "to be shredded." I recorded the shredder, the cardboard box, and began to sift through bank documents stamped "original" with original signatures authorizing wire transfers to H& K Consulting.

The video camera continued to record as I viewed the stacks of Optic-Tech documents that were piled two to three-feet high on the floor of Samson's and Thomas Wu's offices. When I put down my video camera to filter through the stacks, I spotted several documents from our company files, which included blueprints to our machinery and data sheets from our subcontractors on our tensioning and chemical formulations. As I picked up the camera to video documents that I had sorted from the piles, a legal document that I had not sorted all of a sudden appeared in front of my camera lens. Then I heard a heavily accented Chinese voice shouting for me to stop my filming and to leave the premises. The voice was that of Thomas Wu. In his hand was a bankruptcy filing for Marsam Trading Company that they had filed a day before in the Federal Bankruptcy Court. Thomas had thrust this document in front of my camera lens and was using it to block my filming of the evidence that lay before me.

Apparently our replevin raid at Caruso's home did not go unnoticed by Wu or his attorneys. In the week that followed, Wu and his lawyers worked together with his accountants and bankers to draft and file a Chapter 11 Bankruptcy filing for Marsam Trading Company. It was designed to bar our entry for future searches. As Thomas continued to thrust the bankruptcy filing in front of my camera lens, Wu was standing behind him talking on the cell phone with his lawyer. At his lawyer's instruction, Wu handed the phone to the Dade County sheriff's deputy. The lawyer explained that the law dictated that bankruptcy filings stay all replevin actions. The sheriff's deputy handed back the phone to Wu and informed me we had to leave.

I was shocked. I argued with the sheriff that we had caught them red-handed. Stolen documents from my files were there. Piles of evidence were being assembled for shredding. It was clear to me that if we were forced to leave, much of what we had seen would never be seen again. The sheriff then shook his head and shrugged his shoulders and said, "I know, but that's the law."

"What kind of law grants protections to thieves to destroy evidence?" I objected in disbelief.

"Our law," he said as he escorted me out of the building.

THIRTY-EIGHT

After learning of the bankruptcy stalling the replevin, John notified me that I would have to retain bankruptcy counsel in Miami. This was not a field that John specialized in. He was convinced we needed someone local who had specific knowledge and prior relationships with the bankruptcy courts. I immediately called our former local SEC attorney at Greenburg Traurig for a referral. He gave me the name of a senior partner at Greenburg Traurig in charge of the bankruptcy practice in Miami. I quickly signed the partner on, desiring speed rather than efficiency. He then quickly ran up our bill to an astronomical amount to review the case and represent us at the initial hearing.

John flew down with me to attend the initial bankruptcy hearing before Judge A. Jay Cristol, U.S. bankruptcy judge for the Southern District of Florida. Wu was present with his recently hired local bankruptcy counsel, David Softness, from the firm of Ackerman Sunterfitt. Ackerman Sunterfeit had also represented Wu at his initial civil hearing, which they failed to overturn the court's temporary restraining order and preliminary injunction several months earlier. Mr. Softness was a very ethical attorney who later chose to drop his representation of the Wu family as soon as it became apparent what their true actions and motivations were. Also present were two men that I later learned were from Ocean Bank. One was very openly hugging Wu before everyone gathered in the courtroom and standing by his side with his arm around him while listening to the proceedings. Wu and his bankers would often flash harsh stares in our direction or alternatively smirked at what they felt were our bankruptcy counsel's impudent attempts to overturn the stay on the Marsam Trading search and seizure.

The scene was very puzzling to me. Here were officers of a major Florida bank who had just submitted documentation to the bankruptcy court claiming that they were owed more than $5 million dollars by Wu's company, Marsam Trading Company. For a bank allegedly imperiled with losing $5 million of its depositor's funds in this pending bankruptcy filing, the bank officers looked more like Wu's cheerleading section than his creditors. Their mean stares in our direction were only overshadowed by their verbal threats when they approached John and I. Their public display of allegiance to their debtor client Wu, looked more like a scene out of the movie the Goodfellas where fellow Mafiosi display their fealty to their brethren.

The bankers swaggered as they approached John and myself with Wu in tow. One made a very challenging prediction. "You guys won't get a dime, not a dime." He emphasized his statement with great confidence in order to shake our resolve.

John did not even blink, he responded with a long, piercing stare that would have turned flesh to stone. He slowly removed his cigar and then caught the banker off guard when he responded, "You are probably right, but how much do you want to bet me that your client will eventually wind up in jail?"

The banker seemed taken aback by this thought and for a moment released his supporting grip around Wu's wide shoulders. John, sensing blood in the water, leaned in further and said, "Well, you're a banker, aren't you? You have got money, don't you? How much do you want to bet?"

The bankers and Wu just responded with a sheepish smirk and made their way out the door. The scene was not lost on me. The bankers and Wu looked just too cozy for them to be joined at the hip at a bankruptcy hearing. If Wu's financial situation had been as dire as they had informed the court, the bank should have been seriously worried about their relationship with Mr. Wu. Their behavior was quite the opposite.

After Wu and his brethren from Ocean Bank left the courtroom, we turned to our local bankruptcy legal counsel for his input. After all, he was the senior partner at one of the largest bankruptcy firms in Dade County; surely he could now offer us guidance or words of wisdom. All that our local bankruptcy attorney accomplished at the initial hearing was to confirm what we and the Wus already knew; we could not engage in replevins against Marsam Trading Company as long as they were in bankruptcy. He then informed us why he was too busy to offer us a lift to the airport, but was most willing to point out where we might find a taxi on the street outside the courtroom. He also reminded us of his bill that was already due.

"What no kiss?" muttered John under his breath.

"I am usually offered at least a kiss before I am fucked, at least at these prices, don't you think so Brett?"

John had already echoed my sentiments. My first decision was to fire this counsel and do my homework this time to find a more proactive local counsel, perhaps a small boutique firm that specialized in bankruptcy that did not have such a high overhead and billing rates. My second decision was to press John to come up with a creative solution to my problem on his own, so perhaps I ultimately would not have to rely on the services of another yet-to-be proven counsel.

I resolved the first decision by contacting several friends of mine in Miami who referred me to friends of theirs in the legal community. Many of them came back with the same name—Arthur Rice of Rice and Robinson. Arthur Rice was a rough and tumble attorney whose face and demeanor showed his years of battle. Arthur's strategy was simple. He was either going to "win this case or wear them down to make the bankruptcy procedure so inhospitable that they will voluntarily dismiss themselves from the process." His idea of "voluntarily" was something that they would choose to do after he would make their life a living hell.

Arthur Rice eventually succeeded in his endeavor. He used the bankruptcy law to force them to turn over financial documentation that Wu ultimately would not be required to provide in the existing trade secret civil proceeding. Rice compared this discovery process to a proctologist making an examination by using a sewer pipe instead of an endoscope: "Very painful," he said with a harsh laugh and a grin.

The Wus did not like being placed in a venue where they would have to provide information on their finances and assets. Days before the court imposed deadlines to produce their financial records they decided to voluntarily withdraw from the proceedings. But this was months after John resolved my previous problem. John, after being suitably disgusted with the initial results of the previous bankruptcy attorney, turned to his own devices to attempt a solution. He again employed his genius to allow me to legally kick back open the door of Wu's facility.

THIRTY-NINE

⚭

I was able to return to Wu's Miami warehouse just a
few weeks later with two new Dade County Sheriffs and a
locksmith. John found a creative way to regain my entry to
the premises without violating the bankruptcy filing. John
decided to simply re-submit another ex-parte motion for me
to enter the building on a replevin of Optic Tech. Optic
Tech, a separate and independent corporate entity, was
listed as a corporation domiciled at the same address.
Marsam was in bankruptcy, but Optic-Tech was not. Probably a detail that was overlooked by Wu's very hurried legal
counsel who was fending off simultaneous civil and criminal
attacks against his client. In the time between the two
replevins, I decided to hire Brinks Security and Investigations Service in Miami to keep an eye on the warehouse to
make sure nothing significant was overlooked or "disappeared" during my undesired absence.

John ceremoniously removed his well-worn cigar from
his mouth as he placed the new replevin documents in my
hand. "Have I got just the job for you young man! Happy
hunting Brett." John said with a wink and a nod. As I left his
office I could overhear John and Joe chuckle about what
they have just unleashed on poor old Wu. They made it
sound as if they have just unchained a hungry pit bull and
had thrown a steak in front of him. They were right. I
wasted no time booking the next flight to Miami, I coordi-
nated with the sheriff's office on my cell phone as I drove to

the airport. I agreed to pay overtime charges for the two officers so they would meet me the next morning at 8 a.m. at the warehouse on Saturday. I had also arranged to rent a truck in Miami to cart back whatever I could find. Our second replevin action took place on the Saturday morning, just after Thanksgiving of 1999. Staging the raid on a holiday weekend caught them entirely by surprise. After the locksmith picked the lock, I ran into the building. I first went into the offices and opened all the file cabinets. Every single file relating to fiber optics and Optic-Tech was empty as were all the financial file folders. I guess we caught the Wus before they were able to destroy everything; however, I was at least able to videotape the empty file folders that still remained with labels affixed to the jackets. The piles of documents on the floor were gone and the previously disheveled office looked neat and broom clean. This was no surprise, I expected as much.

This time I was able to run into the warehouse with my camera. Inside I saw dozens of huge garbage bags filled with shredded documents. I also saw a gargantuan pile of fiber-optic cable covering rows of pallet racking inside the warehouse. I was awestruck. They had literally duplicated millions of dollars of Super Vision product and it was all sitting right there right in front of me. My hands shook as I panned the long line of cable laden pallet racking and filmed it with my video camera. There was going to be no way they could lie about or deny this later. Doubtless in their arrogance and celebration that they had thwarted our first replevin attempt at the warehouse, they were confident that their bankruptcy-protected warehouse would serve as a safe haven for the counterfeit products.

As Wu raced into the building with Winkler in tow, they voiced their outrage that their "rights" were now being violated. My lawyer was now already on the cell phone with the Dade County Sheriff deflecting all of Wu's objections.

Unless The Wu Family Enterprise or their lawyers could come up with a bankruptcy filing for Optic-Tech that day, the search and seizure was to continue. Since the courts were closed on the weekends, we knew they would not have time to get one.

I recorded rack after rack of counterfeit product. They had not only copied our cables but also every single one of our fixtures and fittings. The Chinese copied exactly, leaving no license for creativity. It would be easy to prove these were exact copies and knock-offs. While I was filming inside, Wu and Winkler carried out the many bags of shredded documents and threw them in the dumpster outside. I had previously complained of all the evidence they had destroyed since the first replevin action and was starting to videotape the pile of garbage bags that were still sitting in the warehouse. Wu and Winkler carried more bags of shredded documents to the dumpster where they thought they would be less noticeable. I ran outside and was able to film Winkler and Wu throwing the garbage bags into the dumpster. Wu would stand at the top of the warehouse stairs at a side door and throw bag after bag of shredded documents to Winkler who would then carry them from the foot of the stairs to the adjacent dumpster. Soon the dumpster was overflowing and could hold no more. I filmed further the confused faces of Wu and Winkler who both milled around for a while trying to figure out what to do with the remaining bags.

Upon leaving, I was warned by Winkler, who was now on the cell phone with his company attorneys, that I had better not trespass on his property again and that this dumpster was off limits to me as well. I thanked the two sheriffs for their assistance and headed to my rented van out in the parking lot with as much cable, light sources, and fixtures that the van would carry. But I could not stop thinking about the shredded documents. I decided to call my lawyer

Joseph Tamborello at home. The "Human Computer" came up with the answer almost immediately. "Trash in a dumpster is not private property," Joe confidently informed me. "I can even cite case law on this if you like. This is how FBI and private investigators routinely obtain their evidence. It's fair game." My mind was racing now. I did not have either the time or interest to hear the Human Computer rattle off case law. I had something else in mind.

No sooner had I hung up with the Human Computer I dialed the local Brinks Security office. They had watched the building for me earlier and were not surprised by my request. A few of their investigators had already had run ins with Wu and his staff when they were found not so inconspicuously parked outside Optic-Tech's parking lot. They scooped up all the bags of shredded documents from the dumpster that evening and placed them in protective storage in one of their warehouses.

If we ever can figure a way to piece all these back together, I thought, we would have a great case for destruction of evidence.

I called Joe and shared my thoughts with him. The Human Computer, true to form, informed me that the proper term and civil claim we would later seek at trial was "negligent destruction of evidence." I told Joe that there was nothing "negligent" about it. This was "deliberate." I could almost hear Joe chuckling on the other end of the line as he again tried to restrain the pit bull that they unleashed: "Brett," Joe implored me, "this will be up to the judge and jury to decide, not you and not me."

FORTY

After we asked our private investigation agency in Miami to recover all the shredded documents from the dumpster, the calls from Wu's lawyers came in predictably to Judge Baker on the next business day. The Wus' attorneys were furious at this terrible travesty of justice I committed and the violation of their client's "rights." The lawyers didn't bother to call Judge Kirkwood because it was he who had issued the order several weeks ago. They sought refuge in Judge Baker who by now was presiding over this case and routinely showed a predilection toward protecting their rights. Judge Baker hemmed and hawed at John's legal display of creativity and tenacity, which Judge Baker opined may have crossed the line or at least into a grey area of the law. However, the Human Computer was again right on point. The case law he cited showed that prior court opinions clearly and consistently ruled on our side. After Joe rattled off the long litany of cases on point, we got nothing more than grumblings of disapproval from Judge Baker.

I have often wondered why Americans have allowed themselves to grow accustomed to a society whose laws offer more protection for the criminals than they do for their innocent victims. In far too many court decisions, the criminal gets off on a technicality at the expense of the safety and security of the victim. How is justice served when we allow legions of lawyers in our legislatures to create bodies of law geared towards keeping themselves employed rather than keeping criminals behind bars? Our system has no longer become "by the people, for the people" but rather "by the lawyers, for the lawyers."

As the pig said in the book, *Animal Farm*, "All animals are equal, but some are more equal than others." I have often marveled at the hypocrisy of the words carved in stone found above almost every courtroom in the nation, "Equal Justice Under the Law." People with more money in this country are "more equal" under our law. Often it is not the just cause that is protected, but the individual with the most money who is able to hire the best lawyers. This is evidenced by the fact that a hungry young inner city kid who steals lunch money from one individual is more likely to go to jail than a middle-aged corporate executive who steals the life savings of thousands. The fact that the majority of the original executives at Enron, WorldCom, and Tyco are still walking free is testimony to this. Such a system cannot possibly achieve justice or equality. It was the same in our case. However, I also learned that people who simply don't follow the law, become even "more equal" in most court proceedings.

Throughout the two and a half years from the date of the injunction to the time of the trial, it appeared that our adversaries and our opponents had all but one strategy: to use the U.S. legal system to wear Super Vision down. They did not care how much evidence we uncovered or how much proof we obtained. They did not hesitate to destroy evidence, file false statements, and threaten witnesses. Even when we achieved a contempt order against them for these violations and were awarded our legal fees, they ignored the court orders again and refused to pay the fees. Every attempt to bring any meaningful sanctions against them were thwarted by their attorneys. Our laws provided plenty of "out" clauses for defendants who had sharp legal representation. The Wus' main strategy was to tie us up in hundreds of hours of discovery and deposition requests and to make sure we ran out of money prior to the trial date. The lawyers for the Wus constantly pushed out the deadline for the trial date to make sure it never came.

The lawyers who were so adept at deflecting any attempt to bring the Wus to justice specialized in defending white-collar criminals. The firm of Snyderburn, Rishoi, and Swan established itself in Winter Park and eventually relocated to downtown Orlando. Philip Snyderburn, the senior partner and lead attorney, was a slightly built and balding man with a penchant for fine suits and ties. Snyderburn also had a well-defined talent for looking people in the eye and relaying information provided to him by his clients as if it were gospel. However, even when our capable counsel caught him relaying to the judge what we later proved was obviously false information from his client, John tried to mitigate any direct accusations against Snyderburn by stating that it was "obvious that he could not have known this in advance." Joe Tamborello, John's ever-present assistant at these proceedings, would just stare at Snyderburn in disbelief. *Some facts are undeniable and bad for your client,* Joe thought. *Just because a client wishes they were different, doesn't change the bad facts.* Law school had taught him to accept them and deal with them head on. The client should always be the one to pay the price for lying. Not the lawyer. And although Snyderburn was not exactly lying to Joe, he did appear to be deluding himself a little bit by preaching his client's view as gospel.

John, a longtime courtroom veteran, did not seem to share Joe's indignation. Whether it was John's true belief that Snyderburn was just passing on information from his client or deliberately misleading the court, I will never know. John, however, exhibited tremendous deference and decorum to Snyderburn as a fellow legal counsel. He did not seek to discredit his opposing counsel. Snyderburn had a long history of being successful in getting individuals accused of white-collar crimes off the hook. His offices on a

high floor in a sleek new downtown office building over-
looking Lake Eola served as ample testimony to the fees people were all too willing to pay to achieve such results.

In Judge Kirkwood we had a bright, no-nonsense judge
who was able to see through all the ploys and fabrications.
He did not allow their eloquent and well-funded defense
attorneys to continue to cloud the issues. Judge Kirkwood
upheld his preliminary injunction order and seemed
inclined to offer us the right to a speedy trial. We discovered
that we would receive just the opposite from Judge Baker.
After Judge Kirkwood had provided the initial temporary
injunction order and presided over the preliminary injunction hearing, John fought hard to keep Judge Kirkwood on
our case. John thought it would also be much more expe-
dient to keep a judge in place who has already heard several
hours of testimony and was already familiar with the case.
But the court rules provided for the judge selected by the
draw to be the judge who would take the case to trial. Only
if Judge Baker would accede to Judge Kirkwood's willingness
to continue with the case would we be able to remain with
Judge Kirkwood. But Judge Baker refused; he wanted to
preside over this case. From that point forward, both the
case and our "luck" changed dramatically.

FORTY-ONE

The individuals who wield the most power in our judicial system are the judges. The judges are given latitude to exercise discretion, but they are also bound to uphold the letter of the law. Herein lies another great contradiction in our legal system. Different judges often provide different interpretations and administration of the law. Although Congress and state legislatures have been trying to remedy this problem by imposing mandated sentencing guidelines, the outcome of a case can vary dramatically, depending on which judge was picked to preside over it. Often the outcome could come as much from the luck (or bad luck) of the draw as much as it could from the skill of the attorney. The judicial selection process is somewhat akin to a game of Russian roulette. The outcome can also be as disastrous. This was very evident in the analysis of the actions of the judges who presided over this case.

Our "good luck" at first was to have Judge Kirkwood preside over the decision to grant a preliminary injunction order and a temporary restraining order against the defendants. Judge Kirkwood listened carefully, questioned our counsel thoroughly, and later granted his motion. As confident as John was to see that a "good judge" would rule in our favor, he was equally confident in predicting that Judge Baker would later rule against us. John's premonitions of the most negative scenarios to unfold in Justice Baker's courtroom became all too accurate. John knew this and thought Judge Baker would rely on his own personal interests and knowledge in making his decisions rather than the facts of the case. John warned me in advance that this would come into play. What John did not warn me of was the other antics that would play out in his courtroom.

During our first hearing before Judge Baker, his honor seemed more intent on reviewing information on his computer screen than listening to the final arguments of the lawyers from both sides that were standing before him. In the middle of a heated debate on the motion before him Judge Baker slowly rose from his bench, looked at his watch, and headed out the side door of the courtroom. As the seconds ticked by into minutes, the defense attorney faced the judge's legal assistant and court reporter and asked, "Are we finished?"

"Yes," said the judge's legal assistant. "I think that means the judge is done for the day."

"He could have told me we were over, or at least let me finish my argument," complained the now red-faced defense attorney.

"Well that is the judge's way of letting you know," replied the legal assistant.

"Great," said the defense lawyer as he turned to my counsel. "John, I guess we get to fight on another day."

Joe lifted his head from his pile of meticulously organized and tabulated evidence and case law to see what had gone on. The Human Computer looked around and asked, "Where is the judge?"

John replied "It looks like the Judge has decided to leave."

"Is that allowed?" replied Joe with astonishment.

"Apparently in this courtroom it is," said John, as he smiled and winked at the court clerk. He then turned and nodded his head with a slight bow in a gracious goodbye to his fellow counsel. "I guess we shall fight again another day."

Justice Baker was prone to more than just simply disappearing in the middle of testimony. He would often get bored with the debate and engage in endeavors on his computer, while the attorneys droned on. Judge Baker felt he was of superior intellect to all who entered his courtroom. The arguments and evidence mattered little. He believed he was able to assess the facts through both his instinct and his intuition supported by his intellectual prowess.

Judge Baker seemed to almost disdain the fact that he even had to sit in the courtroom and listen. He preferred to do the lawyer's jobs for them. He would rather serve as judge, jury, and advocate all rolled up into one. *Much more efficient,* he must have thought.

FORTY-TWO

ᥫᣞ

Justice Baker absolutely terrified me, not just because he acted crazy, but because he was self-right-eous and pompous. This made him even more dangerous, as dangerous as another judge that I had come in contact with in my past, Judge Lewis T. Babcock. The biggest legal mistake that I had made in my life was not insisting that Judge Bab-cock be recused from my case when we were in litigation with ADTI in Colorado more than a decade earlier. I was deter-mined not to make the same mistake with Judge Baker. I knew I could never get a fair trial, even if I received a favor-able jury verdict, because of Judge Baker's predilection to overturn juries in favor of his higher intellectual judgment.

It was clear that Judge Baker's judgment was already leaning towards the side of the Chinese. Judge Baker was skilled in the Chinese language and Chinese history. He also proudly boasted in court of being equally skilled and knowledgeable in his theories on trade secrets. He stated publicly in our court hearing that he doesn't understand what the big deal is with trade secrets. After all, "even if someone does steal the secret recipe for Coca-Cola, it really doesn't matter much... it's all about marketing anyway." With Judge Baker claiming that it was basically OK. to steal any trade secret, even the most famous trade secret in Amer-ica, I knew we were good as dead with him presiding in our case.

Judge Baker's statement reminded me of Judge Lewis T. Babcock's opening statement at our trade-secret hearing before him in 1988, when he said, "Before this case came to me, I never heard the words or term fiber optics before, much less an image magnification device." With that said, Judge Babcock determined he was still competent to rule on technical issues in our case, despite our pleadings to appoint a special master to determine if any of the claims of our competitor were true in our industry. Judge Babcock later went on to rule common tools in the fiber-optic industry such as winding wheels, clamps, and glue were all trade secrets of my competitor. In his conclusion, where he upheld his previous ex-parte injunction, he stated, "I find Brett Kingstone to be 100% incredible. I do not believe a single thing he says." With those words, I not only lost my company, but America lost another promising new technology. George Gilder later wrote in his article, "Severed Heads and Wasted Resources," in *Forbes* Magazine, that with this decision "A federal judge in Denver dealt a puzzling setback to U.S. efforts to compete with the Japanese in big screen TV." It should be noted that to this day, there is not one single television produced in the United States by an American company. Judge Babcock's ruling helped assure that fact.

The truth finally came out in a FBI investigation of Cap Rock Savings, which was one of the largest Savings and Loan frauds in U.S. history. Two years after Judge Babcock's fateful decision was read, the U.S. Attorney indicted the President and CEO of ADTI, Mukesh Assumoll, who financed the quirky "inventor" Steve Sedlmayr and masterminded the court case against me. Assumoll apparently was using ADTI, among other investments, to launder funds he plundered from the bank. He overstated the value of his stock and real-estate investments and loaned himself and his cronies tens of millions of dollars of the bank's money using the soon to be worthless stock and inflated real-estate assets as collateral. Apparently, Assumoll was a man way ahead of his time. He effectively preempted Enron and WorldCom by more than a decade in utilizing the same ruse they had used to fleece their shareholders and investors.

I learned more about Assumoll and his teammates in the ensuing *Dallas Morning News* articles. An Attorney Richard Zadina, was quoted in the case referring to Assumoll as a "smooth, articulate con man." The article reported how at times Assumoll would refer to himself as "His Royal Highness" at Caesars Palace and other similar establishments during his frequent high rolling gambling trips to Las Vegas. The reference was understandable. Assumoll, a dark and exotic-looking man of Indian decent, did somewhat look the part of royalty.

He certainly encouraged the assumption with his arrival in sleek Learjets, accompanying flashy entourage and enormous tips that he showered on those who attended to his every wish.

The bank depositors, however, paid for Assumoll's regal lifestyle with their life savings.

As for Assumoll's colleague and partner, the alleged "inventor" Steve Sedlmayr, was later reported by former employees as claiming his inventive capabilities "stemmed from divine intervention." He further explained that the event that caused him to discover the process for creating fiber-optic display screens was not his meeting with Dr. Glenn and review of his processes, but the result of a car crash in which his Corvette sports car skidded off a cliff and his "head was severed and later reattached by angels who infused him with divine inventive fire." So much for Judge Babcock's judgment of credibility.

Assumoll was sentenced to five years in prison by Texas Judge Jerry Buchmeyer without the possibility of parole for wrecking hundreds of families' lives, as he had my own. He could have received up to 10 years in prison, but federal prosecutors recommended that he receive a reduced sentence because of his cooperation against the other co-conspirators. U.S. Attorney Jennifer Bolen, with supporting testimony from Assumoll, prosecuted several of the bankers and lawyers that assisted in this massive fraud that was estimated to cost U.S. taxpayers in excess of $100 million. Ms. Bolen made it clear in her opening statement at trial that the bankers and lawyers who assisted Assumoll were equally guilty of fraud and deceit: "Everybody knew, everybody got paid, and nobody asked any questions." The jury agreed and the no-nonsense Texas Judge, U.S. District Judge Barefoot Sanders, delivered prison sentences to Assumoll's accomplices.

I never entirely blamed Assumoll for my fate. He was a criminal and hence it was both in his and in his associates' natures to lie and steal. I blame Judge Babcock for allowing him to do it. I also blame myself. I wanted Judge Babcock recused from my case, but my white-gloved lawyers from a very prestigious law firm of Holland and Hart worried that this tactic would just injure their own reputation with the judge. If they were to have other cases before him, this might harm them in later rulings. This was my first experience with the legal system and, not having the confidence or experience to object more forcefully, I let the lawyers call the shots even though my instincts told me otherwise. I was determined not to make the same mistake with Judge Baker.

I knew Judge Babcock's arrogance would never allow him to reconsider his prior decision. I also knew Judge Baker would never change his mind as well. I insisted that John recuse him at all costs. My good fortune was that John was more concerned for the welfare of his client than for his reputation with the judge. The only problem with a recusal request is that it must first initially be ruled upon by the judge you are trying to dismiss from the case. If the judge follows the rules, a motion for recusal that has a legitimate basis must be granted. Fortunately, Judge Baker soon provided a legitimate basis for his own recusal. Unfortunately, he was not too eager to rule on it. Until we were able to obtain a ruling of recusal, we were destined to endure a lot more pain in Judge Baker's courtroom.

FORTY-THREE

For more than two years we were dead in the water in this case due to Judge Baker's continued upholding of the defendant's Fifth Amendment privileges. We could not take any meaningful discovery or depositions in the case to build evidence because all defendants were taking the Fifth. We could not get information on where to look for documents or our stolen property in any of our interrogatories because all defendants were taking the Fifth.

We could not find out where any of the documents that I saw in the first replevin action disappeared to. These documents were never submitted in the discovery requests and the defendants wouldn't answer questions about them because they were taking the Fifth. Any other valuable evidence or information was most probably in that giant pile of garbage bags filled with shredded documents that we found at Wu's warehouse and later reclaimed from his dumpster. It was maddening.

Over the course of the entire year in 2000 we took the depositions of the Wus and their co-conspirators. One by one they attended the depositions only to respond affirmatively to the statement of their name, in every question thereafter they read from a 3" by 5" cue card provided to them by their attorney:

"Pursuant to the advice of my counsel, my constitutional right against self-incrimination and the order of Judge Baker acknowledging my constitutional right, I respectfully declined to answer the question."

First Samson, then Thomas, and then Susan Wu, Samson's wife, read from the cue card in response to every question while being recorded on video camera at their deposition. In between our depositions of the Wus, their attorneys would get their crack at our witnesses and employees. We answered all their questions and provided copies of all the documents they required us to produce.

At one deposition of Thomas Wu, the hypocrisy of this case must have finally overwhelmed even the great John Fisher. After Thomas Wu cited his Fifth Amendment privilege for the tenth or twelfth time, John suddenly exploded: "You know, is this a great country or what? You come here, you steal our technology, hijack it to China, turn around and sell it, and then come over here and invoke the Fifth Amendment privilege of our Constitution and not testify!"

"Is there a question pending before the witness?" Snyderburn responded.

"Yes." Bellowed John. "Is this a wonderful country or what, Mr. Wu?"

"I am going to object on the grounds that the question is argumentative, and instruct the witness not to answer," replied Snyderburn.

"Withdrawn!" Sputtered John. " I don't want to hear him invoke our Constitution again."

Caruso later sat down for his deposition. You could tell that he was dying to talk, but remained firm in his response by reading his cue card with the greatest gravity and expression he could muster when hinting of his disagreement or displeasure of the question put before him. Caruso stared and smiled into the camera. He tried to make light of the situation and went out of his way to try to belittle the proceeding. If Caruso could not show off to prove how smart he was in front of the camera, the best he could do was to smile at his ability to thumb his nose at our attorneys and

American justice. His facial expressions and defiant demeanor did not win him any friends among the jury when his tape was played back later at trial.

It was in April 2000 when David Winkler finally presented himself before John and the video camera for his deposition. Before the court reporter could even fill her dictation machine with the first roll of paper, Winkler had his 3" x 5" cue card out. He placed it down on the table, conspicuously in front of him and smiled at me and John as if to say that this will be yet again another colossal waste of our time. John asked his questions, after providing nothing more than his name. Again and again Winkler gave the same answer. As with the other defendant before him, Winkler would not acknowledge or respond to any question about his residence, citizenship, birth date, social security number, much less about the case. Winkler's deposition came after literally dozens of hours of similar repetitive depositions by all the other members of the Wu Clan. John felt compelled to ask the same questions over and over again, despite the well-known and monotonous response, because in civil cases the exercise of the Fifth Amendment privilege allows the court and the jury to take an "adverse inference" at trial.

By "adverse inference" the rules of procedure in civil cases means that the judge and the jury may assume that no response under the Fifth Amendment privilege can be assumed to be a negative one. Thus a question such as "did you or someone you hired steal the blueprints from the facility of Super Vision" being responded to with the Fifth Amendment assertion could be inferred as a response equivalent to "Yes." John told me that although it was boring as hell to ask all these questions and sit through all these same answers, he wanted it recorded on record that the defendants were not cooperating.

He could later play back this fact to the jury and issue

instructions on the adverse inference accordingly. Since we were not going to get any cooperation from the defendants to develop our evidence, then their very refusal to respond would at least later work in our favor.

Midway through Winkler's deposition, John was beginning to tire and show the strain of these excruciatingly long and monotonous deposition sessions. At one point he leaned over and told me that he feared that the fatal disease of "death by boredom" may set in if the jury had to view all these videotapes. In frustration he finally decided to add some levity to the proceedings:

"OK. Mr. Winkler, since you won't tell me anything about the case, perhaps you might enlighten me on something else—anything else for that matter," growled a clearly frustrated John.

"Who do you think is going to win the American League Pennant Mr. Winkler?" chimed John, now regaining his positive demeanor with a brief rush of adrenaline and a smile.

Winkler paused for a moment as if to think, raised his eyebrows, and nodded at John, then picked up his card and read:

"Pursuant to the advice of my counsel, my constitutional right against self-incrimination and the order of Judge Baker acknowledging my constitutional right, I respectfully decline to answer the question."

FORTY-FOUR

Although my rights as a victim were being
trampled by people who routinely violated every law on the
books, the criminal's rights were of grave concern to both
their counsel and Judge Baker.

For a while it seemed that the defense lawyer's strategy
would work; they would just wear us out financially until
there was no plaintiff in existence to appear at trial. Time
after time, we would bring up our desire for a trial date to
Judge Baker, time after time we were lectured on the importance of the defendant's "rights" under the Fifth Amendment. While our adversaries were hiding our stolen property, violating the injunction order overseas, and shredding
evidence domestically, this judge somehow still seemed more
concerned that "their rights" would be protected.

For the Wus to hide behind the Constitution of the
United States for protection seemed the height of hypocrisy.
While they violated almost every known law of the land, they
were thumbing their noses at the very process that was protecting them.

At one time, an exasperated John asked Judge Baker:
"How long do they intend to take the Fifth Amendment?"
He protested that after more than a year of taking the Fifth,
the defendants were now only using this as an excuse to
delay the trial. Judge Baker predictably responded that the
defendants were entitled to their constitutional protections
as long as they chose to exercise them.

After the hearing I asked John, "Who is going to protect the rights of my staff and my company?" He just shook his head. At the moment the great legal advocate had no answer.

While Judge Baker was still presiding on our case, I had what was the most difficult meeting during the course of the entire litigation with John. With Judge Baker tying up our ability to move forward on the trial, the destruction of evidence and the wanton disregard for every injunction put in place, it seemed that we were just running in quicksand. Despite all our efforts, not only weren't we getting anywhere, but we were drowning in litigation costs. The FBI had called occasionally to ask a few questions, but there was absolutely no indication that we were going to see any action from them that would positively impact our civil case or break the deadlock we were experiencing. By this time, in mid 2001, Fisher Rushmer had three attorneys assigned almost exclusively to our case and their costs were mounting. To date, they had invested more than 1,000 hours of the firm's time, with no hope for recovery in sight. One day, John called with a very grave voice and asked for a meeting with me at my office. I did not like the sound of his voice, and the message I heard at the meeting sounded far worse.

John had initially agreed to take on our case on a contingency fee basis. This was based on his belief that the FBI would file indictments and make arrests soon and that the opposition would later fold and cave in to our demands to settle out of court. As we both learned, this was a gross miscalculation on our part. More than 1,000 non-billable hours later, John found himself visiting my office to inform me that he had to change the 100% contingency arrangement into a partial fee/contingency agreement. John said with great gravity and much sadness that this was the first time in his firm's history that he had to renegotiate a contingency fee agreement.

"We are both about to become embroiled in a long protracted battle and neither one of us wants to run out of ammunition." Neither John nor his partners could continue to justify making such a large investment in prosecuting a case in which the opposition showed both unlimited resources as well as little desire to settle the case. The fact that the FBI and the U.S. Attorney's Office had not made a single arrest nor filed any indictment in the last six months further indicated that this case would be much more of a challenge than had been expected.

The news hit me like a ton of bricks. Our firm was just beginning to recover, but we were still losing money and I saw that with this conclusion our losses could only escalate. Part of me considered giving up the fight altogether to try to preserve our cash and maintain payroll. I talked with Roy Archer and other staff members overnight to see how they felt. Roy likened the process to "wrestling with an invisible bear." We were tangling with large wealthy opponents and they were as difficult to get a hold of as the evidence we were seeking to find.

This was a big decision, one I felt we had to all make together because it would affect all our lives. I kept thinking about my burning passion for justice and the lessons of persistence drilled into me by my father and grandfather at an early age, but then I also looked at the worried faces of my staff. It was clear they were weighing the risks to their jobs and their family's future by continuing the suit. The discussion was not our normal passionate and lively debate, it was thoughtful and grave. You could see on the staff's faces that they understood the importance of their decision and what impact it would have on their future. During the hours we discussed whether or not to pull out of the case, I reflected back on the lessons from my patriarchs.

FORTY-FIVE

Every day my grandfather would tell me to "thank God that you live in America." In my early years of childhood Daddy Pop Max would tell me of the pogroms in Russia and eastern Europe where there was no freedom of religion. My grandfather was convinced throughout his life that the Russians would eventually attack the United States at any time. He hid his guns everywhere througout his house and his small mattress factory. Years after his death, factory workers were still uncovering hidden guns behind pallet racking, underneath conveyor belts and above ceiling tiles. Grandpa wanted to make sure that if the Russians ever did come that he would have his guns close by and within reach.

Not many people on my mother's side were confident in Daddy Pop Max's sanity, but my mother's Grandfather Teddy and Grandmother "Bubbalibila" who saw the persecution in Russia with their own eyes would always speak out in Daddy Pop Max's defense. They would also chime in unison "thank God you live in America."

My Grandfather fought in World War I. My father volunteered to fight in World War II. He was young and filled with fury at the stories he heard of what the Germans were doing. He was Max and Martha Kingstone's only son, but Daddy Pop Max could not, and would not, hold his son back from his service to his country. When I would work at the mattress factory after school, the factory workers would tell me the story of my father's return after the war. On his first day back home, he was still proudly wearing his uniform. On that day a truck driver delivering crates of mattress inner springs from a factory in Alabama blocked the driveway to the facility. He knew my grandfather and the driver had made deliveries to the factory before, however, he kept his conversations to a minimum.

My father approached the truck driver to move his truck from blocking the driveway. My father asked him respectfully. The truck driver was standing by the front door to the showroom in front of the plate glass windows that showcased the retail furniture. The driver looked at my father standing before him in uniform. He didn't have the accent of my grandfather, but to him he was still as much an alien as the old man from the old country.

"Go to hell you Jew bastard."

"How dare you talk to me that way, I fought for my country," my father responded.

"You are just another kike in a uniform, that's all."

Ike Ellington, my grandpa's foreman for 35 years, told me how my father struck the driver with an upper cut under his chin so hard that he lifted the man off the ground and knocked him through the plate-glass window. Two other loyal factory workers somberly nodded their heads in unison as Ike told me his recollection of the sound of the strike and the crash of the showroom window.

Ike added with a gaping gold tooth laden smile: "Always knew the old man was crazy, but didn't know until then that it passed on to your father."

From the time I was five-years-old, my father and grandfather would take me down to the basement and put on boxing gloves and alternatively take turns sparring with me. Both my father and grandfather would yell at me constantly: "Attack, attack, attack….never give up...attack!" They would never get angry at me if one of their punches would get through that I clumsily failed to block. They would never get angry if I fell down. They would only voice their harsh disapproval if I seemed to tire or give up.

After boxing practice my father would read me inspirational stories. *The Count of Monte Cristo* was first read to me by my father at age four. I did not understand all of it at the first reading but one thing I did understand, the Count was wronged and he had a burning passion to avenge himself and reclaim his rightful name and honor. During many cold lonely nights after I was publicly proclaimed by Judge Lewis T. Babcock to be both a liar and a thief, I thought often of my father's reading about the Count. My burning desire to exonerate myself was often the only thing that kept me warm at night.

By allowing these predators to steal my company away from me again was tantamount towards giving up. Super Vision was not only the rekindling of my dream but my vehicle to avenge the unfortunate misdeeds of the past. By constructing yet another successful fiber-optic company, I believed it would give me an opportunity to redeem and exonerate myself. Something I was not able to do in litigation or on appeal due to lack of funding years earlier. There was much more, however, than my desires to consider; many members of our team worked hard to build the company to the level it was today. Many had dedicated their lives on the company's success and their futures depended on it. Their needs and desires deserved equal importance to mine.

Many members of my staff often wondered what drove me during all those years to pursue the litigation against Wu and his cronies. Some thought I was simply pursuing my sense of justice, others thought I was possessed by some demon. Several of my directors were privately questioning my sanity. A few directors were making analogies of me and this case to Captain Ahab with his harpoon plunged into Moby Dick, locked in a death grip as they both sank to the bottom of the ocean. I was not really sure myself if it was my own personal drive or the programming from my patriarchs that was drilled into me. I reflected on this during the many hours that the Super Vision staff debated the future of the litigation against the Wus.

Hours continued to pass and finally a decision was made. Although the staff knew they were risking their payrolls by continuing on with the suit, their burning passions for justice overcame their concerns.

"We have come this far, Brett," Roy said. "You're no quitter and I sure as hell am not either."

The next day I told John we would agree to sign his new contingency-fee agreement, which included a reduced hourly fee in exchange for a reduced-recovery rate. John cautioned me before signing that even at this reduced rate, we would probably be looking at spending several hundred thousand dollars in fees even before we would get to our first day of trial. As bad as things seemed then, I had no idea how much worse they were about to become.

FORTY-SIX

❦

My father's generation had a day in which all of them could remember where they were and what they were doing that day. It was a day when time stood still, and the whole country was locked into a combination of shock and grief. It was the day they shot President John F. Kennedy. Prior to the Fall of 2001, our generation did not yet have such a day. Monica Lewinsky's servicing of our President Clinton and "the day of the stained blue dress" would hardly qualify. There were the usual trials and tribulations over the last few decades. We had a few wars and periods of peace. We mourned the deaths of several celebrities and world leaders. But we did not have a day when time stood still and the country united in one collective feeling which every American would forever remember.

After we had replaced the previous management team, I assumed the additional role of international sales manager in addition to that of president and CEO. Our overseas sales had been decimated during 1998 and the early part of 1999. Since I was the one who originally signed up most of our international distributors, I felt responsible for them. My first step was to determine what we could do to help our existing international distributors grow their sales of our products. My second step was to add new international distributors in territories we were not covering. The best way I knew to do this was to go out and see them. We would then make sales calls with local architects, designers, and construction companies. This would stimulate new business.

In September 2001, I scheduled another visit to our Russian distributor, Vladimir Karpov. My last meeting with Vladimir was a few winters earlier. I vividly remembered the brutal, terrible cold air that ripped through my nostrils and froze the back of my throat and tongue. *Thank God the Czar wasn't so crazy about my grandfather's religion*, I thought, *or I would have been permanently freezing my ass off there.* Russia had changed a great deal since my previous trips when it was still the USSR. There are no more great restrictions on travel and business, no more floor ladies taking notes of your coming and goings in the Intourist Hotels. In fact it has become quite the opposite. It was more like the no holds barred Wild West. Although I am a devout capitalist, I was disappointed to see that the newfound brand of Russian capitalism has brought mostly poverty and misery to the masses and riches to only a well-connected few.

Our distributor, Vladimir Karpov of Advertising Agency A, a large bear of a man, was there to greet me at the airport with another one of his famous Russian bear hugs…

"Strastvi, Brett!"

"Vladimir, your cracking my ribs. Let me go and get me to the hotel."

It was a long, terrible flight and I wanted to get some decent food and a few hours sleep. Upon arrival at the hotel, the Raddison Slavenskaya, a section of the entryway was completely sealed off with what looked like some sort of police barricade and security tape. There was also what looked like a big bloodstain in the middle of it. I turned to Vladimir and asked what had happened.

"Russian partner of hotel had disagreement with American partner of hotel," stated Vladimir somewhat matter of factly.

"Oh I see, but back home they use lawyers for that sort of thing," I said.

"Lawyers take too long. This way more popular in Russia presently, more efficient," mused Vladimir with a wry smile.

"Remind me not to have a disagreement with you," I responded with a somewhat tired smile and nod.

Vladimir, together with Victor and Valery (the "three Vs" as I would call them), owned an advertising agency, Advertising Agency A, that sold space on billboards that they owned throughout Moscow to prominent local entertainment facilities as well as brand name American companies. They also built signs and engaged in lighting design and installation for nightclubs and casinos. Those businesses catered to the wealthy and well connected in Moscow and often money was no object for these establishments. The $50,000 multi-colored fiber optically lit chandeliers, which would seem both pricey and gaudy for even the most liberal and well-heeled American establishments, were purchased without hesitation by these companies.

Vladimir had set up meetings with his customers and again reserved a famous spa facility in Moscow where we could alternatively steam ourselves, jump in the cold plunge, and sing Karaoke while feasting on Caspian shrimp and Georgian Vodka. During the trip, I decided I would also visit our Turkish and Greek distributors on the way back home. They had been calling and asking for someone from the head office to come out and support them. As Vladimir drove me to the airport for a connecting flight on the way to Istanbul, I looked at the fiber-optic sign Vladimir installed at the main terminal. I wondered if my great-grandfather would ever have believed that someday I would be back in his birthplace, conducting business, and looking back on the airport sign that his great-grandson's technology had illuminated?

FORTY-SEVEN

❦

It took only two connections to get to Istanbul. Our Turkish distributor was waiting impatiently for me and was anxious to get to his first meeting. His name was Hilmi Oneran, a short, slightly stout man with dark eyes and thinning hair. He had a particularly large museum project with the national museum in the works to light a huge collection of ancient antiquities with fiber optics. Hilmi believed a visit from the company president might just be enough to help push the project in his favor. I agreed to visit him during the second week of September.

During a previous trip to our United Kingdom distributors, I had visited the giant British construction conglomerate, Bovis Lend Lease. Bovis was in partnership with British Petroleum. "BP Bovis," their partnership, was responsible for constructing BP's new gasoline stations and convenience stores worldwide. Part of its design was the implementation of LED border tube that would replace the previous neon highlighting used for gasoline station awnings and convenience store façades. The worldwide publication of our trade secrets, courtesy of the Wus' patent lawyers, had already eroded much of our competitive advantage in fiber optics. We decided, therefore, to move to a new application to bolster our sales, using LED instead of fiber-optic lighting. LEDs are light-emitting diodes, which were then a relatively new form of lighting technology using solid-state technology. Since Super Vision had by now entered the

LED market with its line of FlexLED and Border tube products, I decided to meet the Bovis Lend Lease people in Istanbul during my trip to Turkey.

Hilmi drove me to the offices of Bovis Lend Lease in downtown Istanbul in the early afternoon of Sept. 11, 2001 so we could set up our presentation in the conference room before the architects arrived. I opened my laptop computer and clicked on my PowerPoint presentation while Oneran plugged in my serial port to the LCD projector. The architects entered about a half hour later. Less than an hour into my presentation, which was interspersed with frequent questions on past projects, a large man in a dark suit entered the room and said, "I understand there is an American in the room." I indicated that it was me.

"Come with me," he said.

At first I hesitated. I was in the middle of a presentation. I asked if it could wait. He explained he was the managing director of this Bovis Lend Lease Office and I needed to come with him right away. Oneran and I were dumbstruck, but neither of us wanted a fight with the head man. We followed him out the door of the conference room.

The managing director of the BP Bovis Istanbul office walked me across the lobby and down the hall to his office. He did not say a word during the 30 or so yard walk between the conference room and his office door. As we entered the office, I could hear the strained and hurried reports of journalists who were trying to explain the inexplicable. I walked around his desk to look at the CNN report on the TV screen beside his computer. It was already simultaneously displaying the same image shown on MSNBC on his computer over and over again. The sight of the first airliner crashing into Tower 1 of the World Trade Center, followed later by another crash into Tower 2, looked surreal. It was like a Hollywood-made for TV movie.

The news broadcasts continued showing the decimation

and wreckage. The piles of debris caused by the initial impact coupled with reports of hundreds, perhaps thousands of people who might have been killed or injured still had not fully registered with me. The whole event was so massive and unexpected it seemed beyond comprehension. I was not feeling anything, neither shock nor pain, just disbelief.

It wasn't until I saw one image that I finally started to understand the true pain and human toll of this tragic event. It was the image of a lone man hanging out the window just above what was left of the 80th floor where the initial impact had occurred. Smoke was pouring out the window behind him, as he sat and waved for help while perched outside on the windowsill. In the background, the yellow and orange glow of the flames were clearly visible. The heat must have been unbearable. The man turned toward the flames and then turned toward the scene of the city below. He pushed himself off the ledge and plummeted to his death.

You could only imagine what went through his mind during the few seconds it took for his body to drop passed the nearly hundred floors and impact the ground. What horror he must have faced to choose between the approaching flames and certain death from the fall. As I saw this eerie image repeated on television of his body floating down the entire height of the building, as if in slow motion, my feelings of disbelief were now replaced by pain and anger. This man, I thought, probably had a family and now his wife and children were now seeing how these murderers stole his life from them. It was that single act of desperation, the terrible plight of that single man, that finally enabled me to grasp the stark reality of this monumental disaster.

I was told by the Hilmi, and his son, Medar, that all the airports in the U.S. were closed. I would probably be stuck overseas for at least another week. I tried calling home to check in with my wife, but all the lines were jammed and I could not get through. Finally at dinner that night, Hilmi lent me his cell phone and I tried again. Maisa had taken the kids out of Hebrew school and brought them home fearing more attacks. She understood my delay, but urged me to come home soon. My Muslim distributors could not have been more supportive and sincere in their sorrow for what had happened to our country. Turkey took great pride in being an ally of the United States. My distributors shared this feeling. As the news reports rolled in that the bombings were the work of Islamic extremists, my distributors did all they could to show their solidarity with the U.S. and concern for my family. This was not the act of the religion that they believed in. They said, "These people were criminals and these criminals must be severely punished."

I did not have one night's sleep during the week that I waited to return home. The image of that man falling replayed over and over every time I tried to close my eyes.

September 11 actually turned out to be a benefit for Wu and his cohorts. September 11 also had a marked effect on the prosecution of our criminal case. Again we were relying on the FBI to pursue the Wu Family to corner them and make them more vulnerable to our attack on their opposite flank. After the September 11 tragedy, it became clear that we could not rely on any help from the FBI or U.S. Attorney's office. They had been ordered to cease all actions on all cases not immediately related to national security and preservation of life of U.S. citizens.

Kevin Hogan called me a few weeks later to tell me that he had been ordered off our case. The pursuit of terrorists within our borders will now be his full time job. As he told me of his new mission, there was some genuine regret and sadness in both his voice and remarks. With everything going on, it was quite understandable that our case was going to take a back seat to our national security. What surprised me that even with this obvious new change in priorities, Agent Hogan's sense of justice still gnawed at him to bring closure to the Wu case. Kevin almost apologized for the fact and told me that from this point forward we would basically be on our own. I told Kevin not to worry. He had a much more important job ahead of him. "Go out and protect our families and bring these bastards to justice."

FORTY-EIGHT

❧

With my legal bills mounting and no hope for help from the FBI, our situation looked pretty bleak. We were so desperate we even provided settlement offers through counsel to some of Wu's cohorts, including Winkler, in order to get even one of his current cadre to testify against him and provide us with banking information. But each offer was just stonewalled without a response. We realized that during all the delays achieved by the Wus' abuse of the court system, the Wus were using the time to squirrel away all their assets overseas. In so doing they were guaranteeing that regardless of the outcome of the trial they would become judgment proof. I knew I had to do something to make sure that Super Vision would somehow recover at least part of the judgment if we would ever get one. I thought back to the words I had read from U.S. Attorney Jennifer Bolen, who stated at the trial of the bankers and lawyers who assisted Mukesh Assumoll in stealing over $100 million from depositors in the Caprock Savings and Loan case that: "Everybody knew, everybody got paid, and nobody asked questions."

The Wus' lawyers, accountants, and bankers made it possible for Wus to file patents on our technology, use multiple corporations to hide their illegal activities, and transfer money outside the U.S. They all knew and they all certainly did not bother to ask questions while they assisted the Wus for a fee. If ultimately I couldn't collect from Wu, then I decided I at least would collect from the "professionals" who aided and assisted them. I made up my mind to go after each and every one of them: the lawyers, the accountants, and the bankers.

During his tenure at Super Vision, Caruso built up his persona as one of a nocturnal creature. In addition to having strange stories and exhibiting unusual behavior, Caruso kept strange hours. Particularly during his last few months at work, Caruso would often work until four or five in the morning. When he would roll in about the crack of 10 or 11 the next morning, the second and third cabling shift staff would confirm the reason for his late arrival to management. He had been up all night "working" on what Caruso said was his new "research projects." He claimed he worked better at night, it was quieter, and he had fewer interruptions.

During the discovery process we did not find any of the copies of the documents that Paul had given us related to faxes sent from Caruso at 5 a.m. to the Wus and their associates. Most likely they had all been shredded. But in the demand for documents from the Wus' patent lawyers, Allen Dyer, we found plenty. At first Allen Dyer repeatedly refused our discovery requests for documents citing "attorney-client privilege." Attorney-client privileged information is protected by law. It refers to the correspondence that is transferred between an attorney and its client, which under law is not subject to the discovery process in civil matters. It is available for discovery if the judge rules that this information was in fact stolen or part of a criminal conspiracy that would be therefore ordered as evidence.

We believed that the documents that Caruso faxed in the early hours of the morning from our facility containing drawings of our manufacturing systems, including our cabling and extrusion machine and formulations and tensioning data, was not subject to this attorney client privilege.

After several protests from the attorneys, a later judge agreed with us. Finally, the patent attorneys were ordered to turn over their files. Bingo! The documents submitted to us by Allen Dyer contained a complete set of drawings of our key cabling-machine components with details on our twisting and tensioning systems as well as the entire description of our process. Even better, the fax header at the top of all pages were still visible: "5:53 a.m. Super Vision." The patent lawyers had received these documents faxed by our employee from our facility at 5 a.m. and then filed patents on behalf of a Chinese competitor with the U.S. Patent Office.

The drawings were such exact copies that we held them side by side to the equipment from our factory and took photos of them. They were identical. We knew this would be of help at trial. There would be nothing left to the jury's imagination at trial once they saw the drawings that Caruso had faxed to the patent lawyers in large blown-up photographs side by side with our equipment.

Our staff looked at all these drawings and documents sent to the patent attorneys and shook our heads. Some of us vented our anger. We could not believe that any law firm would file such information with the U.S. Patent Office and risk disbarment if not prison. But it later became clear to us that some lawyers would do anything for a fee. Copies of the billing statements also came in during discovery. They clearly showed that many months prior to them receiving this information they had billed Wu for reviewing both his "employees'" confidentiality and non-compete agreements with Super Vision. The billing statement also revealed that even months before Brian Gilchrist asserted under oath in Judge Komanski's courtroom that his clients were not "having anything to do with optics because they are not." Gilchrist's firm was billing his clients to review and file patents for that very purpose.

We now had evidence that the lawyers of Allen Dyer not only filed stolen information with the patent office, but now also had proof they had lied to a state court judge in order to get the original case filed against their clients dismissed. The judge was convinced by the attorney's repeated assertions that their clients were not involved in the development or manufacture of fiber optics. Thus, Judge Komanski, without further proof or evidence to the contrary, agreed to deny an injunction.

Much of the information that we later submitted to Judge Kirkwood for our later successful injunction was obtained from files turned over to us by Paul Koren that predated the Komanski hearing. The Wus' patent lawyers deliberately misled Judge Komanski and aided in the cover up, much in the same way the lawyers representing Sedlmayr and Assumoll relayed their client's misrepresentations to Judge Babcock about the origins of ADT's fiber-optic television display technology. We suspected that the accountants who prepared the business plan and the bank who assisted in the bankruptcy filing had similarly conspired with the Wus to defraud the court but we did not have the evidence. At the time, the only smoking gun we uncovered had the prints of the patent lawyers.

When I first raised the issue with John he looked at me in disbelief. He put his hand on his head and he disapprovingly furrowed his brow and shook his head: "Haven't you had enough litigation yet?!"

John basically counseled me that I had an oversupply of energy and an undersupply of wisdom. He felt I was going to spread myself out too thin by trying to simultaneously attack so many targets. He was not willing to add the other parties to the case; he had his hands full with the Wu family and their lawyers.

I told John my strategy and pressed him to consider what this would mean if we could not recover a judgment from the Wus after all the work he had invested in the lawsuit and trial. I asked him to reconsider. John told me he would not and could not be counsel to a suit against the lawyers, since Allen Dyer had been a client of his in the past when he represented them on behalf of an insurance company in prior cases. His prior representation would disqualify him from being their adversary under both Bar Association rules and his own moral precepts. I again pressed John, "If you could do it, would you?" John just thundered back, "No!"

It was clear that was his final word on the subject. We did not talk about it further, but my sense was that John was simply not fond of suing other lawyers. In the same way he did not call Snyderburn before the judge on charges of blatant misrepresentations before the court, John did not want to engage in what would appear as similar aggressive behavior against fellow members of the bar. John was a gentleman and he probably saw it as unsportsmanlike. As for the accountants and the bankers, he did not think we had enough hard evidence yet to tie them in as co-conspirators. Even if we did, John did not want to further dilute his firm's resources on another round of contingency-based or discounted-rate pursuits. He had made a tremendous investment in the Wu case and his focus was seeing it through.

Although I appreciated John's position, I felt that he was thinking more like a lawyer than a business strategist. At the end of the day, if we couldn't collect from the Wus, all our efforts would be wasted. If we at least were able to hold those who assisted them, firms, which had assets in the U.S. and could not easily escape judgment, at least we would get John and Super Vision a recovery of the fees and expenses that we had spent to date. I knew I had to take my pursuits elsewhere and I had to find someone that would pursue them for me.

1. SVI facility at night.

2. Coca-Cola and AT&T spectaculars.

3. Coca-Cola bottle under construction.

4. AT&T sign under construction.

5. Brett Kingstone, Roy Archer, and John Gonzales.

 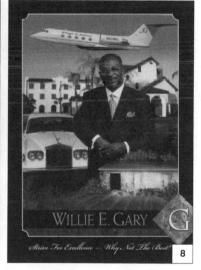

6. Super Vision staff photo in lobby.

7. Brett Kingstone and "The Cable Guys" David Vaughn and Rob Fishell.

8. Willie Gary.

9. John Fisher and Joseph Tamborello.

10. Pepsi globe, Caracas, Venezuela.

11. Moscow Airport.

12. Super Vision Pool and Spa lighting.

13. Tokyo Dome, Tokyo, Japan.

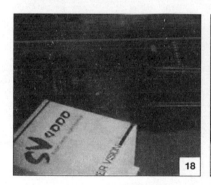

14. FBI raid—Samson and Thomas Wu to the left of FBI agents.

15. Samson and Thomas Wu and Jack Caruso.

16. Removal of boxes from closet during replevin action.

17. Cable found in closet behind boxes during replevin.

18. Light sources found during replevin action at Caruso home.

19. Marsam Trading/Optic-Tech Miami warehouse during first replevin.

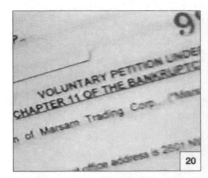

20. Marsam bankruptcy petition blocks camera lens.

21. Empty files filmed during second Marsam/Optic-Tech replevin.

22. Shredder with shredded documents filmed during second replevin.

23. Dumpster overflowing with shredded documents.

24. Entry to U.S. customs bonded Marsam warehouse.

25. Spools of fiber-optic cable in bonded Marsam/Optic-Tech warehouse.

26. Samson Wu closing door on giant vault at Marsam/Optic-Tech warehouse.

27. Private Investigation surveillance video at Shanghai restaurant (James Li-left, Jack Caruso-right).

28. Shanghai Qualong Optic-Tech factory in Shanghai, China.

29. James Li seals and signs Ted's "confidentiality agreement" and bill of sale.

30. Counterfeit cable demonstrated and sold in Shanghai factory in violation of U.S. court orders.

31. Chinese-made components are compared side by side with Super Vision's U.S. patents.

32. James Li opening door to warehouse in Shanghai with Chinese "customs in bond" products.

33. James Li selling "China customs in bond products."

34. Taxi driver receiving package of optics and sources from Ted.

35. Cocoa Bay, Panama—Samson Wu's current residence in South America.

36. Wu family owned retail stores in Panama City.

37. The Wus' showcase with $100,000+ of gold watches in one window.

ALLEN, DYER, DOPPELT, MILBRATH & GILCHRIST, P.A.
Attorneys At Law

255 South Orange Avenue, Suite 1401
Orlando, Florida 32802
(407) 841-2330
FAX (407) 841-2343

March 30, 1998

Mr. Paul P. Koren
MAAS INDUSTRIES, INC.
110 S. Magnolia
Sanford, FL 32771

S T A T E M E N T

Matter: 020488   Prod: JSW
MISC. GENERAL MATTERS
Client: MAAS

For Professional Services Rendered:

03/18/98 BRG   Conference with Jeff Whittle; research
                 on non-compete agreement.
03/18/98 JSW   Conferring with Mr. Koren regarding
                 non-compete agreement; analyzing and
                 conferring with Mr. Gilchrist regarding
                 same.
03/23/98 BRG   Prepare memorandum; conference with Jeff
                 Whittle; legal research
                           Total Professional Services $ 755.00

For Disbursements Incurred:

03/24/98   photocopy charges - March 1998 $ 0.40

                           Total Disbursements Incurred $ 0.40

39

---

38. The Wus' Stefanie S.A. headquarters in Panama.

39. Allen Dyer March 30,1998 billing statement.

I. SUMMARY of THE INVENTION

A: IT IS Therefore AN object OF THIS INVENTION TO PROVIDE A METHOD IN WHICH TO PRODUCE A SUPERIOR LATERAL LIGHT EMITTING FIBER OPTIC CABLE.

B: IT IS A Still further OBJECT OF THIS INVENTION TO PROVIDE A METHOD TO CONTROL LIGHT EMISSION UNIFORMITY BY MEANS OF MICRO-FLEXURE TO THE INDIVIDUAL STRANDS OF FIBER OPTIC (P.M.M.A)

40

FILING RECEIPT

UNITED STATES DEPARTMENT OF COMMERCE
Patent and Trademark Office
ASSISTANT SECRETARY AND COMMISSIONER
OF PATENTS AND TRADEMARKS
Washington, D.C. 20231

APPLICATION NUMBER	FILING DATE	GRP ART UNIT	FIL FEE REC'D	ATTORNEY DOCKET NO.	DRWGS	TOT CL	IND CL
09/215,079	12/18/98	2874	$0.00	21008	5	24	5

JEFFREY S WHITTLE
ALLEN DYER DOPPELT MILBRATH & GILCHRIST
P O BOX 3791
ORLANDO FL 32802-3791

RECEIVED

JAN 2 5 1999

A.D.D.M.& G.

Receipt is acknowledged of this nonprovisional Patent Application. It will be considered in its order and you will be notified as to the results of the examination. Be sure to provide the U.S. APPLICATION NUMBER, FILING DATE, NAME OF APPLICANT, and TITLE OF INVENTION when inquiring about this application. Fees transmitted by check or draft are subject to collection. Please verify the accuracy of the data presented on this receipt. If an error is noted on this Filing Receipt, please write to the Application Processing Division's Customer Correction Branch within 10 days of receipt. Please provide a copy of the Filing Receipt with the changes noted thereon.

Applicant(s)

PINHAS P. KOREN, ORLANDO, FL; JACK CARUSO, ORLANDO, FL; THOMAS T. WU, MIAMI, FL.

CONTINUING DATA AS CLAIMED BY APPLICANT—
THIS APPLN IS A CIP OF 09/079,576 05/15/98

* SMALL ENTITY *

TITLE
APPARATUS FOR FORMING LATERALLY LIGHT EMITTING FIBER OPTIC CABLE, LATERALLY LIGHT EMITTING FIBER OPTIC CABLE AND ASSOCIATED METHODS

41

---

40. 5:53 a.m. fax on April 13, 1998 outlining patent based on Super Vision's trade secrets faxed from Super Vision's fax machine.

41. Allen Dyer patent filing—Dec. 18, 1998, based on continuation of earlier May 15, 1998 filing.

SUPER VISION INTERNATIONAL   Multi-Page™   **HEARING-JUDE KOMANSK**
VS. MAAS INDUSTRIES, INC.   9-29-98

Page 17

1 WISH A MAKE A BRIEF RESPONSE?
2   MR. GILCHRIST: YES, I WOULD, YOUR HONOR.
3 THIS IS A SITUATION WHERE THE PLAINTIFFS ARE OUT
4 TO PUNISH FORMER EMPLOYEES AND THEY SIMPLY
5 JUMPED THE GUN.
6   WE'VE GOT TWO CORPORATIONS HERE, OASIS AND
7 MAAS. THEY PRODUCE POOLS, WATERFALLS IN POOLS.
8 THEY DON'T MANUFACTURE OR DISTRIBUTE, SELL,
9 REPAIR ANYTHING TO DO WITH FIBER-OPTICS. WE
10 HAVE NOW AN OVER-ZEALOUS INVESTIGATOR WHO ASKED
11 THEM TO BUILD A SIGN. THEY THREW UP SOME
12 ARTWORK. DRAWING UP ARTWORK IS NOT A VIOLATION
13 OF AN AGREEMENT. AND AS THEY HAVE DONE IN THE
14 PAST THEY WERE GOING TO BUY THE COMPONENT PARTS
15 FROM SUPER VISION.
16   SUPER VISION OFFERS FOR SALE THE
17 INDIVIDUAL COMPONENT PARTS. THEY HAVE SOLD TO
18 THESE SAME INDIVIDUALS THEIR OWN SIGN THAT THEY
19 DISPLAY. THE COMPONENT PARTS. THEY HAVE SOLD
20 THEM TO THE BISTRO THAT ONE OF PRINCIPALS HERE
21 OWNS. THERE IS SIMPLY NO COMPETITION.
22   . THIS IS A SILLY CASE IN LARGE RESPECT. WE
23 CAME HERE ON A DAY'S NOTICE OVER A $450 PIECE OF
24 ARTWORK THAT HAD NO OPTICS, THERE WAS NOTHING
25 INVOLVED IN THE SALE OF OPTICS. THEY HAVE NO

Page 18

1 EVIDENCE MY CLIENTS HAD ANYTHING — HAVE
2 ANYTHING TO DO WITH OPTICS, BECAUSE THEY DON'T.
3 THEY FOLLOWED THEIR NONCOMPETE TO A TEE. THEY
4 ENTERED INTO — WHAT THEY DO IS THEY MAKE
5 WATERFALLS.
6   THESE ARE THE SPILL-OVER EFFECT. YOU PUT
7 THEM IN THE POOL DECK. THEY SPILL OVER. AND
8 THAT'S ESSENTIALLY WHAT THEY DO. MAAS MAKES
9 DRAINAGE SYSTEMS FOR THE DECKING. THIS IS A
10 POOL BUSINESS. IT'S NOT A FIBER-OPTIC
11 BUSINESS.
12   AND THE CONFUSION, OBVIOUSLY, BY THE
13 PLAINTIFFS, IS ONE OF PLAINTIFF'S COMPETITORS
14 ASKED IF OASIS CAN DESIGN THE SPILL OVER THAT
15 WOULD HOUSE THE COMPETITOR'S FIBER-OPTICS. MY
16 CLIENT DOESN'T SELL THE FIBER-OPTICS. THEY
17 ENTERED INTO AN AGREEMENT THAT SPECIFICALLY
18 SAID, WE'RE NOT GOING TO SELL ANY FIBER-OPTICS.
19 WE'LL LET YOU PUT WHATEVER YOU WANT IN OUR
20 SPILL-OVER. WE'RE NOT SELLING ANY
21 FIBER-OPTICS. AND THAT'S WHAT THE EVIDENCE IS
22 GOING TO SHOW.
23   WE CAN TALK ALL DAY LONG ABOUT TRADE
24 SECRETS AND WHETHER IT WAS TRULY A TRADE SECRET
25 OR WHETHER MY CLIENTS KNEW OR CAME IN WITH

Page 19

1 KNOWLEDGE OF THE TRADE SECRETS. WE CAN GO ON
2 LIKE THAT FOR DAYS. BUT THE BOTTOM LINE IS
3 THERE ISN'T ANY BREACH OF THE AGREEMENT, NOR ANY
4 EVIDENCE OF BREACH OF THE AGREEMENT.
5   THIS WAS AN EFFORT TO SET UP FORMER
6 EMPLOYEES. THEY HAD SOLD THEM SOME SIGNS IN THE
7 PAST. THEY SENT AN INVESTIGATOR IN TRYING TO
8 TALK THEM INTO BUYING A SIGN. BEFORE THEY COULD
9 GET THE COMPONENT PARTS FROM SUPER VISION, THEY
10 WERE HIT WITH A LAWSUIT LATE FRIDAY SETTING FOR
11 HEARING TODAY. ESSENTIALLY ONE DAY'S NOTICE TO
12 COME DOWN HERE AND EXPLAIN PAGES AND PAGES OF
13 DOCUMENTS. I WAS HANDED THE MEMO THIS MORNING
14 MYSELF.
15   BUT SIMPLY PUT, THIS IS NO COMPETITION.
16 WITHOUT A BREACH OF THE AGREEMENT WE'RE ALL
17 WASTING OUR TIME HERE.
18   THE COURT: OKAY. WHAT SAY THE
19 PLAINTIFF? DO YOU WISH TO ANNOUNCE ANY TYPE OF
20 WITNESSES OR PLACE ANY EVIDENCE?
21   MR. HORNREICH: WELL, YOUR HONOR, THERE
22 SEEMS TO BE VERY LITTLE CONTROVERSY. THEY'RE
23 NOT CONTESTING THE ENTRY OF THE INJUNCTION.
24 THEY SEEM TO BE ADMITTING THAT THEY'RE WILLING
25 TO ALLOW THE INJUNCTION TO BE ENTERED BECAUSE

Page 20

1 THEY'RE NOT DOING ANYTHING IN VIOLATION OF THE
2 AGREEMENT. AND I DON'T KNOW THAT THIS COURT'S
3 TIME WILL BE WELL SPENT HEARING EVIDENCE WHEN
4 THEY'RE BASICALLY AGREEING TO ALL ELEMENTS OF
5 THE MOTION.
6   THE COURT: MR. GILCHRIST.
7   MR. GILCHRIST: I'M NOT AGREEING TO ANY
8 ELEMENT OF THE MOTION. THE MOTION TAKES THE
9 POSITION THAT ANY INVOLVEMENT WHATSOEVER WITH
10 FIBER-OPTICS IS A VIOLATION OF THE AGREEMENT.
11 THAT IS SIMPLY NOT TRUE. THE AGREEMENT CALLS
12 FOR NONCOMPETITION FOR FIBER-OPTIC SIGNS OR
13 DISPLAYS, VIDEO WALL DISPLAYS, PROJECTION
14 TELEVISION SYSTEMS WITH SCREENS IN EXCESS OF 60
15 INCHES AND IN SOME CASES ROBOTICS. IT HAS
16 ABSOLUTELY NOTHING TO DO WITH A WATERFALL.
17   THE COURT: GO AHEAD AND PROVE YOUR CASE.

SUPER VISION INTERNATIONAL, INC.,
A FLORIDA CORPORATION,

                    PLAINTIFF,

    —VS—   CASE NO. CI 98-7737
                                  DIVISION NO. 33

MAAS INDUSTRIES, INC., A FLORIDA CORPORATION,
OASIS FALLS INTERNATIONAL, INC., A FLORIDA
CORPORATION, RICHARD HEINER, INDIVIDUALLY,
JARROD HEINER, INDIVIDUALLY, VINCENT BURNS
A/K/A FRED BURNS, INDIVIDUALLY, AND JACK
CASTRO, INDIVIDUALLY,

                    DEFENDANTS.

SEPTEMBER 29, 1998
10:00 O'CLOCK A.M.

42

42. Transcript of Brian Gilchrist's comments before Judge Komanski

Case no. CI 98-7737 Sept. 29, 1998.

FORTY-NINE

§?

I first met Willie Gary in the hallway outside the courtroom where he was trying one of his most famous cases. John had heard that Willie was trying the famed billion-dollar Walt Disney Epcot Center Case just a few floors above us. We were having one of our early pre-trial hearings and during a break he suggested that we go upstairs to see the master at work. As proud as John was of his own abilities, he also had a healthy respect for other great lawyers. Willie, John told me, was "a man to be reckoned with".

As soon as John and I exited the elevator, we saw a short, square, and muscular bulldog of a man pacing the hallway outside the door to the courtroom. As we approached within feet of Willie, he continued to pace the hallway back and forth gesticulating with both arms and hands as he walked. Willie would mumble a few words, and then grunt, and stab his index finger in the air as if to complete the thought and prove the point. Often after making that final gesture, he would smile with self-approval. John and I must have witnessed at least three passes back and forth down the hallway until he noticed we were there.

"Hi Willie," John said as Willie finally glanced up and acknowledged us.

"John, you old dog, how are ya?" Willie fired back with his broad, trademark grin.

"How's it going in there Willie?"

Willie leaned back and flashed a broad smile to the

heavens. "John, we be barbecuing them in there. I'd surely hate to be Disney right now!"

"Willie, I would like to introduce one of my clients, Brett Kingstone. I've explained to him that you're almost as good a lawyer as I am."

Willie leaned even further back, this time bending his knees slightly as he let out another broad grin. "You been lyin' again, John? Boy, don't listen to a thing this man says." He then thrust out his hand and shook mine in a vice-like grip. We both squared off our shoulders and stood toe to toe as our eyes met, like two pit bulls eyeing one another before a fight. This man, I thought, would represent me one day.

Willie was definitely a man who would take on any adversary, any foe. He would grab his adversaries by the throat in the same vice-like grip that he held my hand and when the opportunity presented itself, he would clamp down even harder. John was a brilliant intellectual in the courtroom; Willie was a street fighter. What John accomplished with skill, Willie achieved through raw power and persistence.

Willie would often say that he might not be the smartest lawyer in America, but he was definitely the hardest working. I identified more with Willie's style. Willie couldn't care less about the Marquis of Queensbury rules of engagement or the Old Boy network. He would rather rip the old boys out of their club and kick their asses outside in the parking lot. When Willie went to trial, he would put in more hours than any lawyer alive. His wife would often comment in interviews that before a trial she rarely get to see him. What Willie lacked in Ivy League polishing, he more than made up for in pure passion and persistence.

Willie owns two Lear Jets—Wings of Freedom I and II—a many gabled mansion, and a limousine large enough to accommodate a football team. He grew up as the son of a poor black sharecropper in Florida. Much of his childhood was spent working hard in the fields with his family or washing dishes in a local hotel. Though poor, he was determined, so determined that he hitched a ride to a local black college and fought to enroll even though he did not have enough money to pay the application fee. While football players fed him scraps from the training table, the college agreed to wave his application fee and offer him admittance. Willie won a football scholarship later and ate regularly at the training table himself. Willie was fond of saying that he "repaid his debt to Shaw University for waving his $10 application fee by giving them a check for $10 million." He also later bought the hotel where he washed dishes and turned it into his own office building for his growing legal staff.

In addition to bankrolling Shaw University with his $10 million dollar donation, he made an additional donation large enough to guarantee the football team's expenses in perpetuity. Willie remembered the football players who brought him food when he was too poor to pay for his own meals.

Willie's rise from a farm worker in the Deep South to one of the world's wealthiest lawyers is a modern day Horatio Alger story. He is a living legend, although he would be careful never to say as much himself. Willie praised hard work and God for his success. Willie sensed the deeper meaning and value of his success. He knew he had a mission. He preaches the gospel of self-reliance and hard work regularly on nationwide television. He frequently visits poor inner city and rural school districts. When he arrives in his enormous limo and clad in his spectacular silk suits, he captivates his audience with his dazzling lifestyle. This enables him to reach into their hearts and minds with his less than glamorous message of hard work and persistence.

"Never, ever, never, ever, ever, ever give up, NEVER!" Willie chants to the schoolchildren seated in front of him. "To get ahead you got to work hard, I mean hard, real hard!

If you follow the path of hard work it will lead you to glory. I know, I've been where you are and I got to where I am by hard work. You got to want it. You got to dream it in order to see it and have it." I would see the same sort of coaching from Willie with his son Seiku. There was never any doubt in my mind that Willie's son was going to be a great success like his father. With the same inspiration and determination that he would infuse to the throngs of schoolchildren that he would visit, Willie would chant over and over again to all his sons: "never, ever, ever give up!"

I had the opportunity to sit next to Seiku for lunch when Willie was delivering one of his famous inspirational speeches. This speech was before the annual luncheon of the Orange County Bar Association. Willie was the featured guest speaker and even the audience of normally cynical and sarcastic lawyers were rapt. Seiku had heard the speech about a hundred times, but you could see that his father's words still had an effect on him. Seiku's eyes welled as his father retold the struggles of his days in poverty and his determination to build a better life for his family. After the speech I turned to Seiku and told him what a great man he had for a father. He responded with a big warm hug.

With the same passion he preaches, Willie practices his profession. Willie's hard work paid off in the Disney case as well. Although there was a question in the legal community as to the validity of the claims of Willie's clients in developing the concept for EPCOT Center, Willie left absolutely no room for doubt in the minds of the jury. The jury awarded his client $350 million dollars, another record-making verdict in the Florida courts.

Many had previously believed that due to the size of his adversary, Willie would never succeed in getting the case to trial much less result in such a verdict. But Willie was always confident in his belief that he would succeed. With his well-known passion and characteristic self-confidence, Willie was prepared to take on anyone. Willie feared no adversary; he was the only lawyer who was bold enough to take on the lawyers that assisted the criminals that stole our technology. While most other lawyers feared suing one of their own and the subsequent implications it would bring to their reputations, Willie jumped at the chance to bring a few pompous and errant members of his profession to the woodshed and give them a proper thrashing.

After I approached him to handle our case he graciously accepted and promptly assigned two of his best staff members to the case, Madison McClelland and Linda Weiksnar. Madison was a tall, young clean-cut blonde country boy. He kind of looked like an overgrown version of Opie from the TV show *The Andy Griffith Show* set in Mayberry. Linda was an attractive and curvaceous, curly-haired blonde who favored formal business suits in stark contrast to the more casual attire of her fellow Stuart, Florida colleagues.

While Madison was jovial in his approach, Linda was serious and all business. The two made an interesting team. Madison was the talker and Linda was the legal researcher. They immediately began sifting through the mountains of evidence that we had already collected for the case and prepared their pleadings against Allen Dyer and Rothwell Figg, the two patent-law firms that assisted the Wus in patenting trade secrets that had been stolen from Super Vision. They also brought a civil action against Spencer and Klein, one of the law firms that were all too happy to instruct Wu in the art of using multiple corporations, both domestically and overseas, to carry out their endeavors.

Madison and Linda reported back to Willie that there was enough evidence to potentially make the law firms liable as accomplices to Wu's trade-secret theft. Willie then prepared his plan of attack with Madison and Linda to bring the law firms to justice.

FIFTY

For a while it seemed that the defense lawyer's
strategy would work; they would just wear us down financially until there was no plaintiff in existence to appear at
trial. Time after time, we would bring up our request for a
trial date to Judge Baker, time after time, we were lectured
on the importance of a defendant's "rights" under the Fifth
Amendment. While our adversaries were hiding our stolen
property, violating the injunction order overseas, and shredding evidence domestically by the dumpster load, this judge
somehow still seemed more concerned that "their rights"
would not be violated.

It took three attempts to recuse Judge Baker. The first
two requests, Judge Baker denied. Coincidently, during the
time of our third request, Judge Baker was later brought up
on charges by the JQC (Judicial Qualifications Committee)
for violating court ethics and rules. Apparently Judge
Baker's famous ex-parte contacts with witnesses and
"experts" outside the courtroom were getting him in trouble
in a few other cases. We had already caught him in similar
contacts with potential witnesses in our case. When the
lawyer assigned to review all of Judge Baker's other cases
finally got around to ours, John was chosen to be a witness
in the JQC's hearing on Judge Baker's alleged impropri-
eties. Judge Baker called John after he was selected as a witness for the JQC "to talk." After all the warnings, he still
tried to engage in ex-parte contact with a witness, especially

in his own defense. Baker announced his "retirement" later that year, but not before he finally "voluntarily" recused himself from our case.

For Super Vision, the removal of Judge Baker was something akin to divine intervention. It allowed for a much reasonable judge and ultimately a much saner trial, but not without a few twists and turns along the way.

FIFTY-ONE

⚭

With Baker recused, we were passed around to a few judges for awhile until a new trial judge could be found. One judge did not quite know what to do with our case, although she was very impressed with the repeated presentation of "evidence" questioning my credibility, which consisted of a copy of Judge Babcock's opinion of more than a decade ago. Fortunately, we were later transferred to another justice, Judge Spencer. At a hearing on the matter, John presented the subsequent evidence on the case and the criminal indictments that followed. Judge Spencer agreed that Judge Babcock's opinion was irrelevant, and therefore, ruled it was inadmissible.

We also were not sure whether or not any of the new judges would continue to buy the Fifth Amendment argument, which Judge Baker had allowed to delay our trial for almost two years. These delays were costing us greatly in time and money. In early 2002, our case fell to yet another justice, Judge Ted Coleman. Judge Coleman was a tall and distinguished advocate with a powerful disposition and a strong southern accent. He appeared as someone who would absolutely not stand for any nonsense, no matter how eloquently any lawyer attempted to serve it up. After a rather long speech by Snyderburn on his client's constitutional rights to continue to invoke the Fifth Amendment, and the great disadvantage to his client's rights if they were forced to go to trial while they were still invoking it, Judge

Coleman turned to John and said, "What have you got to say on this matter?"

John's answer was short and to the point. "They have been invoking this right for the past two and a half years, judge. In what century do we plan to allow my client his right to get to trial?" John also further pointed out the repeated injunction violations of the Wus while they were hiding behind the Fifth Amendment. Judge Coleman responded, "Well, it looks like the inmates have been running the asylum here." And he then set the trial date right then and there. We were finally going to have our day in court.

I was almost in tears as I left Judge Coleman's office. After years of discouragement and having been saddled with an impossibly difficult judge, I finally saw a ray of hope in our case. I was very grateful that another judge was able to see through the Wus' tactics and shared equal dismay at their banal attempts to elude justice. I was on an emotional rollercoaster that entire evening, filled with the relief and anticipation that we would finally get to have our "day in court."

With almost all the current trial judge's calendars completely booked, including Judge Coleman's, we were assigned yet another judge who was able to accommodate a trial scheduled for several weeks. Judge Thomas Spencer, a justice who previously filled in our case to assist on a ruling, was called out of retirement to accommodate the busy court docket. Judge Spencer was not particularly regal looking, nor did he carry himself with the same arrogant and self-important air that was so obvious with Judge Baker. A polar opposite of Judge Baker, Judge Spencer was very humble and low key. Judge Baker would often sport bowties as he ruled from the bench, taking great care in his appearance. Judge Spencer would often wander in the courtroom with crumpled suits. Judge Spencer had a full head of silver hair and a calm and pleasing disposition. He sort of looked like a modern day Will Rogers and talked in the same simple and assuring manner that won Will Rogers great respect and acclaim among the common man of his day.

Judge Baker would stride into the courtroom only after his court clerk would announce his impending entry and instruct all in attendance to rise. Judge Spencer would unceremoniously enter the room, often with his black cloak draped over his arm, and wave off the attendees that decided to rise, often encouraging them to take their seats. After taking a brief minute to slip into his black judicial gown, Judge Spencer would take his seat and immediately launch into the business of the day. His demeanor was more like a busy CEO of a private company than a bureaucrat.

Judge Spencer seemed to have a deep understanding that his role was more of a public servant than master. He focused less on pomp and circumstance and more on the substance and efficiency of the proceedings. Most importantly, Judge Spencer also seemed to care about the victims and the impact his rulings would have on them.

Judge Spencer had a staunch work ethic. He was always available for every hearing and trial date and sat through all the testimony until it was completed. The only time Judge Spencer took a break was when his son returned home from active duty in the Iraq War. Throughout many of the hearings after trial that took place during the buildup and subsequent invasion of Iraq, the judge never once even hinted that his son was on active duty on a Navy destroyer patrolling the Persian Gulf. The cruise missiles from Thomas Spencer Jr.'s destroyer later found their marks. These missiles and the impending barrage from surrounding frigates and carriers helped pave the way for the land invasion of Iraq. With the mission completed, Tom Jr. returned to homeport in Jacksonville. The only time Judge Spencer left his post for even a day was the day he left to greet him.

Judge Spencer made it clear he was ready to prepare his calendar for trial, but he also made it clear that both sides better have their evidence prepared, for when he set the date and calendared the courtroom, the case would move forward without delay. Judge Spencer also seemed to have as healthy a respect for the taxpayer and he would not stand for costly delays or rescheduling. We knew that once we had a court date set we'd better have our evidence in order. This was a concern for us since we knew most of the evidence was either destroyed or hidden in China. Although we wanted to rush to trial, we also wanted to make sure we would be prepared to ensure a victory. Under the law, the burden of proof was on us.

I was convinced that in Judge Spencer, we had found a judge who would be fair. I was also convinced that with this judge we also better be prepared. John Fisher and Joe Tamborello had the same thoughts and we began to ponder what we must do before the trial date. "If we walked into Judge Spencer's courtroom and just shot blanks," said John, "we will lose." Our thoughts turned to evidence gathering prior to trial.

With our opponents responding to every deposition question with an invocation of the Fifth Amendment, it was clear we were getting nowhere fast with litigation. All they had to do was to continue to destroy documentary evidence, hide the stolen goods overseas, refuse to answer questions and refuse to provide meaningful documentation (whatever was still not shredded at this point) and we were going to go to trial with nothing but third-party accusations and hearsay. Our only eyewitness, Paul Koren, we were told, would be easily discredited by the defense counsel since they would try to make Paul appear as a double turncoat, who betrayed both Super Vision and Wu. Without independent witnesses or some real "smoking gun," we may even lose in a summary judgment hearing before trial.

I had a hunch that what they took great efforts to hide and destroy in the U.S. would be maintained without fear of confiscation in China. I knew we needed to do something outside the normal legal procedure to finally get the evidence we needed against Wu. This would probably have to come from someone who was versed in covert operations or "black ops." A man who was fearless, well trained, and capable of going into the very heart of the Wu family's overseas operations. I decided to search for just such a man.

I searched the Internet the next evening for Hong Kong law firms. I called every one that specialized in commercial litigation, which included counterfeiting and overseas judgment enforcement, to get a referral on a private investigator who could infiltrate the Wus' Shanghai factory. It just so happened that one of the law firms I contacted, the Hong Kong office of the British law firm Lovells, was investigating the same Wu family for another client in the U.S. Just by coincidence, their investigator had already made contact and had ongoing "operations" against the Wus. They agreed to set up a meeting for me to meet this man.

FIFTY-TWO

⹌⹃

The 17-hour flight to Hong Kong from
Orlando was grueling and the landing, as usual, was terrify-
ing. The Hong Kong airport was surrounded by mountains
capped with hundreds of towering apartments and office
buildings. The plane skimmed the rooftops of the buildings
and then immediately dropped between the mountains onto
a short and narrow runway. There is not much room for anything in Hong Kong, much less airport runways. During my
first visit to Hong Kong, I made the mistake of checking into
one of the airport hotels. The constant thunder of the airplane's engines kept me awake all night. They seemed to all
but shatter my hotel room windows. I opened the drapes to
see that the planes passed within less than a 100 feet of the
surrounding buildings. They came close enough to my window that I could clearly read the insignias on the fuselage.

I lost an extra day while traveling across the International Date Line. I had left on Sunday night and I arrived
Tuesday morning Hong Kong time. I just had time for a
shower before I met for lunch with my local distributor Alex
Yeung and C.K. Lam of Thorn Lighting.

As soon as I exited the plane I felt my hair start to curl
from the humidity. The weather in Hong Kong soaks your
clothes so they cling to your body. The climate is tropical
almost year round with a few periods of torrential rain-
storms the locals refer to as Monsoons. I checked into the
Sheraton on Nathan Road in Kowloon. Both sides of Hong

Kong, the downtown Hong Kong side and the mostly tourist and retail Kowloon side, straddle the dramatic ports lining the Hong Kong harbor. After I met with my distributors and visited a few customers, my internal clock had still not yet adjusted to the time. It was now night in Hong Kong, but my body was still sensing morning in Orlando. I decided to take a long walk down Nathan Road to tire myself out. Maybe then I could get a good night's sleep prior to meeting the investigator early the next morning.

Throughout all of Hong Kong and Kowloon you witness one massive crush of humanity. The crowds of people filling the streets of Nathan Road made it difficult to walk; you are constantly surrounded by people. Hong Kong is also a city of many great contrasts. As I headed just two blocks down Nathan Road from my beautiful modern hotel, I saw a young beggar, probably in his teens, lying on his side in the middle of the sidewalk holding out a small plastic bowl in his one arm as a constant stream of people navigated around him. His other arm was cut off at the elbow and both his legs were severed from the knee. He was therefore forced to maneuver himself by wriggling on his side using either his good arm or the stump of his other for balance. The sight seemed to be in stark contrast to the thousands of gleaming high-fashion shops that lined the streets and the sleek glass and steel buildings that towered above.

As I stopped to drop a few coins in his cup, I remembered the similar sights I encountered during one of my earlier trips to China. Maisa joined me on this trip. It was Maisa's first trip to China and Hong Kong. Our first stop was to attend the annual trade fair in the city of Guangzhou to exhibit our fiber-optic products at the show's lighting section. We stayed at a hotel just across the street from the trade fair. There was a bridge that crossed over the road that led pedestrians to the main entrance of the trade fair. It was a very strategic bridge because virtually all the guests at the surrounding hotels would have to use it to get to the trade fair. Most people who used this bridge were foreigners and most of the local inhabitants were aware of this, particularly the most vile members of local society.

As we crossed the bridge we saw a row of several children sitting in the middle of the bridge holding out their hands or a cup begging for money. The children ranged in age between approximately two to five years old. Maisa's heart tore open. She made me put a coin in each child's hand. She talked to the children but they did not respond. They seemed dazed, almost comatose. Their eyes had blank stares and they did not respond to Maisa's voice nor seem too cognizant that we were even there. Their hands just grasped the coins when placed in them, almost as if a reflex action or by instinct. After seeing that she was not having any effect on the children, Maisa sadly walked off toward the main hall with me. As we walked away I turned back to look at the children still sitting motionless on the bridge. I then turned back to Maisa and saw tears streaming down her face.

We quickly set up our booth at the show and plugged in the power cables to our fiber-optic light sources. Soon the small 10 foot by 10 foot booth was alive with color and light. As soon as the show started, I wanted to talk with every passer by about my product, Maisa wanted to talk about the children. With every Chinese that passed by the booth Maisa hoped to find a local that would explain to her why those children were on the bridge and what would become of them. Finally Maisa found someone from Guangzhou who told her that the children were kidnapped by local bandits and drugged so they would sit still all day and beg for money.

She stormed out of the booth, no longer teary eyed. I knew this look. Now she was determined and mad. She ran to the first person in uniform in the convention hall that she could see. She mistook a guard for a policeman and delivered him a stern tongue lashing for allowing those children to exist by the fate described to her earlier. The guard did not speak English but he seemed to be both worried and perplexed by Maisa's furor. Finally he radioed for another security officer who spoke English to join him.

The other guard explained to Maisa that the reason neither they nor the police bother to remove the children is the fact that as soon as they remove the children they will be replaced by another group of children that would be kidnapped. The whole endeavor would be pointless. If they did not beg on that bridge they would perhaps beg in a more dangerous location on the street, or an inconvenient one by the front entrance. The guard said the best way we could combat this type of activity is to not give money to the children because that money just goes into the hands of the criminals that kidnap and drug them. It only encourages more activity like this.

Although the English-speaking security guard seemed very sincere and took great efforts to try to explain, Maisa was totally unsatisfied with his response. From that point forward Maisa did not give them money. She just brought them food. Some were too drugged up to even feed themselves. Maisa would hold the sandwich for them as they took their bites. Seeing their condition, Maisa became overwhelmed with anger. She commanded me to stand on that bridge all night and "bash in the heads" of those who returned to collect them. I stood on that bridge until two in the morning, waiting and ready to deliver the justice my wife demanded. No one came. The children continued to sit motionless. A police officer walked by and in broken English asked me what I was doing there at that hour. I explained, he laughed at me and said, "No one come, no one come while you or I here. Bandits very smart."

As I stared at the cup of the beggar lying on the sidewalk of Nathan Road, I wondered who was going to collect from him the following morning. I wondered whether his injuries were from a previous accident or the deliberate work of bandits who mutilated him to make him seem more sympathetic to passing tourists. Such contrasts between unspeakable acts of barbarism against a backdrop of modern buildings and shopping centers that line the major roads of this city seemed almost incomprehensible. Perhaps part of the contrast is due to the almost 100 years of previous British rule over this colony which infused a mixture of culture and values from both East and West.

Only steps away from the plush windows featuring Dior, Prada, and Fendi, you will find the handcarts and rickshaws that seem as if they should be both miles and millennia away. Tired, but not yet ready to sleep, I wandered down the alleys and side streets to see the "old China." The side streets are where the locals shop from carts laden with lower cost, locally made goods, destined for the legions of hotel, restaurant, and dock workers. There are also market stalls that sell exotic ancient Chinese medicinal potions made from crushed herbs and roots that are prepared for almost every kind of ailment imaginable. Rows of duck, chicken, swine and snake carcasses hung from hooks in open stalls or glass windows of the butcher shops. The stench that filled the alleyways was overpowering at times. My eyes teared as I held my breath and quickly walked down yet another alleyway.

I picked up a red Chinese dress imprinted with golden dragons for my daughter, Victoria, at one wooden stall. At another I picked up a soccer outfit with the embroidered design and logo of a famous British soccer club, Manchester United. Both cost me less than $5 each. The vendors in traditional Chinese "pajama suits" thanked me in Cantonese, "mm-goi." I then walked out of the alleyway and returned to Nathan Road to get a handbag for my wife.

Realizing I needed more in the way of an apology to my wife for taking such a long trip without much advance warning, I decided on purchasing both a pair of shoes and a matching belt for the handbag. The bag, belt, and shoes were all made in Italy, at least it said they were. They all had fine hand-made detailing on supple light-brown leather. The combination set me back a few hundred dollars, but I realized that in a shop on the Spanish Steps in Rome or the Duomo in Milan, just the shoes alone would set me back this much. The attractive young lady dressed in a mini-skirt, leather boots, and halter-top behind the counter thanked me for my purchase in English laced with a British accent. I left with the package satisfied that upon my return I would not have to share the couch again with my dog Luis. I headed back to my hotel pleased with this accomplishment. Although tired, I lay in bed for hours unable to sleep. My imagination was racing with thoughts of what type of man I was going to meet the next morning.

FIFTY-THREE

I sat waiting at a table beside a lavish buffet in a
hotel alongside the Hong Kong harbor. The man I planned
to meet instructed me to meet him there for breakfast. "Be
on time," I was told. I looked out the giant floor to ceiling
windows that faced the harbor. A mass of boats ranging
from sleek hydrofoils to ancient Chinese junks were navi-
gating the churning waters as they made their way to port.
Minutes after I had started reading the menu I looked up
and saw a man staring down at me with a bit of a sarcastic
smile. It was clear he was amused by how easy it was to sneak
up on me and stand over me while I perused the menu. Ted
Kavowras was tall and large man, neatly dressed in a pair of
tan pants and a white button down shirt. He had the look
of someone whom you could not easily place. In Hong
Kong he clearly was a foreigner, but Ted might have well
been a foreigner almost anywhere. His long black hair and
beard, dark features and indistinct accent gave Ted an
exotic and mysterious quality.

Ted Kavowras, aka Ted Johnson aka Ted Smith aka The
Sheik of Dubai, was allegedly born in New York City to a
Jewish mother and Greek father. He dreamed of being a
cop throughout his childhood and joined the NYPD (New
York Police Department) immediately after college. After
only a few months on the job, he fell down several flights
of stairs while chasing a suspect and his back injury led to
his immediate retirement from the force.

In the years that followed, Ted took the few odd jobs that law enforcement would allow for someone with ruptured discs and a cracked vertebrae. He was as a federal marshall appointed to serving papers and, in another post, was sent overseas as a body guard to diplomats in the Middle East. It was there he learned about Arab trading companies and the ins and outs of operating shell corporations in Dubai for profit and for surveillance purposes.

Government agencies or private businesses that did not want to reveal the true nature of their business or their ownership would set up front companies in trading centers like Dubai.

Often the "offices" would be only a phone number linked to a line at an answering service, and an address that was nothing more than a drop box at a mail forwarder. Ted also acquired a few other interests such as photography and Asian culture, which led him to a photo expedition to mainland China and a chance meeting with a Chinese woman who became his wife.

They settled in Hong Kong where Ted networked with officers in the Hong Kong Police Department, getting referrals here and there for "private jobs" that could not be handled by officers on the public payroll. He named his private investigation firm Panoramic Consulting, an inappropriate name I thought until I heard the whole story.

Word of Ted's skill were passed on from corporate litigators and intellectual property attorneys. The litigation and patent firms turned to Ted to obtain photographic evidence establishing the counterfeiting of their clients' products, particularly the fraudulent reproduction of name brands from the U.S. and Europe. He proved effective in documenting such illicit activities both in Hong Kong and China. His ability to disguise himself and to gain entry into criminal enterprise became legendary. The recordings he made with hidden video cameras provided winning outcomes in both local and overseas courts.

Horace Lam, a lawyer in the intellectual property department of the Hong Kong branch of the Lovell's law firm in Hong Kong introduced me to Ted Kavowras. Coincidentally, Horace was familiar with the Wus and already had a client who was engaged in investigating them. But before he could disclose any specifics to me, he had to check with his other American client for clearance. Only then could he share information and introduce me to the investigator who had already devoted almost a year infiltrating the Wus' operations. The "American firm" none other than Bulova Watch, a subsidiary of Loews Corporation, a *Fortune 500* company controlled by the Tisch family of New York, N.Y. and traded on the New York Stock Exchange.

I became tied up in knots with both anticipation and excitement. What a tremendous opportunity, I thought, to engage someone who already had penetrated the Wus' den of thieves. However, I was also very nervous. What if such a big corporate client would prefer its privacy over assisting a stranger? I had tremendous hopes, but I also braced myself for more disappointment.

Horace called back the next morning. It was about midnight my time. He had already talked with Loew's chief legal counsel, Warren Neitzel, and told me that his client would be more than happy to allow us to engage his investigator to take action on the Wus' crimes against our company. This was a magnanimous gesture, since most *Fortune 500* companies would have demanded secrecy. I later learned that Mr. Neitzel's tremendous sympathy for fellow victims of counterfeiting, was only equaled by his fury with the Wus and their accomplices. He wanted to see our company saved as much as he wanted to see the pirates shut down.

Between mouthfuls of steamed noodles and quail eggs, I felt as if I was engaging in an intellectual cat and mouse game with Ted. His objective was to learn as much about me while telling as little about himself. I was desperate to pry out everything he had already discovered about the Wus before the clock on my billing meter with him would start ticking. We both smiled at each other between rapid-fire exchanges of questions, each realizing what the other was up to. Ted seemed to be doing more than just interviewing me as a potential client; he was sizing me up, determining whether or not I could be trusted. When I later learned how dangerous his work was, I understood why. At times he would be putting his own life and the lives of his associates at risk. If news of his operations would leak from a careless client and reach his targets, he might not return from the investigation. Guns were outlawed in Hong Kong and China, however, some of the smugglers who dealt in both human and illegal product trade had them, the rest did their work with knives. I later found out that in Southern China meat cleavers were the Triad (Gangster) tool of choice and called "Choppers."

It was not until our second meeting that Ted agreed to take on our investigation. He then not only graciously opened his offices to me but also his home. We then walked a few blocks from our second meeting at the hotel to Ted's apartment facing Hong Kong harbor. The panoramic view from his living room window reminded me of the name of his company, Panoramic Consulting. A few minutes after the housekeeper served us tea, his wife emerged with their newborn baby. She used no makeup, she didn't have to. Her large almond shaped eyes were framed by dark eyebrows and graceful long lashes. Her soft features and rose petal colored lips were enhanced by her long coal black hair. Her silky skin glistened in the sunlight that streaked through the living room window. Their daughter had her mother's features, but her father's disposition. She too seemed to be sizing me up before she determined if she would grant me even a shy smile.

Ted ushered me into a room beside the living room which he used as an office. His main office was elsewhere in Hong Kong, but this room was where he prepared himself for "operations". Strewn throughout the room were several computers and all sorts of miniature video cameras and recording devices. Ted showed me a small camera lens about the size of a button linked to an even smaller wire that led to a miniature video recorder about the size of a pack of cigarettes. It could easily be clipped on a belt like a case for a pair of glasses or cell phone. There were also several sets of glasses, hats, and other disguises. A small mirror was set beside them so Ted could see how each one of his persona's appeared before meeting his quarry. He would then strap on one or more of multiple cell phones that were labeled by each investigation. It must be difficult, I thought, for him to keep track of who he was supposed to be in each investigation. I would have probably made the mistake of not remembering which role I was playing and answering the wrong phone with the wrong persona accordingly.

Ted explained to me how he was able to video record the criminal acts in progress. He also explained how other cameras hidden in suitcases held by his associates would also capture him on film negotiating the illicit transactions with his targets as his associates stood by. Ted explained that he would continue his operations against the Wus for Super Vision, just as he had done for Bulova watch in the past. This time instead of focusing on video taping the counterfeit watches and watch tags that the Wus were manufacturing and selling to other watch dealers and counterfeit manufacturers, Ted would now focus on capturing the Wus and their associates on tapes with our counterfeit fiber-optic products and processes. He again offered the same overconfident and somewhat sarcastic smile as he told me that he would deliver the legal equivalent of both the "bloody glove and the video tape," referring to the one piece of evidence in the O.J. Simpson trial that was the only thing lacking to secure a conviction: a videotape catching him in the act itself.

Ted was completely confident that he would deliver documentary and irrefutable evidence of the Wus' crimes against Super Vision. He continued to show off his high tech equipment with almost the same pride that he introduced his daughter. Ted's world was fascinating, but as I learned later, it also was very dangerous.

It is amazing how greed can sometimes dull the senses. To engage the Wus, Ted assumed the persona of Ted Johnson from Dubai. He looked slightly Arabic, having long black hair, dark features, and long, black, dark beard, but for some reason no one questioned his name, "Johnson." He regularly engaged the Wus with a completely unbelievable accent in which he sprinkled a few Arabic words every now and then for good measure. Perhaps the Wus thought that "Johnson" was only his assumed name, that he too had a shady past and present that he desired to protect. In any event, he shelled out plenty of money to buy plenty of counterfeit watches. They probably couldn't have cared less if he were a Martian.

Ted had all the accoutrements of a rich Arab Sheik, a solid gold diamond encrusted Rolex dangled from his left wrist, and an endless supply of tales of clandestine business dealings worldwide that he later asked to be kept "private." Ted hinted that he was from one of the branches of the Emirates royal family, but "a distant branch and one that preferred its privacy." The Wus very willingly agreed to be sworn to secrecy, they showed great sincerity in the "trust" that could be placed in them. The more Ted expressed his concern for protecting his own illicit business dealings, the more willing the Wus were to open up their closely guarded and walled in facilities for tours of their illegal operations.

FIFTY-FOUR

❦

Soft, soothing music filled the air at the Tea Garden Restaurant at the Ritz Carlton hotel in Shanghai. Rows of neatly set tables with fine linen cloths, napkins, and china sat waiting for guests. It was early Saturday morning and most of the business crowd, the regular hotel guests, had already returned home for the weekend or the holiday season.

The restaurant was almost empty. Several neatly combed and freshly pressed waitresses in their white shirts and black skirts hovered over the remaining guests who were nursing their cups of coffee at a few scattered tables throughout the restaurant.

At table seven, two men waited for their guests to arrive. Through the lens embedded in their leather portfolio sitting on the table, a blue crystal goblet could be seen blocking much of the view. Occasionally a waitress would come by with a pot of coffee, asking in English and then in Chinese if anyone needed a refill. One of the men nodded in response to the question in Chinese. The other sat silently, completely focused on his approaching quarry.

"Good morning, sorry we are late," said a Chinese man with a perfect American accent who introduced himself as James Li and extended his hand to each of the two waiting men.

"We had to go shopping first," said the grinning American who accompanied him. He was eager to show off his purchases: Vitamins, American coffee, Swiss chocolate, and Cuban cigars, basically all the staples required by an ex-pat.

"Normally you cannot get any of this good stuff in Shanghai, but I found a place," beamed Caruso. After showing off his acquisitions, he extended his hand and introduced himself to the two men at the table.

The Chinese man who had been sitting at the table then introduced himself in Chinese and offered his card. He stated that he was the man in charge of China operations for his very important client from Dubai who sat beside him. The gentleman from Dubai, Ted Johnson, was already known to Caruso and Li. They had previously participated in a number of watch transactions at which time Ted had made it clear that both his identity and his transactions in counterfeit watches were to remain secret. He could not afford for his clients to know that the watches he was selling at high premiums in his luxury stores in Dubai, were actually knock offs from China. "He had," of course, "his reputation to consider."

But this time their business was not watches, Li and Caruso had come to introduce Ted to their fiber-optic business. Earlier, Ted had responded to their inquiries about their other products with requests for quotations for several "large projects" at the homes of Dubai Sheiks and business magnates.

"Marhaba, Salaam Alechem," said Ted.

"Alechem Salaam," said Caruso with visible pride in his ability to utter a few Arabic words.

Ted looked at his watch and commented that since they had gotten a late start, and time was of the essence before he had to fly back, that they should just get to the business at hand. As Ted talked softly, Caruso and Li had to lean forward so that now their faces became clearly visible in the video lens and were not being blocked by the blue goblet.

Ted, noting the fact that Caruso was American, felt compelled to express his views that America was an overbearing worldwide policeman that somehow brought the September 11 tragedy upon itself.

"I don't mean to be disrespectful, but America is a big place and they feel they can walk all over anyone else's place. This is not correct, it make people angry," Ted said in his halting, heavily accented English. It was a poor attempt to mimic an Arabic speaker, but they accepted it. His previous tens of thousands of dollars he paid for counterfeit Bulovas spoke louder than his words.

"Oh I agree," Caruso crowed in support. "I don't agree with everything my country does, in fact I have a lot of disagreements with my country right now. If someone does not bother me, I won't bother him. Unless he comes into my home and bothers me why should I bother him?"

The more Caruso agreed with Ted that September 11 was somehow the fault of the United States; the more he discredited himself as a traitor as well as a thief. But He would not just stop there. He then launched into his own off-beat political opinions.

"This whole mess started with Hillary Clinton and her Lesbian lover Janet Reno. Oh yes," Caruso said with his eyes wide open for emphasis "They are Lesbians you know and they want to rule the world."

Sensing he had an opening to further toy with Caruso and wanting to give him more rope to hang himself, Ted then suggested, "I thought the problem in America was with black people. We do not like your black people in the Middle East. Black people from Africa, good, but black people from America, not good. They steal and cause problems."

Caruso then launched into his own diatribe about American blacks. With every new sentence, his portrayal became more exaggerated and hateful.

Unbelievable, Ted thought, *this guy is not only a thief, but now I have got him on camera confirming that he is a traitor and a racist as well*. Ted fought the urge to smile as he prayed that there would be at least one African-American member on the jury who would one day watch this. He then collected himself and moved to the business at hand. He started asking questions about his guest and his company's capabilities to light up the beautiful palaces in Dubai.

Caruso was all too eager to dive in and offer Ted any type of fiber-optic lighting products that he or his clients could imagine. Caruso described SideGlow cable to outline restaurants and retail stores as well as landscape lighting and star-field ceilings for elegant homes.

He pulled out Optic-Tech brochures from his briefcase and pointed to counterfeit Super Vision products. He could deliver and install them anywhere in the world, even in Dubai, or he'd train Ted's staff so they could do the work themselves.

Ted smiled as Caruso handed him the brochures in full view of the camera. *Strike one and two*, Ted thought, *engaging in the sale and transfer of counterfeit products and violation of the court injunction orders.*

But Caruso was not yet finished. The more Ted seemed eager to listen, the more Caruso was eager to talk. He launched into descriptions of all the 12 international patents he held and the installations he'd done in the past to bolster his credentials. These included work for the Disneyland "Main Street USA" in California as well as the SpectroMagic Parade for Disney World in Orlando. He crowed about the fiber-optic Coca-Cola bottle in Times Square, the pool lighting in Sylvester Stallone's house and then, in a never-ending effort to impress, he talked about the spectacular installation he did in the bedroom of a "dirty, old man who wanted to impress his young wife."

He and his Optic-Tech team had climbed above the ceiling rafters of the "dirty, old man's" bedroom and drilled firework patterns and placed fiber optics through them. A start button was then placed right beside the headboard so "at the moment of climax the old man could push the button and fireworks would appear on the ceiling." Caruso smiled as the video camera continued to roll. Ted meanwhile had shifted the portfolio so that the recording now captured an unobstructed full frontal view of Caruso as he continued to extol his handiwork.

Ted did not know it at the time, but none of the projects Caruso was referring to were not accomplished by Caruso or his Chinese company. They were all produced by Super Vision. As for the "dirty, old man," this was a combination of fact and Caruso's imagination combined. The project was real; however, it had been produced by me, years before Caruso even joined us when our payroll consisted of only three people. The project was for a building contractor, Roy Lathan Sr. The beneficiary was not his "young wife," but his wife of 25 years, whom he took on a two-week cruise while we completed this anniversary present at his home. After the job was completed, I was so inspired that I promised Roy that I would hire him to build our factory someday. Seven years later, Roy's construction company, Lathan Construction, built our 80,000 square foot facility.

Ted smiled and even chuckled at Caruso's enthusiastic descriptions, but he made it seem as if he was still not yet convinced:

"Ah yes, these were projects that you did in the past, but what have you done more recently, lets say in the past few months for instance."

Caruso leaned forward and rubbed his hands together and with a wide-eyed frenzy launched into descriptions of recent projects including the Communist Museum and several hotels and restaurants.

Strike three, Ted thought, *recent sales of stolen technology*.

Ted smiled and leaned back as Caruso bantered on. He did not wish to show that he was won over by stories alone. He needed to make them understand that further proof was necessary, such as a tour of their facility. Once there he could record the actual counterfeit products. He would then have the proof necessary to seal the Wus' fate with the judge and jury. Ted also wanted to capture on video an actual sale of these products.

As Ted continued to lean back in his chair, Caruso pressed on.

Ted then interrupted: "We have a saying in my country, first we make friends, then we make business later. We also need to see these things with our own eyes. All what you say is interesting, but we need to get to know you and your company better before we are comfortable introducing your new products to our clients. We want to make sure we can have trust before we do business."

Caruso all but cut Ted off: "I don't cheat. You want to cheat me, OK. that's alright, you will only get to cheat me once." He then looked across the table and in the most sincere look that he could muster, Caruso said, "Whenever you cheat someone, it all comes back to you in the end."

With that said, Caruso then informed Ted that "Of course we would be happy to show you our showroom and our factory so you can see who we are, it's about two hours away."

Ted again glanced at his watch. He knew he only had about a half hour left of recording tape and that this visit could yield the most crucial evidence.

"It is late and I have to go to my plane, perhaps we can schedule this for next week sometime. Please call my assistant and make the necessary arrangements."

Ted then stood up and said his goodbyes, sprinkling in a few words of Arabic: "Shukran, Ma-Salaama my friends."

Caruso, with another one of his trademark self-satisfied grins chimed in, "Salaam Alechem."

"Until we meet again," replied Ted as he turned to leave. Ted had to muster all his strength not to smile as he left. He turned to his Chinese staff member and winked. His fellow investigator nodded his head in approval.

FIFTY-FIVE

❦

Ted's other work was keeping him tied up. He tried to delay his trip to Shanghai until the third week of January, but Caruso and Li kept insisting on an early visit. So Ted decided first to send his Chinese investigator. The investigator would gather the necessary information and draft the paperwork to accomplish their first purchase. Ted would then come later to pay for and pick up their order.

Ted's Chinese associate was extremely tall. He towered over his counter-parts and as a result he had to wear his buttonhole camera on the lowest buttonhole in his jacket to avoid shooting over their heads.

Investigative Operation 2: Jan. 6, 2002

Jack Caruso was there to greet Ted's man at the door and quickly gave him a tour of the showroom. Caruso then ushered him into the office where James Li sat typing a contract and invoice for Ted's signature.

Prior to this visit, Ted and Caruso had pretty much agreed on a list of fiber-optic cable and light-source products that Ted would purchase. The showroom tour was just a formality. The documentation was being prepared to be carried back for Ted's review, prior to his visit only a few weeks later.

Ted's investigator made sure to hold up the contract he was handed about waist high so his hidden camera could get a clear view of every page. This would definitely establish the sale and purchase of pirated fiber-optic lighting products.

The visit to the factory lasted less than an hour in total. Caruso and Li did not offer to show the investigator anything beyond the showroom and a few offices. What lay in the warehouses would probably have to wait until the next visit.

FIFTY-SIX

Investigative Operation 3: Jan. 27, 2002

Ted adjusted the miniature microphone and tucked the cable and transmitter inside his shirt while trying to maintain his balance in the rumbling and rickety Chinese taxicab. His Chinese assistant seated beside him reviewed the image from the hidden camera in his briefcase. He had a two-inch diagonal LCD monitor in one of the file folder sections of his handbag. He used this to check the quality of the image being recorded. The wide-angle lens gave an excellent picture. He could clearly see Ted fumbling with his microphone and transmitter in the back seat beside him.

The taxi passed in front of a long wall situated in front of a cluster of two and three story factory and office buildings. It slowed at an iron gate, manned by a guard in the adjacent gate-house. The guard came out to check on their credentials. The Chinese investigator explained the nature of their visit in Mandarin and the guard opened the gates and motioned for them to enter. The rear door of the taxi swung open.

"OK. lets go," Ted turned towards the concealed camera being held by his investigator with a wink and a smile: "It's show time!"

They walked toward the three-story office building, as they were previously instructed. He found Li waiting in the lobby to greet him as he stepped inside. Ted played his role as a wealthy Dubai businessman with characteristic bravado, but his concern had now risen. He had noticed that the guard outside was in the uniform of an officer in the Army of the People's Republic of

China. *The government is somehow involved in this operation,* he thought. He dared not fidget now with his hidden microphone. If caught he would not be brought before any court as we know it. Once turned over to whoever controlled the officer at the gate, this operation could well be his last.

Li gave Ted a more in-depth tour of the showroom that had been offered to his investigator earlier. With great pride Li pointed out all the fiber-optic signs and samples of fiber-optic cable and light sources that covered the walls, floor and ceiling of the showroom.

"All our cable is manufactured in the States using our secret formula," he boasted.

Ted inquired about the nature of the formula, how he'd obtained it and how long they'd been in the fiber-optic business.

"Continuously from the States and here for nine years. Caruso has been with us for seven," James said. "Jack since 1995-'96, was working for someone else in the states before we poached him."

"You poached him?" said Ted with a smile.

Li smiled back. "Yes. And we patented his process in China which created a cable that gave us more light. This is unique."

He then walked Ted and his associate over to the next room. It was locked. Li unlocked the room and immediately showed off the bright cable that his company manufactured. The illuminated coils were lying all over the floor. But something on the table in the center of the room caught Ted's eye as he tried to focus the camera. It was a highly specialized machine custom-made for the focusing and assembly of fiber-optic lamps in a reflector system. James, oblivious to his guest's attention to this equipment, was completely caught up in bragging about his secret twisting process that resulted in the "world's brightest fiber-optic cable."

The camera managed to record a close enough view of the equipment so that its individual components were identifiable and clearly in focus. The camera then panned back to James' impassioned sales pitch in which he continuously held up the fiber-optic cable, shaking it for emphasis.

"We have a patent protection on our way of twisting 1 mm fiber, nobody else does, and we have special machines we use in the States," stated Li.

"I cannot tell secrets absolutely, people steal in China and you cannot protect your product."

Li then guided his guests to a conference room with a long dark table and several chairs. A television set was at the front. Behind them was another showroom with fiber-optic cable wrapped around two simulated Roman pillars. A secretary brought in tea while Li left to retrieve the contracts and the secrecy agreement that Ted had sent via fax prior to his visit.

The signing process took place with great ceremony and for-mality. Li placed his red-chop stamp on the table and carefully inked the chop with his Chinese name. He then stamped it in red ink on all the documents.

Ted reemphasized his need for secrecy and his concern that Li and his associates tell no one of his dealings or the nature of his purchases. In further confirmation of Li's commitment to this, Ted asked that in addition to his Chinese stamp he attach a pho-tocopy of his driver's license and passport.

"Sure, of course," the accommodating Li chimed in, "I'll get it at once."

The camera recorded Ted's smile. Nothing now would be left to chance as to who signed this contract when the case would finally get to trial.

"Here is a copy of my passport and I have already faxed a copy of our contract and invoice to Debbie and Ruby Wu in Hong Kong."

"Great," said Ted. "So they already know of our transaction."

Li nodded. Yes.

"How about Thomas Wu?"

Li again nodded and said, "Yes."

Now we can implicate the other family members, Ted

thought; *we can now tie in Wu's mother and sister, as well as the brother, into this conspiracy.*

"Your order is being boxed up now, why don't we take a tour of the warehouse and factory?"

"Good idea."

Ted and Li walked through a series of warehouses with Ted's investigator trailing close, but not too close, behind. He wanted to get a panoramic view of the two having discussions and of the surrounding racks of counterfeit Super Vision products that filled these warehouses.

At first, Li proudly showed off cardboard boxes filled with bags of counterfeit Bulova watch tags. He bragged of their quality, indistinguishable from the originals. They sold thousands of these to Ted on tape, just as they sold thousands to other watch counterfeiters in China.

The next warehouse was noted as being special. Li explained this as he stood outside its locked door over which two pieces of broad tape in a large X were plastered. This was a bonded customs warehouse, for export only (similar to one they also had in Miami).

"Technically, products in this warehouse cannot be sold here in China, they are for export or re-export only under Chinese tax law."

Ted and Li then entered. Ted's assistant captured a great shot of the pallet loads of fiber-optic light sources and giant spools of fiber-optic Sideglow and end glow cable. The warehouse contained more than a million dollars of counterfeit product.

Ted studied the labels on the light source boxes and the stenciled label on the wooden spools of fiber. They showed Optic-Tech's address with "Miami, FL USA" in large bold letters.

"How can you have a U.S. address on China goods?"

"It's all made by our U.S. company," said Li.

"So you just shipped it back here and ship it out again?" Ted asked, hoping to now again confirm the violation of the court orders to remove any evidence including all inventory in the Miami warehouses.

"Yeah we just cut it all up and ship it out." Li then proceeded to take a few boxes and a few cut lengths of cables and handed them to his warehouse worker who packaged the product for Ted's sale.

Li explained how they brought in products for "re-export," but in fact they snuck them out, sometimes in broad daylight, under the noses of the local Chinese tax authorities allowing them to sell the products locally, tax free.

As they walked out together, Ted watched Li lock the warehouse door and replace the large taped X. The tape had been stripped off and reapplied so many times that it was now drooping over the doorframe. It did not have enough glue left to provide a proper seal.

Ted turned to Li, "How does the local customs people allow this, aren't you worried about getting caught?"

Li held up his hand and rubbed his thumb and two fingers together and laughed, "You give them something and they look the other way."

Ted's assistant was standing at a perfect angle; he caught it all on tape, gestures, comments, drooping security tape, and warehouse door.

Interesting, Ted thought. *The Wus sell bonded merchandise designated for export in broad daylight in violation of China's tax laws, so now I've caught them violating China law as well as U.S. law. For these thieves, no laws are sacred.* Ted thought this would be a great clip to burn them with the Chinese government. Unlike the U.S., China doesn't have much in the way of jurisprudence. You steal from the Chinese government, you and the local officials involved may well face a firing squad the day after you are found out, with no Fifth Amendment to hide behind and no trial by a jury of your peers.

They then walked back to the office where Ted's assistant recorded the payment made in cash. The money was clearly visible as the hundred dollar bills were counted out and placed in Li's hands and the signed and chopped copies of the invoices and secrecy agreements were placed in Ted's. They then walked to the waiting taxi and placed their purchases in the front seat.

While Ted leaned over to place the last box into the cab, a sharp, loud crack was heard. The noise echoed throughout the parking lot. The transmitter attached to his microphone had fallen out of Ted's shirt and hit the pavement. Ted, facing the open door of the taxi, had his back to the guard, but the guard was right behind him.

The microphone was still attached to Ted's shirt and the cable was dangling in front of him. Ted panicked, grew flush and broke into a sweat. Although he was sure they could see the small and square black transmitter on the ground, he was not sure if his body had still hid the microphone cable dangling from his shirt.

The guard moved closer to investigate as Li's blissful expression faded to a look of concern. Ted had caught everything he needed on tape. He was only steps away from the factory gate and now his successful investigation was about to unravel.

Just before the guard could reach down to pick up the transmitter, Ted deftly scooped it up and tore the microphone and cable from his shirt. He quickly coiled the cable in the palm of his hand and feigned trying to hook the device that he kept concealed in his hand to his belt loop. He then turned to his hosts in disgust and shook his head and said "these damn cheap Taiwanese pagers keep falling apart, one of these days I am going to buy a good one, made in America or Europe!" He shook his head and shoved it in his pocket as Li translated to the guard and they both laughed.

Ted now grateful that his ruse worked joined them in their laughter.

As they climbed into the taxi, the driver turned to Ted and his associate and looked puzzled and somewhat upset.

During Ted's faux paux, the taxi driver had a full frontal view of Ted and his transmitter, mike, and cable. The few moments that he continued to stare at Ted with his arms folded, while refusing to start the cab, felt like an eternity.

Ted's Chinese investigator then looked at his watch and commented out loud in Chinese on how late they were for their flight and how large a tip they were willing to pay if they could get to the airport on time. The investigator even suggested an amount equivalent to several times the rate of the meter.

The driver then smiled, unfolded his arms, and turned to start the engine.

The last image caught on tape was the view from the passenger window as the taxi passed through the open gate and drove past the walls of the factory complex. A slight sigh of relief was also heard in the background.

FIFTY-SEVEN

It was only several months later, when Ted flew out
to visit us with the results of his investigation, that I learned
of the danger he subjected himself to in his work. Chinese
law calls for the death penalty for almost all acts of espionage and often does not distinguish between corporate or
government sponsored acts. Although the $40,000 to
$50,000 we paid for his research and services seemed huge
at the time, it paled in comparison to the risk he took. The
videotapes that Ted brought back with him were the most
valuable evidence in our entire case, more valuable than
legal research obtained at more than 10 times the cost in
deposition and discovery. This fact was not only recognized
by me, it was also later duly noted by our esteemed counsel.

For John, Ted probably was not only the most valuable,
but the most beloved of the cast of characters with whom he
worked with on the case. When it came to adventure and
tales of daring, both inside and outside the courtroom, John
and Ted were kindred spirits. Ted was a real "secret agent,"
an adventurer. There were times when I suspected John
would have liked to leave his legal practice and join Ted in
his exploits. A few months after I had hired Ted, he flew out
to Orlando with the recorded results of his investigation to
authenticate his work and testify at the contempt of court
hearing we had before Judge Spencer. We knew the Wus
were violating the court orders, now with Ted's video and
testimony, we had proof.

During the dinners we had together at the Del Fresco's Steakhouse in Orlando both before and during Ted's contempt of court hearing and later trial testimony, John and Ted would sit across from each other and take turns giving each other a hard time in a rapid fire of humorous assaults.

"What do you mean by that?" John would quip as he furrowed his brow and poked his cigar within inches of Ted's face.

"So are you gonna make something of it, because we can settle this right here," responded Ted with a broad smile.

John and Ted would practice arguing over nothing and subtly threaten each other for absolutely no reason other than to have some playful sparring. These two men really admired each other; they were both at the top of their craft, great at their professions, and were not too humble to remind each other about it. There were times at those dinners when I thought my importance and that of the case took a backseat to the color of the wallpaper in the restaurant.

Joe Tamborello just sat quietly beside John and witnessed the spectacle. As a new junior member of the firm, he did not feel it was his right to participate in such sparring or horseplay until his position was firmly established. I was just too busy trying to keep up with the rapid-fire assaults being leveled across the table. Joe was like the new pledge, carefully watching the older fraternity brothers revel in their games. He definitely was not going to take any risks in crossing swords with either John or Ted, although occasionally he would dart subtle looks in my direction in order to indicate as to who he thought scored a point or two at any given moment.

Joe would become absolutely rapt as Ted would describe, in between courses, how he would play many roles like an actor to engage many different targets that he was investigating. I later asked the very serious and seemingly one-sided Human Computer why he was so fascinated by Ted's stories of the roles he would play. It was then that I first learned that the Human Computer had more than one dimension, his true love was acting. He and his wife were thespians who practiced their craft during the evenings and would occasionally participate in local plays on the weekends. Joe said that memorizing case law was just like memorizing his lines from the plays he studied. Joe was absolutely fascinated by Ted's ability to play these roles in real life situations with individuals who were not reading from the same script. In Ted's world, however, a misstep in the performance could mean much more dangerous consequences than a bad review. To Joe, Ted was a real-world artist.

Like a brilliant artist, Ted was able to take fabrics from many different looms and somehow weave together a beautiful design. His unrelated training in photography proved to be a hallmark in his evidence-gathering skills for his private investigation firm. His past experience in Dubai became his secret weapon in creating believable front companies to gain entry into companies under investigation in Hong Kong and China. At times the Wus called Ted on his Dubai cellphone number, thinking he was in Dubai on business, it was actually only a forwarding number that rang to one of the specifically labeled Hong Kong cellphones that Ted would carry with him at the time.

During breaks in our discussions with Ted, we would watch Ted's surveillance tapes in John's office and shake our heads in wonder. It was almost unbelievable how easily Ted would so easily gain the confidence with such corny portrayals while investigating some very sharp criminals. You would think they would be smart enough to see through the excesses of his performance. But one thing Ted had was a tremendous amount of confidence. What he lacked in acting talent, he more than made up for in self-confidence. We learned at another dinner of one of Ted's operations in which he was cornered by a criminal who did not believe his cover story. Ted challenged the criminal to prove who he was before he would even consider answering questions about himself. The criminal backed down and the investigation continued.

We now had a tremendous amount on footage showing the Wus engaged in all sorts of counterfeiting, but there was one thing we saw while reviewing the tapes with Ted that was earth shattering. In one of these visits, Ted had caught the famous missing optical bench in operation at the Wus' Shanghai facility, which had been stolen from our lab. To us, these videotapes were akin to the finding of the "Holy Grail."

FIFTY-EIGHT

During the past two and a half years of litigation, injunctions, and court orders, we had heard that Wu and the rest of The Wu Family Enterprise accomplices were still conducting business as usual in China, counterfeiting our products, operating our stolen equipment, and utilizing our trade secrets. Now, with Ted Kavowras's videotapes, we had proof. The question was would the judge allow the tapes into evidence and if so, even if we won a contempt hearing, would Wu just lie and ignore the judge's orders as before? We were very frustrated by now and equally angry. Even if Wu's banker's previous threats were right, "you will never see a dime," we at least wanted Wu and his cohorts thrown in jail. John agreed that although this is something he normally would not do in a contingency case, he would file papers for contempt of court and ask the court to jail the defendants. Both his frustration level and sense of justice demanded it.

We ultimately had the hearing on contempt of court violations for The Wu Family Enterprise's breach of the injunction order three weeks prior to the trial date. At the hearing, Ted's videotapes were provided as the main evidence. By law we were required to present the videotapes to the other party's counsel prior to the hearing for review. Their legal rights dictated that they needed time to review all evidence against them prior to the hearing. Immediately, Snyderburn objected to showing the judge the videotapes. He knew his client had been caught red-handed and that if the videotapes were shown, his client was toast. Knowing he had nothing to defend the behavior on the tapes; he moved to find legal loopholes that would allow him to bar the evidence as inadmissible.

First, Snyderburn claimed that the tapes were taken surreptitiously without his client's knowledge, therefore they violated his client's constitutional rights to privacy. John mockingly retorted that the tapes were in fact taken in China, so only Chinese law would bar their use, if any. He doubted if either he or Snyderburn were experts in Chinese law and; regardless, we were now in an American court where Chinese law did not apply. He further noted for the Judge several Florida Supreme Court cases that the Human Computer had researched in anticipation of Snyderburn's objections. The Florida Supreme Court determined that, even in cases of videotapes or recordings taken in the U.S., if they were taken of someone committing a crime without their knowledge or consent, it is still admissible as evidence. The act of the crime itself was not protected by the expectation of privacy and thus the recordings are allowed to be submitted into evidence.

John read Joe's meticulously prepared brief: "Society has a higher moral justification in such cases to protect itself and the safety of the majority, which should not be sacrificed at the expense of an individual's perception of privacy." This was one issue, John added, "where common sense and case law shared common ground."

Perhaps the most dramatic case was the "State of Florida v Anthony Paul Inciarrano." In this case a lawyer, Michael Anthony Phillips, agreed to meet a client who had previously threatened his life in his office. The lawyer kept a tape recorder in his drawer, which he used to record important meetings. He turned on the recorder before the client, Inciarrano, entered the room. The hidden tape recorder ultimately recorded the brutal murder of the attorney. The tape was later found by the police.

At trial, the defense attorney tried to have the recorded evidence thrown out of court due to the fact that his client's rights to privacy had been violated by the improper recording that was taken without his client's knowledge. The Circuit Court admitted the tape into evidence, which resulted in a 25-year to life sentence. However, The District Court of Appeal reversed the decision based on the denial of the tape into evidence on grounds that the tape had violated Florida's statutes against unauthorized recordings.

The prosecuting attorney brought this case before the Florida Supreme Court. In its opinion, The Florida Supreme Court cited that society deserves a right of protection against such acts and that State laws regarding privacy protections were not designed to protect illegal acts or murderous intentions. In citing the unanimous opinion, Florida Supreme Court Justice Alderman stated: "The conversations between the victim and Inciarrano regarding a business deal in which the victim no longer wanted a part, the sound of a gun being cocked, five shots being fired by Inciarrano, several groans by the victim, the gushing of blood, and the victim falling from his chair to the floor were recorded on a tape found by the investigating officer in the victim's desk." Justice Alderman concluded, "Thus, here, if appellant ever had a privilege, it dissolved in the sound of gunfire."

The Florida Supreme court ruled the tape was admissible as evidence, regardless of whether the victim had permission or knowledge from his murderer. Accordingly, the District Court of Appeals decision was overturned and the 25-year to life sentence of the Circuit Court was upheld.

The Human Computer had meticulously highlighted the key sentences in Judge Alderman's opinion being read by John. As I sat beside him I could hear Joe mutter that opinion word for word from under his breath as John read the opinion before the court. Judge Spencer agreed with the case law and the Florida Supreme Court that individuals who engage in criminal acts should have no reasonable expectation of privacy. Judge Spencer then denied Snyderburn's request to quash the tapes of Wu and his co-conspirators.

We did not want to waste the judge's time wallowing through 16 hours of videotapes, so I made an edited version of the tapes the night before at Century III Communications near Universal Studios. The Century III staff assisted me in editing the 16 hours into an hour summary of the key scenes where our stolen equipment, most notably our optical bench, and the illegal sale of fiber-optic products were caught on camera. There was one other piece of editing that I was required to have Century III accomplish and this request came directly from Ted. Ted insisted that in all frames that his face was visible we needed to electronically mask his face from view. When I asked why, I was again reminded of just how dangerous Ted's job was. Although Ted's profession was always to carry out tasks for private industry, rather than government, "sometimes" Ted said in a very uncharacteristic dour tone "the Chinese government does not distinguish between the two." The penalty for such covert operations could mean death.

After the tapes were edited and presented to the judge, Snyderburn again objected, this time because his client's rights to review the edited version were denied. John insisted that this was simply an edited version. Everything on these tapes was taken from the 16 hours of video that Snyderburn had already had ample time to review. Snyderburn still insisted his client would be at a disadvantage if he was not able to review theses tapes before they were presented in the hearing. Out of an abundance of caution, the Judge granted Snyderburn's request. John's take on the decision was that the judge did not want to provide fuel for an appeal for what we hoped would be a harsh verdict against the sins to be shown on the tapes. The hearing was adjourned until the next day.

We returned to the courtroom the next morning. John and I came in extra early to test the court's new video play-back system. The video system provided for a display screen at the judge's bench and one at every juror's seat. There were also two large overhead screens so everyone in the courtroom would be able to see them. This made for a dramatic presentation at trial, but at this hearing there were just the lawyers, bailiffs, and myself as well as the judge and his clerks who served as the audience.

The judge asked Snyderburn if he had reviewed the tapes. He again asked him if he had any objections. Snyderburn repeated the litany of objections he had made earlier of invasion of privacy and other constitutional rights of his client that were violated by the tapes. The same old objections, more or less. Not hearing any new objections, the Judge turned to John and said, "proceed."

John had brilliantly time coded the videotapes so that he could stop the tapes at precisely each frame where another violation of the injunction order had occurred, or where another member of The Wu Family Enterprise did something that directly contradicted statements made in their corporate court filings. Although all the individual defendants were asserting their Fifth Amendment privilege and refusing to testify, their corporations, who were also defendants, were required to respond to our court pleadings and interrogatories. Individuals are allowed to assert the Fifth Amendment protection against self-incrimination, corporations are not. All we had gotten from the corporate responses to date was denial that they had been engaged in any illegal behavior whatsoever.

John had prepared 3 feet by 5 feet tall charts showing copies of the injunction orders. He highlighted the very language of the order that the defendants had violated in each scene of the video. The video showed the defendants selling fiber-optic products more than a year past the date of the injunction. John stopped and compared each offense shown in the video against the chart's three-inch tall words from Judge Kirkwood's injunction order effectively saying "Thou Shalt Not."

John took particular pride in freeze-framing a picture of our stolen optical bench in Shanghai and holding up the blow-up of the interrogatory response from the Wus' counsel stating, "they do not have an optical bench" and do not know that Super Vision had one stolen. He also played the videotapes of the first replevin action showing the mountain of counterfeit products as well as the wholesale shredding of evidence. John contrasted this to the Shanghai video showing that much of the fiber-optic products that were illegally manufactured were subsequently sent to the China facility. This was yet another violation of the court order that barred the "transfer, dissipation, or sale of Super Vision's assets or the sale of fiber-optic products incorporating Super Vision's trade secrets." John was able to provide the subsequent evidence on the case, and the criminal indictments that followed Ted's video recording of the money, receipts, and products changing hands left little to the imagination.

By the time John was halfway through his presentation, it was clear that both the bailiffs and the clerks present wanted Wu and his cohorts hung on a tree outside the courtroom. Before John was finished, the judge raised his hand as if to say he had had enough and asked Snyderburn for a reply. The judge ruled that Wu and the original group of defendants known as The Wu Family Enterprise had violated the injunction and were therefore found in "Contempt of Court." The judge further ordered the defendants to pay all legal fees and expenses for the contempt hearing, which later proved to be $80,000. The judge immediately ordered the shipment of all counterfeited products and stolen property, including the optical bench, back to the United States. Barring receipt of the money and products ordered, he said he would place all the defendants in prison.

Snyderburn, sensing the judge was clearly angry with his clients, did not try to object, but volunteered that his clients would comply with the court order within a week and return all the products to a court-appointed storage warehouse in Orlando.

"Very well," boomed Judge Spencer, "Then we understand each other. Everything will be returned here in a week's time or your clients will be incarcerated."

As we left the hearing, John was not in a celebratory mood. He really wanted Wu and his crew jailed. He felt he failed in achieving this objective. During the five-block walk from the courthouse to Fisher Rushmer's offices, John and the Human Computer engaged in a debate as to the likelihood of Wu following the judge's order. Even if he risked another round of contempt hearings and possibly jail, nobody could be sure if Wu would transfer back in physical form what amounted to the smoking gun itself. The stolen property would obviously later be presented at trial just two weeks from now. This debate raged all the way to Fisher Rushmer's front lobby.

One week later we were all called before Judge Spencer for a review of compliance with his order. Still, no optical bench and no equipment. Snyderburn very apologetically told the judge that his client had a problem in the English interpretation of his order and therefore felt it should be "shipped back" within a week, not necessarily that it needed to "be delivered" within a week. Snyderburn indicated that, on the seventh day from the date of the order, Wu had placed the equipment on a container ship heading from the port of Shanghai to Los Angeles. From there, the container would be offloaded in port and transferred to a truck that would drive cross country and deliver the equipment to Orlando. Its arrival would be most likely sometime in October, a month after the trial date.

"Which part of have it HERE within a week did your client not understand, Mr. Snyderburn?" demanded Judge Spencer.

Snyderburn did not have an answer, but argued vigorously that his clients should not be jailed for such an indiscretion; the punishment would simply be too harsh and would not fit the nature of the offense. Judge Spencer, although angry that his rulings were again violated, still showed an abundance of caution to err on the side of any credible argument that Snyderburn presented. He did not want to provide any grounds for any appeal of his order. John wanted incarceration and he again sensed he was losing the battle with the Judge.

"Your Honor, isn't it obvious what is happening here?" sputtered John, "the defendants know this stolen property would be damaging evidence at trial so they put it on the proverbial slow boat from China!"

Judge Spencer was moved, but he felt before incarceration can be ordered he had to give the defendants one more chance. He gave the defendants 10 more days to get the products to Orlando. This would give us the chance for a delivery before trial. Barring that, Judge Spencer was going to throw the whole lot in jail.

Snyderburn protested that it was impossible to remove cargo from a container ship at sea.

The judge responded, "Perhaps that was exactly the intention of your client." The gavel then hit the desk and the hearing was over.

FIFTY-NINE

A week came and went and again we found ourselves in front of Judge Spencer to review the compliance, or
lack thereof, with his order. Again Snyderburn reported that
the cargo could not be moved and would not be in Orlando
until late September at the earliest. Snyderburn then went
into an impassioned speech about his client's rights and how
they would be denied a fair trial if they were to spend their
time during trial in prison. Snyderburn's statements again
struck a chord with the judge. *What if he imprisoned the defendants? What if after three weeks of trial at the taxpayer's expense the
trial was set aside because the defendants could not be present?* This
would yield yet again another hollow victory for the plaintiffs.
John argued that he had already been informed by counsel
that the defendants planned to continue to assert their Fifth
Amendment rights throughout trial so what good would
their physical attendance be if they did not plan to participate or testify?

The judge, however, saw a potential conflict with jailing
the defendants either so close to trial or during the trial
itself. He asked Snyderburn what he would suggest for
punishment in lieu of incarceration.

Snyderburn took a long pause and then half-heartedly
offered, "Well, I guess you can strike their pleadings." Bang
went the sound of the gavel. "So ordered!" said the Judge.

John was smirking and beaming with amusement. He
acted as if we had won a victory, one, which I had yet to

understand. As far as I was concerned the defendants again slithered out from under another chance for meaningful punishment. They were not sent to jail, so we lost.

"What was this strike their pleadings business anyway?" I asked John.

John then responded that it would be the "next best thing to jail time. Perhaps even better." By striking the defendants' pleadings the judge effectively sentenced them to stand trial with automatic guilty pleas; they could not contest the charges against them. This greatly limited their defenses without eliminating them entirely. We still had the burden of proof, but we disarmed them of any defense. If we made our case to the jury the only thing they had to decide was the amount of damages that they would award for each offense.

"This was what I was going to suggest myself," said John. "Snyderburn just made it easy for me. The judge was able to rule after Snyderburn put it into the record that such a strong sanction was suggested by him. This will not be reversed on appeal."

John cautioned me after the victory: "This is just check, not checkmate; we still have a trial ahead of us."

SIXTY

The day before trial, John, Joe, and I all
agreed to visit the courtroom together. This was a ritual for
John, a veteran of many trials. He always liked to visit the
room in which he would present his case and final arguments to the jury. By familiarizing himself with his surroundings in advance he could focus more on the evidence
and the jury. He could also make strategic decisions as to
where to stand in order to position himself to command the
most attention from the individuals who will sit in final judgment of the case.

We all walked the five blocks from Fisher Rushmer's
downtown offices in the First Union Bank building to the
gleaming new Orange County Courthouse completed less
than a year earlier. We were notified that our trial would be
in the main courtroom on the top floor. This was the largest
courtroom in the building, usually reserved for murder trials or trials of public figures like celebrities. The room was
of a size and stature to accommodate crowds of press and
interested on-lookers.

I passed through the line at the metal detector way
behind John and Joe. They were walked right though the
special entry for courtroom workers and legal counsel that
was provided far to the right of the roped-off waiting lines
for the general public. I entered the three-story marble-clad
atrium. John and Joe were waiting for me. For a moment I
hesitated as I looked at the painting of former Orange

County Chairman Linda Chapin's face grinning down at me from the wall of the rotunda.

Why is she grinning? I mused. *This facility was a testimony to the reckless disregard of taxpayer's money due to the many delays and tens of millions of dollars of cost overruns. I could have brought this building in on time and under budget, just like I did our new facility,* I thought, *the difference is I was spending my own money at the time, she was spending the funds of others.*

John became frustrated with my delay and motioned for me to follow. I joined him and Joe in one of the several silver elevators that lined the adjacent hallway.

The trip up to the 23rd floor seemed to take forever. I felt my heart pounding with curiosity and anticipation. I was anxious to see the room where my fate would be decided. We exited the elevator and headed down a carpeted hallway leading to a giant set of mahogany doors. John pulled open one of the doors and immediately I was struck by the grandeur of this spectacular courtroom.

John calmly strutted around the courtroom, continuously chewing on his trademark unlit cigar as he studied his surroundings. Joe and I just stood in the middle of the courtroom, jaws gaping in awe, as we swiveled our heads from side to side and then up and down in an effort to take in the overwhelming impact of the architecture. The courtroom was two-stories tall, with visitor seating on both the first floor and balcony. The courtroom could easily accommodate more than 100 people sitting and standing.

Through the two-story tinted windows that framed the elevated judge's podium like two pillars of light, was a spectacular view of downtown Orlando. Several vultures and hawks would float by these windows. A few would eventually perch themselves on the windowsill and occasionally flap their wings and groom themselves. Above the judge's elevated podium were one-foot tall letters, deeply cut into the concrete wall facing the entire courtroom: "EQUAL JUSTICE UNDER THE LAW."

The mahogany furniture and wood paneling provided a timeless appearance to the new courtroom. However, the electronic control system and multiple flat screen video monitors screamed out 21st century. At each table, for both the plaintiff and defense, were two flat screen video displays with touch screen control systems for use by counsel. At the lectern was a complete audio-visual control system that fed the video, CD, overhead slide or hardcopy to all the screens in the courtroom. There was a screen at the judge's podium and a large overhead screen facing the visitor's gallery. Off to the left side of the room, between the two counsel tables and the judges podium, was the juror's box. Inside the mahogany walls of the juror's box were 12 leather chairs. The chairs were bolted to the floor but they could tilt and swivel in any direction. Attached to each chair was a flat screen video display which had control buttons so each individual juror could either enlarge or shrink the image being displayed to assist each person's eyesight as necessary.

"Mmm, Uh huh, Uh huh," mumbled John deep in thought. He stood with arms crossed looking at the jurors' box and the nearest counsel table located right along side it. "We will sit there," John nodded at the counsel table closest to the juror's box.

"Joe, you will arrive early tomorrow and see to it that we have this table."

Joe nodded at his mentor with acknowledgement. He then turned towards me and raised an eyebrow as if he already knew John's strategy. "The good guys," Joe later told me "ought to be closest to the jury." Joe also later mentioned that John once told him that it would also give him a better chance to read the jurors' faces during his opposition's cross examination and closing remarks.

This was the second time in my life I would actually see

a legal case go all the way to a courtroom hearing or trial. The first time ended in disaster. But this time it would not be one man that would decide my fate, but a jury of my peers. As I stood and stared at the jury box, I let out a deep sigh and wondered who would ultimately be sitting in those chairs during the next few weeks.

SIXTY-ONE

On Sept. 10, 2002 we took our seats in the courtroom to undergo jury selection. Immediately before trial, lawyers from both sides go through a process called "voir dire." The voir dire is the process of selecting a jury, which takes place in the courtroom before the judge. A jury pool of up to as many as 100 jurors are herded by the bailiffs into the courtroom where they all take seats and prepare for a series of questions. The initial questions are very general in nature, often posed in mass, sometimes responded to by a raising of hands for "yes" or "no." Later questions are more specific and presented individually to each potential juror. The culling process of the jury soon becomes apparent, as each legal team queries to seek out jurors that they think will be favorable to their side of the case. Each side has several opportunities to eliminate jurors in this process. Ultimately, the jury pool will be cut down to the required number of jurors and alternates. In our case, the State court civil proceeding called for six jurors and two alternates.

All the jurors were selected by random drawing from the general population, usually from driver's licenses and voter's registration cards. The few times I was selected, I was herded into the Orange County Courtroom jury pool waiting room with a few hundred other people. We would each be called by name and separated into individual groups. This process alone often took more than an hour, and then each group would be sent off to different courtrooms where trials where scheduled to take place.

In that courtroom we would await our fate as to whether or not we would be chosen to spend the next two days to several weeks in court. For some, being selected as a juror was like hitting the lottery. It was a free pass from work, which your employer had to pay for. For others, it was like catching a bout of the plague.

Like most small business owners and professionals, I hoped and prayed that I would be disqualified. Usually the lawyers would be more than happy to assist me in this endeavor for they had no interest in selecting people who would not simply accept their every word as gospel. These lawyers, defense lawyers in criminal trials and plaintiff's lawyers in personal injury suits in particular, were only too happy to get rid of guys like me from the jury pool. What the lawyers wanted were Twinkie eating, Jerry Springer and Sally Jesse Raphael watching, couch potatoes whose hearts would bleed along with theirs for the terrible childhood of the defendant that just stabbed some old woman 72 times for her social security check or gush in the excitement of being able to hand over a winning lottery ticket to some idiot who just spilled a cup of coffee on themselves at the drive-in window of McDonald's. After all, big companies have lots of money and no one thought they would see any impact on their own insurance bills or the costs of products they would purchase in the future.

After several jury notices and appearances, I noticed a pattern. I found myself walking out of the courtroom with the same group of men and women who would achieve early disqualifications. But none of us would feel more than a tinge of guilt for not contributing to the justice process. We had patients to see, customers to serve, classrooms to teach, or businesses to run. Or so we thought, it at least justified our shirking of our responsibilities to our community.

I did not try to hide my desire to get disqualified in the

past. In one case, after the voir dire was being interrupted by the sound of a siren from an ambulance, I shouted out at the personal injury attorney, "Sounds like that's meant for you. Aren't you going to run out and chase it?" Even the Judge chuckled; I was out before the lunch break. In another case I was asked what were my "feelings" about crime. I responded that I felt all criminals should be "publicly dismembered and then their limbless carcasses should be dragged through the streets." I was out in the first 10 minutes.

The tables were now turned. I was sitting at the plaintiff's table with my counsel, hoping the very same people who tried to duck out of the process before would somehow be allowed, or forced, to stay. I had scribbled notes on my yellow pad, trying to keep track of names or seat positions of the jurors I hoped would remain from the jury pool. I would write their answers to both sets of lawyers' questions next to their name. Soon there were stars and asterisks next to the "top 10" and lines crossed over those who I hoped would be excused and sent back to watching Jerry Springer.

Now, sitting in the opposite chair from the one I had been accustomed to in that courtroom, I was surprised to see how seriously many people in the jury pool took both the process and their responsibility. Once John had told them about the case and what this meant, not only to Super Vision, but to the country as a whole, I sensed that the level of interest and commitment of the potential jurors uniformly increased.

There were three jurors that I noted with multiple stars and asterisks that I particularly liked early in the process. One was a construction worker who made it apparent that he did not have any patience with any foreign firms or individuals that would steal U.S. jobs. Another juror, a business owner, who clearly showed his impatience with the jury selection process, also indicated he would show impatience with the defendant. There was also a woman in the jury pool who tearfully recounted the attack on her husband by a criminal who had previously been released from prison for a prior violent crime. This woman felt that no mercy was shown to her husband and made it clear that she would show no mercy to any criminal, white collar or otherwise. I liked this woman too, she was intelligent and articulate.

There were several other jurors that I noted too, some because I felt that their present or past positions suggested that they would be favorable to our cause, others simply because I thought they would be fair. There were two middle-aged black women who held administrative and nursing positions. They appeared very thoughtful and deliberate as they carefully listened to the lawyers' questions and then provided a response, which was brief and direct. My mother worked both as an administrator and a nurse in a nursing home; for some reason I liked the connection. I had no idea as to their opinions on the specific issues at trial, but I felt at least these two women would be fair.

There was also a former police officer in the jury, after 33 years of service he had recently retired. He was large and powerful. When he would fold his muscular arms over his chest and lean back in his chair and cast a disapproving glance at the defense table, he was quite formidable looking and intimidating. I wanted him on my jury, but I felt it would be guaranteed that Wu's lawyers would disqualify him. Snyderburn wouldn't be stupid enough to let a cop on the jury. I also noticed a Head Chef at Disney who ran a large kitchen staff in one of the hotels on Disney property. He previously served as a cook in the Air Force. It was clear this man was a leader. I hoped he would be picked as well.

Another potential juror of note was a shift manager at McDonald's. He apparently was caught up in the jury process in the upswing of the back-to-school season. It was also the high season in which his restaurant drew many of its customers. It was clear he would rather be somewhere else, managing his staff of several dozen people on his shift, but he politely answered the questions with a thoughtful response. He did not reveal any bias regarding any of the specific issues relating to the case. I felt there was a good chance that he would survive the several challenges that both parties were given. I also felt the same about the white middle-aged lady who served as an administrator for our local newspaper, *The Orlando Sentinel*. She stood out as having both a pleasant disposition as well as a genuine interest in the jury process. She also looked like she was a good mother and probably grandmother. I thought she would not present a threat to either side and she too might survive the cuts.

As the jury started to thin with each round of disqualifications, it became clear both my initial favorites, as well as the day-time talk show couch potatoes, were going to be sent packing. As the construction worker was dismissed by Snyderburn and was told he was free to go, he walked by my table and put out his hand, "I sincerely hope you fry these bastards; good luck, man." I shook his hand and thanked him. I was sorry to see him leave. The businessman left his seat and headed straight out the door. The woman whose husband had been viscously attacked wandered slowly out of the courtroom. She seemed as if she was not sure if she should leave even after being dismissed. As she walked out past my table, she glanced at me sadly and left me with a nod and a slight smile of support.

The other six jurors were the ones I had noted. I was not surprised most of them survived the selection process, but I was shocked, as was John, that Snyderburn left the cop on the jury. Apparently, this was not done deliberately; Snyderburn was just more worried about other potential jurors jettisoning his case than the cop. Snyderburn had used up his number of disqualifications on other people; the cop;

therefore, survived among the last six.

Two alternate jurors were then chosen, a systems admin-istrator for Sprint in her 30s and a Publix store manager in his early forties. The alternates were chosen just in case one or two jurors took ill or experienced an emergency that would prevent them from serving out their obligations. John chuckled as he leaned over to me and said that after a three-week trial, one of the illnesses might be "death by boredom." The six jurors and the two alternates then received their instructions as to when and where they needed to report each day of trial.

Halfway through the first day of jury instructions and trial, the McDonald's shift manager asked to speak with the judge during the break. He approached the judge and asked him if he could be removed from the jury. My heart sank. He stated that his boss insisted that he get himself removed from this three-week trial. He could not afford to continue with only two of his three shift managers. His absence was becoming a burden to his business.

I understood the owner's concern; however, I felt this man would make an excellent juror. I was also worried if we lost someone so early in the process we might not make it to verdict with a full jury. Judge Spencer questioned the man about his predicament. He informed him that federal law does not allow anyone to interfere with the obligations of a juror. He then asked the man whether or not he wanted to stay. A long silence filled the courtroom as the man looked down at his shoes and pondered his response. He then lifted his head towards the judge and said, "Your Honor, I think it's my obligation as a citizen to carry out my duty, but I gave my word to my boss that I would ask you to relieve me."

I felt a lump in my throat as I saw how principled this man was. He felt a duty to the process but he also was a man who would keep his word to his employer as well. Here was a guy under tremendous pressure at work who still wanted to do the right thing. I was proud of him, I was proud to have him on my jury. The judge made sure he stayed there and delivered a clear set of instructions for him to carry back to his boss. He made it clear that the juror had no choice in the matter. It was still going to be tough for him to face his employer with the news, but Judge Spencer made it clear that the issue was "non-negotiable." As grateful as I was for the integrity of the McDonald's shift manager, I still felt guilty that I was robbing his boss of three weeks time of one of his key employees. I hoped that at least both these men's sacrifice would result in something meaningful at the end of trial.

The next day, on Sept. 11, 2002, I got up extra early to join thousands of other Orlando residents at the first annual September 11th memorial service downtown in front of the new Orange County History Center. Hundreds of firemen, policemen, and city workers in uniform were assembled alongside local residents to hear the mayor, sheriff, county chairman, and local clergy deliver eulogies for our fallen countrymen. I stood next to one city maintenance worker with a small American Flag on a stick planted in his pocket. Alongside me were two policemen. All of us had tears in our eyes. We were overcome with the wave of emotion that filled the heavy humid air that engulfed the outdoor ceremony.

Judge Spencer made a special point of having the entire jury and all others present to stand for a minute of silence in memorial to the victims and the men and women of our military that were fighting overseas. All of us, with the possible exception of the defendants, realized the gravity of the situation. We understood the great sacrifice, which provided us with our freedom and a judicial system that allowed us the right to a trial by our peers, regardless of its imperfections.

SIXTY-TWO
❦

The most electrifying moment in the courtroom was when Special Agent Kevin Hogan was called to the stand and sworn in.

"Do you promise to tell the truth, the whole truth and nothing but the truth, so help you God?" the court secretary read aloud.

A broad shouldered, muscular bulldog of a man with a closely cropped crew-cut stood ramrod straight with one hand raised and said, "Yes, I do." Agent Hogan then took his seat.

"Mr. Hogan, please state your full name for the Jury," asked John.

"My name is Kevin G. Hogan."

"Mr. Hogan, what is your occupation?"

"I am a special agent with the FBI."

"The Federal... Bureau... of... Investigation?" John enunciated deliberately with a great pause in-between each word as he turned to face the jury. John made sure it was repeated with the proper gravity that it deserved. John raised his eyebrows toward the jury to further emphasize his statement.

"Yes, sir." Responded Agent Hogan.

From my chair at the plaintiff's table not more than a few yards from the jury box, I heard two men in the Jury mumble "wow" under their breath to each other. Two women on the jury simultaneously turned and nodded to each other in both approval and anticipation. The jurors could all sense that his testimony was going to be the high-light of the trial. Here was a real life FBI man. This perfor-mance was going to be something that they would later tell their families had been worth the three weeks of sitting through monotonous testimony.

"Did you, Agent Hogan, in the course of your investi-gation, audio tape the conversations of a certain Jack Caruso regarding certain illicit activities he performed on behalf of The Wu Family Enterprise?" John thundered as he turned towards the jury to emphasize the importance of his question.

"Yes Sir!" Agent Hogan's loud response drowned out the defense's repeated objections.

Predictably, the defense attorney shouted his objections, but regardless of the Judge's decision, it was too late, John had already made his point. It was by now deeply embedded in the jury's minds never to be removed by a ruling chal-lenging that statement.

"And what did Mr. Caruso say during this tape-recorded conversation, Special Agent Hogan?" John again thundered with even greater gravity to draw the Jury even closer in anticipation of some great admissions to unfold.

Agent Hogan was actually much more reserved in his response than anticipated, sticking to the facts and only answering specifically what had been asked of him. He vol-unteered nothing. Having had an opportunity to review the contents of the tape-recorded conversation with Paul Koren, who was in the FBI office making the recorded call to Caruso, Agent Hogan's testimony was actually a bit of an underperformance to what I had expected. However, the performance was received quite differently by the judge and jury who sat on the edge of their chairs absolutely enrap-tured by every small bit of additional information that he provided. Several times, Agent Hogan was forced to respond that he could not divulge certain information due to an ongoing criminal investigation. He stuck to the facts and limited his responses to what the U.S. Attorney had earlier cleared for his testimony.

Agent Hogan did not appear to be taking sides. He was not going out of his way to cooperate with our attorney and just sticking to a cold, calculated, and unemotional portrayal of the facts. This kept the jury more spellbound than if he would have seemed all too eager to tell the whole story after the first few questions. Over time, Agent Hogan gave a clear picture of what the man sitting at the defense table would have to say if he was not taking the Fifth Amendment in the courtroom. Agent Hogan told of Caruso's bragging of all the money he was making from providing information to the Wus and of the $1.4 million he claimed he was paid to date for his efforts. Again, Agent Hogan did not seem to show any emotion or partiality. He was just calmly stating the facts as he heard them. That was of course until the defense attorney made the terrible mistake of angering Agent Hogan in cross examination.

"Agent Hogan, during the recorded conversation between Mr. Koren and Mr. Caruso, at any time, did Mr. Caruso acknowledge that he had stolen any property from Super Vision?" probed defense attorney Snyderburn.

"No he didn't. He made a number of exculpatory statements," Agent Hogan calmly replied.

Snyderburn immediately seized upon Agent Hogan's use of the word "exculpatory."

"When we say exculpatory statements, those are statements some people might call self-serving?" Queried Snyderburn, who now tried to make Agent Hogan's testimony look like he was merely offering his opinion rather than facts. Snyderburn now tried to turn the tables on Agent Hogan and turned his back on him, facing the jury.

"Exculpatory in the sense of him saying he didn't really do anything wrong?" he was now almost admonishing Agent

Hogan in front of the jury.

I understood what the defense attorney was trying to do. Agent Hogan had given some very damaging testimony against his client and he was taking a gamble to find any way he could to discredit this testimony even by turning the witness hostile toward him. This, I knew, was a bad gamble, because I knew Agent Hogan, while Snyderburn did not. Hogan was not a man to be threatened nor toyed with. His response was predictable and devastating. He immediately went from a witness who only responded briefly and concisely with facts to each question to one who was now willing to offer far more than what was asked of him to prove his point.

"Basically, yes" he snarled as he bore down on the defense attorney, "But he also made statements acknowledging that there had been a crime committed and that Paul Koren had left evidence of the crime behind."

Agent Hogan leaned forward in his chair and bore down on Snyderburn: "During the course of that conversation, Mr. Caruso stated in addition to receiving 1.4 million dollars, he stated that he created these products and patents in eight months. And in addition to this, he had received a Ph.D. in physics from the government of China and was selling these products throughout China. At the same time, he's saying that he was paid $1,000 to give them a patent and put the optical bench together. From what my experience as a criminal investigator, if you're part of a conspiracy, you are guilty of the crime also."

The courtroom fell utterly silent. Snyderburn at that point knew it would only get worse for him and his client. Visibly shaken, he took two steps back from the witness stand. He regained his composure and made it back to the lectern to review his notes. Caruso did not help matters much by rising from his chair and urging on his attorney to ask Agent Hogan more questions. He started furiously writing and passing a series of notes to Snyderburn, obviously questions he wanted Snyderburn to ask of Agent Hogan. Caruso's angry glares at Agent Hogan were noted by a now very angry jury. They looked at Caruso as both pathetic in his protests and disgraceful in his refusal to bear responsibility for his actions. Even his own attorney waved Caruso off with annoyance and tossed the pile of notes aside. Snyderburn then looked up from his notes across the room towards Agent Hogan who shifted his weight and leaned forward in his chair with eager and belligerent anticipation.

Snyderburn then somberly shook his head and said, "I don't have anything further, Your Honor."

SIXTY-THREE

§2

If the FBI agent provided the most electrifying moment of the trial, our British distributor Garry Armitage, provided the most humorous.

Garry had a tremendous sense of humor, although much drier and more subtle than American style in-your-face jokes and remarks. When I first drove up with Garry to his home in the English countryside, he would nod over to the grazing sheep lining the roads on the way to his picturesque property and let out a deep sigh and say "ah yes, England, where the men are men and the sheep are nervous." Garry also had a way of making people laugh even without saying a word. The only other man I saw who could do that was the British comedian Benny Hill, who actually looked like a taller version of Garry. Benny Hill would cause me to burst out laughing on his nightly TV show just with a mere wink and a grin. Benny was fond of observing his rather absurd surroundings and adept at making commentary with just his facial expressions. Garry had similar talents.

As he stood before judge and jury, beside the witness chair, Garry Armitage raised his right hand and took the traditional American oath to tell the truth before God. Garry smiled at the judge and then turned to smile to the Jury with a slight ceremonial bow and took his seat. It was clear they already liked him. He then turned to the judge and with his traditional proper British accent said, "Hello there; good morning, your majesty." The judge chuckled and the jury roared. From that moment on, the entertainment began. John must have sensed that Garry's testimony would be quite raucous and thus dispatched his assistant to question him.

Throughout his testimony, Garry, engaged in a "colonial form of humor," would not directly refer to the United States as an independent country. He treated it as if it was still an errant colony of the British Crown, sometimes turning to either the judge or jury to offer unsolicited advice on how we could improve our country and our legal process. Most of this mayhem was in-between breaks in his testimony. At one point Garry said of the U.S. "I know you are just a young country, don't worry, you'll get it right in a few hundred more years."

Joe had Garry review his past dealings with Super Vision and Wu. Garry explained how he became a distributor for Super Vision. He said he first met me, Brett Kingstone, at a trade show and later signed up to sell our products. He flew out for his first Super Vision International Distributor's Conference at the Westgate Lakes Resort in Orlando sometime back in 1996.

It was at that conference and training seminar that he first met Wu. Wu was going around introducing himself to all the Super Vision distributors as if he had another agenda. "Quite a friendly guy for a Chinaman," Garry would muse with a quick wink and a smile to the jury. "He invited me out for a few pints that evening." Sir Armitage continued: "Turns out we went out to one of those establishments on South Orange Blossom Trail." The jury roared and the judge smiled, they all realized that Garry was referring to one of the many strip clubs populating that area.

"Well, you know there is only so much of that naked women and beer business that one can take in a night and about two o'clock in the morning or so, we returned to the car and headed back home." Now Garry leaned forward and cupped his hand over his mouth as if he were about to unveil an important secret: "Bloody Samson was knackered. He spent most of the trip back riding on the roadway medians and dividers, damn near killed us all. I got back to the hotel and I said I'm not going to have anything to do with that guy." Garry looked at the jury and rolled his eyes to underscore his tale of peril. The jury could not help but laugh along with the wacky Englishman.

Garry explained that the next morning Wu approached him to ask if he would be interested in buying fiber-optic signs from him directly. Garry replied that he thought he could only sell those through Super Vision and after all he had an agreement with the company and so did Wu. It was clear to Garry that Wu was just using his distributorship agreement from the start as an entry to Super Vision's products and distributor base. He believed Wu never had any legitimate intentions to honor his agreement. However, it was not until much later that Garry realized that the counterfeit products that were appearing in England through other distributors were actually Wu's work.

Garry's testimony was valuable, not only for the humor, but it sealed the count of Fraud as well as Fraud in the Inducement. To prove Fraud in the Inducement we had to convince the jury that Wu's sole reason for signing the initial distributorship contract was to defraud our company.

At the close of his testimony, Joe, asked Garry a final question: "Since that convention where you met Mr. Wu, have you had any other contact with either him or anyone from his company?"

"Oh dear," Garry replied, "I wouldn't touch him with a barge pole." Snyderburn, sensing he would gain no ground with this witness, particularly after his negative experience with the FBI, declined to cross examine for any extent of time. As the uneventful cross examination concluded, the judge told Garry he was free to go. Garry stood up and jovially strode across the room past the jury box, completely happy that he had said his piece. Just before he passed the jury box, he turned to the jury and said, "Don't worry, all is forgiven for that silly revolution, come back to England, we will forgive you." The jury again chuckled.

Garry made sure that he would leave the jury with a smile both on his arrival and on his departure. It was hard not to like Garry. It was even harder for anyone to like someone he clearly despised. Wu sank down deeper in his seat. He began to see the trial was not going well for him.

SIXTY-FOUR

"The plaintiff calls Brett Michael Kingstone to the witness stand" bellowed John. I was finally going to have "my day in court." I stood before the judge with my hand raised and was sworn in by the clerk. It was the first time I was able to face Caruso directly. My eyes tried to lock onto his, but he just looked away every time I tried to catch his gaze. I knew that the main purpose of my testimony was to verify one of the key "smoking guns," the optical bench that had been stolen from our laboratory. But first, John wanted to engage in a little history lesson about Super Vision for the jury. He wanted to establish the trial, error, and great sacrifice in time, money, and effort that it took to develop our manufacturing process.

"Only then, John had told me earlier, "would the jury understand the value and importance of what had been stolen."

For several hours of testimony I relived the history of Super Vision, from the small apartment to the garage to our public offering and the development of our manufacturing system. The years of trial and error, the months of design work, and the weeks of crawling on my hands and knees with David Vaughn were all described in detail.

We then turned to the stolen documents. Faxes of drawings Caruso had faxed from our office at 5 a.m. to both his cohorts and his attorneys, were compared side by side with photos of the actual equipment. They were clearly identical.

One by one John methodically compared the process that Caruso filed in his patents on behalf of the Chinese, to the photos of the equipment, and descriptions of our process in our warehouse. Each component and every claim proved to be identical. A large photo of our optical bench found at the Wus' Shanghai facility was presented. This photo was copied from Ted Kavowras' video. John held up the photo to the jury, side by side with photos of the remaining optical benches in our laboratory. John asked me to compare them.

"Identical," I replied. However, the jury already had come to that conclusion by themselves just by looking at the photos.

"Objection!" cried Snyderburn, "calls for speculation, Mr. Kingstone can't possibly know that this is identical nor can he prove that his optical bench is missing."

I took Snyderburn's objection as a warning. I knew that I better do homework before the defense was able to cross examine me the next day. Snyderburn's objection gave me insight to his game plan for tomorrow. This was further underscored by Caruso's obvious elation, almost celebration, when Snyderburn objected. Since Caruso was taking the Fifth, he wasn't allowed to talk or take the stand, but you could tell he was desperate to do so. He telegraphed his thoughts and tried to argue his case through gesture and facial expressions from the defense table.

I was now more concerned with why Caruso appeared to be so happy with Snyderburn's objection than with the objection itself. It was obvious that Snyderburn could no longer contend that his client "did not know.....or never had an optical bench" because the video now proved that Wu did. After contemplating Caruso's reaction I began to think that Caruso was so happy because their new strategy must be that we could not prove that either A: our optical bench was stolen or B: the optical bench we videoed in

Shanghai was the one stolen from our lab.

After my testimony with John was over, we breaked for the day. I immediately got on my cell phone at 5:30 p.m. and called our CFO, Larry Calise. I asked him to prepare an inventory report on how many optical benches we purchased and how many we had remaining. Larry then told me we could not prepare such a report because we had never capitalized and inventoried the optical benches. Since this was machinery that was custom made for a specialized purpose, we expensed them at purchase rather than capitalized and depreciated.

I asked Larry who else would have known that we did this. His first answer was Caruso, since Caruso ordered most of the parts for the optical bench and purchased the components required for assembly. Larry also commented that anyone who read our 10Ks and 10Qs would see that we did not carry this equipment as a capital asset on our depreciation schedules. I knew Snyderburn routinely read our quarterly and annual reports because throughout the three years of litigation he would often comment "at the rate you are losing money, you will not likely survive to the trial date."

I now knew why Caruso was so happy and why Snyderburn thought he would be able to invalidate my testimony. "So Larry, how do we prove that we bought four optical benches and that we now have three?" Larry thought for a minute and consulted our accounting manager Deidre Chin See who had been with the company for more than eight years. Deidre suggested that we look into the original purchase order requisitions and compare them to the corresponding invoices from vendors in the files. She believed we could also verify the check numbers that we paid for these items in our accounting program called Macola. I asked Larry if this could be prepared tonight in time for my testimony tomorrow.

Larry was hesitant since much of these records were by

now in dead storage boxes piled up on the factory floor. Just to move them would take hours, searching the contents would take hours more. I explained why this was important. Both Larry and Deidre agreed to work through the night.

In the meantime, I had Roy Archer take pictures of himself holding that day's newspaper right alongside the three remaining optical benches and had him and all the engineers sign affidavits that they knew of four optical benches constructed by Super Vision and that only three remained in the laboratory. Roy and Steve Faber were able to pinpoint the time when one of the optical benches was discovered "missing" within 30 days of Caruso's departure from the company. Tomorrow, I would see if I correctly predicted what Snyderburn and his client Caruso were so self confident about.

SIXTY-FIVE

I took the stand again, just after the court clerk reminded me that I was still under oath. Snyderburn immediately launched into questions about my past and the history of the company. Since Judge Spencer had already ruled that Snyderburn could not use Judge Babcock's decade old decision to destroy my character, Snyderburn instead launched into a series of questions on our company's finances. He focused on the losses we reported in the past few years and claimed that this action was nothing more than a tactic to blame someone else for our losses.

True, our losses over the past few years continued to mount, part due to our mounting legal bills and litigation expenses, and part due to the fact that my attention was being constantly pulled away from sales. Although I was not firing on all cylinders in the sales department, fortunately Paul Koren was. Our disaster was averted largely due to Paul's single-minded focus on growing pool sales. In his first year back, Paul more than doubled the sales of our ailing pool division. Paul's dedication took up a lot of slack that was created by my constant diversion on the demands of the lawsuit.

I was already aware that Snyderburn would try to use this against me as a weapon. As we neared trial, the losses created by the litigation itself became his newly fabricated motis operandi for our claims against his client. I was ready for him when he hit me with the question.

"So Mr. Kingstone," said a very self confident and

mocking Snyderburn "you haven't turned a profit in the last few years, all I see here is losses….You're not aware of any inaccuracies or any information that's not correct in the statements that you have given to the Securities and Exchange Commission?"

"Everything I read and signed while I was acting president and CEO is accurate, to the best of my knowledge. When we had lost money, we didn't hide it. We reported it. And in most cases, we took great effort to make sure if there were issues of expenses that could be capitalized or spent, we chose the conservative route rather than hide them as companies are doing today." This was only months after the allegations were made public about Enron and WorldCom. Our stock market had been reeling from the stories of fraud, fabricated profits, and hidden losses, which made headlines nationwide. Congressmen in Washington were now starting to call for indictments. I saw that the response struck a chord with the jury. Snyderburn also saw how his attempted attack on my character had backfired. He then immediately launched into his next attack, this one he seemed assured would come as a surprise.

Snyderburn later focused on the optical bench. If he was able to discredit my representation that the optical bench was stolen by Caruso and the Wus, he would then be able to discredit me and my testimony. He felt certain he was going to make me look ridiculous in my assertions. He tossed copies of Super Vision's annual reports on the witness bench and asked me where it stated the number of optical benches that Super Vision possessed at any time in the company history. I informed him that since the optical bench was both custom-made and proprietary, we did not account for it the same way we would do for a piece of equipment that we bought off the shelf. The optical bench was used for lab equipment rather than for production. We did not capitalize or depreciate it accordingly, we simply wrote off the expenses for the components used to build it as we purchased them.

Snyderburn then smiled as if he caught me and stated, "So Mr. Kingstone, do you have any proof that any of these optical benches actually existed much less the original four and now remaining three?" I deliberately hesitated in my response; I wanted to look over at Caruso to memorize that Cheshire cat shit-eating grin on his face before I unleashed our homework from the previous night. The longer I hesitated, the more confident Snyderburn looked and the more visibly celebratory Caruso appeared. In some way, Caruso thought his open antics of glee would show the jury just how innocent he was and how preposterous my claims against him were. Only his previous antics regarding the FBI testimony could have equaled this mistake.

"Actually Mr. Snyderburn," I said, "I do, if the court will permit me to submit these affidavits and reports from our accountants I can specifically prove that we purchased and assembled four sets of components utilized to build four sets of optical benches. I also have photographs of the remaining three benches taken along with our staff yesterday."

Snyderburn immediately demanded to see the reports and affidavits. The judge eventually complied with his demands, but only after he admitted them into evidence and instructed his clerk to stamp them accordingly. Snyderburn angrily reviewed the records as Caruso's smile faded to a frown. The jury was now chuckling at how the overconfident Snyderburn seemed to be completely trumped. Snyderburn then looked up at me and asked me how I was able to gather this evidence in such a short period of time. I then told him that his objection the previous day and his client's visible behavior told me that I better do my homework.

"After your client did almost everything but dance yesterday I decided to call my office. They informed me that your client was probably happy because it was he who purchased the parts for these benches and it was he who knew we did not number or account for these in inventory. What he did not count on was that my staff was willing to stay up all night and sift through all the expense records to prepare this report. The report and receipts clearly show four sets of optical benches were purchased and three sets remain. This information cannot be found in the annual reports Mr. Snyderburn, but it still exists in our records. Your client can stop dancing now."

Snyderburn was dumbstruck. He again looked at the reports complete with copies of all the receipts, invoices, and financial records. He compared them alongside the affidavits from the engineering staff.

While Snyderburn was comparing these documents I took it upon myself to ask him a question, "Any further questions about the optical benches Mr. Snyderburn?"

"Mr. Kingstone, I want to stop talking about the optical bench," Snyderburn replied as he took off his reading glasses and turned to stare at Caruso who was unable to offer any assistance.

"Good," I responded "I would think so."

The jury chuckled in unison as Snyderburn retreated to his defense table, filed the documents, and closed his briefcase.

SIXTY-SIX

David Vaughn was called to the witness stand. David talked of the hundreds of hours of testing, dozens of nights without sleep, and the anguish of all that crawling on his hands and knees up in the loft above the cable machine. When David was told by Joe that Caruso had claimed that he had invented the cabling process, David visibly recoiled in his chair. David made it clear it was a team effort at Super Vision to develop that process and Caruso had no rights to claim it, much less transfer it to a competitor.

David was also questioned about Caruso's reason for leaving Super Vision. David stated that Caruso told him that he was, "trying to avoid paying alimony." Basically he wanted to show no visible income.

After Roy Archer was sworn in, he stared coldly at Caruso from the witness chair. Caruso averted Roy's eyes and nervously fidgeted with his collar and tie while seated at the defense table with his counsel. Roy's conservative appearance and local Southern accent struck a chord with several members of the jury. Roy took the stand "loaded for bear." It was clear to Caruso that this testimony would also not go very well for him. At almost every question for both the prosecution and defense, Roy looked right at Caruso and directed his answers as if he were speaking directly to him.

Joe was becoming more self confident in court after completing several prior examinations of witnesses in front of a jury. He became more bold in his questioning. He sensed that he could do more damage to the defendants with the subject of the optical bench. He decided to open the wound further with Roy's testimony. Photos of the optical bench recorded in Shanghai were again held up side by side with the optical benches used at Super Vision. Joe asked Roy to identify the optical benches and certify if they were in fact identical. Roy asserted that they were. Roy further asserted that the exact components, including custom-made fixtures on the optical bench, were hand machined by Super Vision and its contractors. This made it absolutely certain that the defendants did not buy this optical bench off the shelf from another supplier or anywhere else for that matter. "This bench was stolen," Roy said in a slow, strong, and deliberate tone as he continued to stare down at Caruso. Caruso continued to avert Roy's stare.

The defense lawyer then took his turn at Roy. Snyderburn again found himself in a difficult position. Just as the jury clearly identified with David's earlier testimony, he also sensed that they also identified with Roy. As a home-grown Florida boy, Roy was a likeable and down to earth young man who inspired confidence and trust. Snyderburn knew that any chance he took to try to discredit Roy directly would only further enrage the jury at both him and his client. Snyderburn tried to give Roy plenty of opportunity to state that his testimony had been mistaken, that this may not "exactly be the optical bench that was stolen" or "perhaps he did not recall every single element of an optical bench he had not seen in two years."

Over and over Snyderburn grilled Roy on his memory and the possibility that perhaps he was mistaken. Roy did not flinch. "Perhaps this is an optical bench which my client's constructed on their own Mr. Archer," again pleaded Snyderburn, in hope of creating even a slight hint of doubt.

"Perhaps that is completely impossible, Mr. Snyderburn,

considering that the majority of those components were one of a kind and machined in my machine shop," replied Roy Archer. This highly paid attorney could not make any staff member flinch much less our factory manager. Snyderburn basically threw up his arms and shook his head. He returned to the defense table clearly disappointed.

"Are you through Mr. Snyderburn?" asked Judge Spencer. "Yes Your Honor" responded Snyderburn. "In that case the witness is excused" stated Judge Spencer. Roy rose from his chair and walked across the room, never breaking his stare at Jack Caruso. The jury saw that Roy was full of genuine anger and indignation. As I looked at the jury I could see that they were starting to stare at Caruso and Wu as well in the same unpleasant manner.

SIXTY-SEVEN

Another memorable moment in the trial was the testimony of Paul Koren. The jury had heard in earlier testimony about Paul's previous role with Wu in the theft, and they had also heard about the equally incredible return of Paul to Super Vision. We all knew that Paul's testimony would be crucial to the credibility of our case. Paul kept a calm demeanor throughout most of his testimony. He repeatedly admitted what roles he played in the assistance in the theft of Super Vision's trade secrets. Several times he directly responded to questions put to him about his honesty and accountability for these actions. Paul's forthright response was, "I am no angel, but I know the difference from right and wrong. I know what I did was wrong and I am now trying to put it right."

On one occasion when Paul was asked how he felt about what he had done, he broke down and cried. The jury was not only visibly moved by Paul's sincere anguish and feelings of guilt, but the Judge even offered to give him time for a recess so he may collect himself. Paul denied the Judge's offer for a recess, preferring instead to press on with the case. Paul walked the jury through the contents of the entire discussion that I had with him on the flight to Newark, N.J. to visit Hayward Industries. Paul tearfully recounted how he betrayed his close friend and his colleagues. He told the jury of how I had "sentenced him to 10 years hard labor at Super Vision" as penance for his past acts. It was at that point that the jury not only forgave Paul for his mistakes, but also understood why we had hired him back.

Michelle was then called to the stand. Michelle described a chance meeting she had with Caruso at Wal-Mart just after he left the company. Michelle saw Caruso as she was waiting in line by the check-out counter. Caruso was only too proud to reach into his pocket to flash a wad of cash more than three inches thick to prove to Michelle just how well he was doing. At the same time, Michelle reminded the jury of Caruso's reason for his departure and noted that his ex-wife had called the company several times complaining that she did not have money to buy groceries. Roy also had confirmed that Caruso went around the company, telling everyone, including Roy, that his reason for leaving was that he wanted to show no income so he could avoid paying alimony. These statements, combined with the testimony of a forensic accountant, William Thomas of MBT Consulting, show that in the years prior to trial the Wus transferred $28.5 million outside the United States utilizing methods "consistent with money laundering," gave the jury a picture into the depth of the defendants' deceit.

By this time, the jurors' eyes were burning holes into Caruso's head. Even Caruso seemed to know he was hated by everyone in the courtroom.

Dr. William Glenn was then called to the stand as an expert witness to confirm that the information taken by Wu and his accomplices from Super Vision would qualify as trade secrets. Snyderburn hammered away at Dr. Glenn, trying to get him to make any admission that some or even a small part of the information alleged to have been stolen was not really proprietary in nature and thus did not qualify as trade secrets. Dr. Glenn was unwavering, so Snyderburn then turned to hammering Dr. Glenn for being biased due to his personal relationship with me: "In the 20 years that you have known Mr. Kingstone and done business with him, do you consider him to be a friend?" When Dr. Glenn responded "Oh, Yes," Snyderburn then tried to entrap him by stating that would lead to a bias in his expert opinion. Dr. Glenn was again unwavering. "Well, I am presenting my opinion as an expert witness. It may or may not help him, depending on what the opinion is."

I was later cross examined again by Snyderburn who by now was desperately looking for at least one point to score. It seemed his new plan was to now discredit us as an underdog in this case by showing the jury that we were exaggerating about the Wus' heavy-handed tactics earlier in the case: "Mr. Kingstone, when you talk about all these legal fees for depositions that have gone into bankrupting your company, there were not any depositions in China, where there?"

"No. But you told me that was your intention."

Snyderburn approached closer and raised his voice: "There were no depositions in China, yes or no?"

"No."

"There were no depositions in Massachusetts?"

"No. But you planned to schedule them."

Snyderburn now was admonishing me: "There were no depositions outside the State of Florida, were there?"

"No. But you had threatened us with that repeatedly."

"Now the depositions –"

John interrupted: "Counsel, I don't think he's obligated to give yes or no answers to that."

Snyderburn ignored John's statement and pressed forward: "There were no depositions outside of the State of Florida, were there?"

I turned to the judge and asked: "Can I answer that fully, Your Honor?"

"Yes, you can," Judge Spencer replied.

"You told us we'd never see our day in court. And now you're telling us that even though we have our day in court, your clients will never spend a dime regardless of the jury verdict that I get, because all their money is outside the United States. You told us repeatedly that you would drag all of us all over the world for depositions. You had my employees for dozens of hours. I want to give you a full answer so the jury knows what kind of game you're playing."

John then returned to playing more videotapes of each of the defendant's depositions. Over and over the statements droned on, "Pursuant to the advice of my counsel, my Constitutional right against self-incrimination and the order of Judge Baker acknowledging my Constitutional right, I respectfully decline to answer the question." The defendants read the same pre-written statement to every question asked of them including, "What is your age?" and "Where were you born?"

The only opportunity for levity was when John, finally got to the part in David Winkler's deposition when he asked: "Mr. Winkler, could you at least tell me who do you think is going to win the American League Pennant?" The men in the jury roared, the women just chuckled. Thereafter, they returned to their severe state of boredom. After the video-taped depositions of Thomas Wu, Samson Wu, and Susan Wu stating over and over again: "Pursuant to the advice of my counsel, my Constitutional right against self-incrimination and the order of Judge Baker acknowledging my Constitutional right, I respectfully decline to answer the question," I was beginning to see the jurors' eyes glaze over again with each ensuing tape and each repeated invocation of the Fifth Amendment.

Something exciting had to happen and soon, before the fatal disease that John had warned of, "death by boredom," would set in.

SIXTY-EIGHT

☙

The day and a half of monotonous videotaped depositions almost put the jury to sleep. After hearing every member of the Wu Family and all the officers and directors of their companies repeatedly recite their Fifth Amendment response, I was fearful that John was starting to lose the jury's attention. John explained to me that regardless of how boring it was, he had to enter the defendant's responses to direct questions on the theft into the record. Whenever the defendants recited their Fifth Amendment privilege as an answer in a civil trial, John could legally inform the jury that they could take that response as an "adverse inference" of guilt.

Recording these adverse inferences on key questions relating to each count of theft and liability was critical to securing liability and corresponding damages. John explained that when the jury went into deliberations they could review these responses on each count and vote accordingly. I thought if the jury saw one more Chinese person on videotapes repeating his constitutional right to protection against self-incrimination, they would not only scream but rule against us for torturing them. Thankfully, John turned to a much more interesting set of videotapes and a much more interesting witness soon enough to recapture the lost momentum in the case. That witness, of course, was none other than the one I liked to refer to as the "Sheik of Dubai," Theodore Kavowras.

SIXTY-NINE

It was clearly evident that Judge Spencer was fascinated by Ted Kavowras. Ted's two days of prior Contempt
of Court testimony was a chance to see a real secret agent at
his craft. The judge's appetite had previously been whetted
by Ted's performance and the Judge seemed eager to hear
more. The jury soon became rapt as well.

When Ted first took the stand he looked completely
unkempt and disheveled. He had not slept in two days and
didn't bother to shower or comb his hair. His flight arrived
in Orlando directly from Hong Kong. He was well worn
from the trip. It didn't help matters much that Ted was still
sporting his long hair and long beard that he often used in
his characterizations of the undercover characters he was
portraying. His now raggedy and matted long hair and
beard made Ted look more like a homeless mad man than
a professional investigator. The judge, however, was clearly
happy to see Ted in any shape or form. The jury became
fascinated with Ted as John gave him the opportunity to
talk about his past. The cop on the jury sat up and took
notice when Ted talked about being a former New York City
policeman. Other jurors were interested to learn of his
photography talent and how he named his company. All
the jurors became interested in how this native born son
wound up in Hong Kong and met his bride in China. Ted
might have looked like a street person at the time, but he
was very engaging and witty. When he smiled and answered

a question, the jury smiled as well. But when John later directed Ted to turn his discussions to the Wus and their underhanded methods, the jury had a completely different expression.

First John wanted to establish for the jury how Ted gained the Wus' confidence and ultimately access to the Wus' facility. "How do you do your investigations?" he asked.

"Most factories in China are very much like prisons. They build big walls around them and they search employees going in and out. It's a very much controlled environment," Ted responded. "So how do we overcome that? We have a number of underground techniques which we use with our Chinese agents, which is to do trash searches, approach staff who are going to and from work or going outside the grounds. Now these are big complexes, so most of the staff actually lives there as well in dormitories. They work 12-hour shifts seven days a week. We try sometimes to insert employees, but I find the most effective methodology is to use undercover approaches from front companies we set up around the world and we pretend to come and act as big buyers. Just like narcotic investigations, if drug dealers didn't deal drugs, they would never get caught. If counterfeiters didn't want to manufacture and export counterfeit products, they wouldn't get caught."

John then queried Ted on his cover story and approach. "So you pretended to be a wealthy buyer from Dubai?"

"Yes!" Ted replied. "Sometimes I even dress up in Arabian garments or clothing. I basically go and I work the target."

After John guided Ted through his approach up to the point of his first recorded visit with the Wus he instructed me to play the one-hour summary videotape from Ted's surveillance camera. I was tired and worn from the trial and I put the wrong tape in the video machine. It became apparent to the Human Computer who was following the time-coded script that we had the wrong tape. Ted, who also previously reviewed the edited tape, had become visibly surprised and impatient as the long version of the tape continued to grind on. The jury, however, was glued to the video screens.

In one section, that we previously planned to edit out due to length, Caruso was seen sitting across the dinner table from the then Ted from Dubai. Caruso was all too happy at the dinner table to run down the United States' involvement in the Mideast and Afghanistan in a seemingly never-ending effort to please his dinner guest and future client. This hit a raw nerve with the jury, almost exactly a year after the September 11 attacks. The jury looked at Caruso as not only a thief but also a traitor. From his early clumsy attempts to greet his client in Arabic "Salaam Alechem" to his repeated negative statements about U.S. foreign policy, Caruso was hammering just one nail after the other into his coffin.

In another part of the video, Caruso started his negative rant against black people. This was also part of the video we planned to edit out since we did not want to insult or enrage the jury. The mistaken video poured out Caruso's feelings in Caruso's own words from one outrageous statement to another. John stood from his chair and turned to me red faced during that part of the video. Joe seemed a bit upset as well, making numerous motions with his finger quickly slicing under his chin.

But before the hand gesturing from the prosecution table and the witness stand resulted in a recess to replace the tape, Caruso started to tell his philosophy of life and fairness to his new-found friend and business associate. John saw my hesitancy to rise as this part of Caruso's dialog started to play. Ted, knowing what was to come, calmed down for a moment. John took his cue from Ted and sat back down in his chair.

"I don't believe in cheating, I never cheat in business," said Caruso in the most sincere expression that he could muster "if you want to cheat me, that's fine, you will, but I will never give you a chance to cheat me again. What I have learned in life is that if you cheat, sooner or later it will come back to you."

It was the first time anything poetic emerged from Caruso's mouth in that video. I immediately looked over at the jury and saw them all staring at their video screens, arms folded, and heads nodding almost in unison. The mistaken unedited video had made its point, it was time to go back to the abbreviated version before Ted's wagging index finger and Joe's gesturing hand would fall off.

We took a break to change tapes. The Judge granted a 15-minute recess. Ted strode directly outside the courtroom and took up residence on the couch in the hallway. When the jury returned after their break they were all laughing among each other as Ted wandered back into the court-room. Apparently, the very tired Ted had fallen asleep on the couch during the break. The sight of their witness sprawled out on the couch snoring away was found very amusing by several of the jurors that walked into the hallway for a water or bathroom break. John was kind enough to let me in on the inside joke. He leaned over to whisper in my ear that he had to wake Ted up to get him back on the witness stand.

John then asked Ted to authenticate the tapes we were about to play. The tapes demonstrated further proof of the Wus' misdeeds. It was as compelling on all of the charges leveled against them as were Caruso's earlier near suicidal comments. The jury saw the stolen optical bench, thousands of feet of counterfeit cable and hundreds of counterfeit light sources stored in the Wus' locked custom warehouses. As Ted's tapes rolled, Caruso continued to brag about the sales they made in China in direct violation of the injunction order. Caruso also tried to gain further credibility by even taking credit for sales made by Super Vision prior to his employment. He claimed that he had made these sales and installations himself while working for Optic-Tech.

John stopped the tape and asked Ted, "So were you aware that these projects were actually accomplished by Super Vision?"

"No, not at the time," Ted responded, "but after review of the tape Super Vision made it clear to me that these projects were never accomplished by Jack."

"So," responded John as he turned to the jury, "in addition to Jack stealing Super Vision's products, equipment and trade secrets, he was also stealing Super Vision's reputation and good will as well!"

The jury got it, you could tell by looking at their faces that they now believed he was capable of stealing anything. The tape rolled on only to further confirm the other counts of fraud and theft. John started to sense that the videotapes were making his point. He decided to let the tape play out and avoid further commentary.

After the testimony, the judge would ask to see Ted's hidden camera and asked him questions about his investigation. This went on throughout the time that the jury was let out on break. When the jury returned, Snyderburn was given a chance to put on his case for the defense. It was an anemic defense, after failing to gain any points in cross examination he found himself with little left to explain the now well-documented and videotaped actions of his clients. After less than a day of his uneventful performance, both sides were allowed to present their closing arguments.

SEVENTY

⟨⟩

Sensing the importance of this final
day of testimony before the jury, I invited all our staff to
attend the trial. The rows behind the defense table were
filled with the Super Vision staff. The rows behind the now
sparsely attended defense table were empty, Samson and
Thomas were no longer in attendance. Only Caruso, Susan
Wu, and one of her two daughters remained. Snyderburn's
half hour presentation was a vain attempt to reconstruct history. Even Snyderburn noticed the folded arms and stares
of disbelief with each attempt he made to refute the evidence. In desperation, Snyderburn then tried to once again
attack the credibility of the victim and witnesses in his closing arguments.

He pointed at to me and then to Paul and claimed that
the witnesses testimony was made by a "pact with the devil"
just to try to profit at the Wus' expense at trial. This became
the theme of Snyderburn's closing comments. "A pact with
the devil" to save a failing company in order to profit at his
client's expense.

John had a detailed and thorough closing presentation.
He had practiced it for hours prior to attending the final
day of trial. But the moment he heard Snyderburn's closing
remarks he cast it aside. I was not sure if he did so because
he had strategically sensed the opportunity to seize the
moment to eviscerate Snyderburn or, perhaps, just because
he was just plain angry. But John ripped into Snyderburn

like a hungry tiger tore into prey. "DEAL WITH THE DEVIL?"

John roared at the top of his lungs at he lept to his feet and faced the jury, "Am I the devil?" He then spun around and pointed at me "Is he the devil!" John then swept his open hand in gesture across the sea of Super Vision employees filling the rows of benches behind me, "Are the people from Super Vision that showed up here, are they devils?" he shouted as he again turned towards the jury. John's veins in his neck were bulging and pulsating as he vented his disgust. "If there's a devil in this courtroom and you look around, I don't think it will be on our side of the room. It will be on that side of the room," John intoned as his outstretched arm reached towards the defendant's table. John's anger filled the air and overwhelmed the jury. This was no prepared speech, this was raw passion and anger. The jury knew this. As John paused to regain his composure, it was clear he had seized the moment. You could have heard a pin drop in that courtroom in the 30 seconds it took for John to calm himself and utter his next words.

John turned from the jury and delivered an icy cold stare towards the defense table: "Just who are the real criminals in this trial, Mr. Snyderburn? Have you even been sitting in the same courtroom as all of us have for the past three weeks?" John then went on to summarize chapter and verse each of charges against his clients including Fraud in the Inducement, Civil Theft, Theft of Trade Secrets, RICO, and Negligent Destruction of Evidence. He reminded the jury of the key evidence produced to substantiate every single charge against the Wu family and how these people continued to lie, cheat and steal throughout the entire litigation process and then chose to take the Fifth Amendment throughout trial.

At the end of what by now was a flawless presentation on the charges and the evidence, John reminded the jury why they were all here. "Justice!" John roared. "It took two years of battle to get here," as he faced the jury he pointed his finger back at the defense table, "and they did everything they could to keep us from getting here."

John then turned to Snyderburn and took notice of the several empty seats at the witness table: "I know who the devil is," he said as he turned and stared directly in the eyes of the jury, "and he cares so little for our justice system that he has not even chosen to grace us with his presence in this courtroom."

Caruso and Susan Wu looked pale and squirmed in their seats as John turned from the jury and slowly walked back to the plaintiff's table. Even Snyderburn was visibly shaken. There were many Super Vision staff members who had tears in their eyes. Tears had already been welling up in mine.

Carpe Diem. John not only seized the moment, he had in just 30 minutes summarized all our frustrations and sacrifice during the past few years as well as our present hopes for justice. John had just executed his most powerful performance of the trial. I had always been deeply impressed by his capabilities during all the years he represented me, but this was the most spontaneous and inspiring performance I had ever witnessed from him. As John arrived at the plaintiff's table he was still bristling with fury. Joe and I were speechless. We did not say a word to him as he sat down beside us.

Judge Spencer then turned to address the jury: "As I indicated earlier, you have to select one of your number to serve as the foreperson of this jury. Your verdict must be unanimous. All the exhibits will be brought in to you."

The judge then turned to the two alternates: "Mr. Litsinger and Ms. Brooks, you are the two alternates, and your services are now completed. I want to thank you for being with us. I hope you don't think your time has been wasted because you have not had a chance to participate in the deliberations. You have to realize if someone had gotten sick or just decided they didn't want to come back and go home, if we didn't have an alternate, we would have started this trial over again. So it's very important we have alternates. I thank you for your service." With that Judge Spencer released the alternates and let out the jury to deliberate our fate.

After the presentation of the videotapes, followed by John's powerful closing argument, I thought the decision of the jury would take just a few minutes. Unfortunately, this presumption proved to be wrong. As the hours ticked by I became both worried and shaken in my confidence in the verdict. We were later informed that the jury would retire for the evening. They took most of the day to continue their deliberations. As the morning faded into the afternoon, the lack of a resolution became maddening to me. I started to reanalyze the entire trial in my mind and look for where we might have possibly gone wrong.

SEVENTY-ONE

The jury entered the courtroom after almost two full days of deliberations. All of us had been standing by on cell phones to hear notice that the verdict had been reached. I had been very confident that we should win by a landslide, but the fact that the jury took two days to decide worried me. I was very nervous when they entered the room and took their seats. My stomach felt like it was full of butterflies trying to escape.

I looked over at the defense table. It was empty, with the exception of the Wus' lawyer, Phil Snyderburn.

It was very symbolic that the Wus and Caruso, who sat through most of the trial, chose not to bother to sit through the verdict. They did not plan to be held accountable for the verdict, so I guess, regardless of what the jury found, they felt it would be of no consequence to them. It was the final act of thumbing their nose at our justice system after several years of abuse and violations. My stomach was churning in a combination of anticipation of the verdict and disgust that neither the Wus nor Caruso cared enough about the outcome to even show up.

The judge turned to the jury foreman and asked him had the jury reached its verdict.

"Yes, your honor," replied the McDonald's shift manager.

John took out the jury form whereby each count against Samson Wu, Debbie Wu, Ruby (Wu) Lee, Jack Caruso, and

292

Thomas Wu was listed with a space beside each count to check off the word either "Guilty" or "Not Guilty." On subsequent pages, the jury form had the names of all defendants listed with blank lines listed under each count against them where they would list money damages they had assessed for those charges.

As the judge's clerk read the jury form handed to her by the jury foreman, John Grocholski, John, Joe, and I sat poised, with pen in hand, waiting to write down the results:

On the count of fraud, the jury finds the defendants:
Samson Wu—**Guilty**
Thomas Wu—**Guilty**
Debbie Wu—**Guilty**
Ruby Lee aka Ruby Wu—**Guilty**
David Winkler—**Guilty**
Jack Caruso—**Guilty**
Travis Ponchintesta—**Guilty**
Marsam Trading Company, Inc.—**Guilty**
Marsam Trading Company, HK—**Guilty**
Optic-Tech International, Inc.—**Guilty**
Shanghai Quailong Optic-Tech Inc.—**Guilty**
Cosmic International—**Guilty**

As the judge's clerk read on to cover all 10 charges including negligent destruction of evidence, tortuous interference with contracts, fraud in the inducement, civil theft, misappropriation of trade secrets, and violation of the Florida RICO Act, the words rang out again on every charge for every defendant: Guilty.

After taking more than 15 minutes to read all the charges and all the guilty verdicts, the judge's clerk then turned to the monetary damages. By this time, John and I were not able to keep up. It fell to the Human Computer to list all the monetary damages and add up all the numbers.

Joe's pencil point marked up page after page with dollar amounts besides the names of each defendant. Every single defendant was charged with multi-million dollar judgment amounts; Caruso in particular was singled out for the largest sum, probably a reflection of what they thought of him as a human being as well as to what they thought of him as a conspirator in this case.

Joe nervously tallied the amounts. It was the first time I had seen the normally stoic Human Computer visibly flustered and overwhelmed. This was his first case and his first jury verdict. He arrived at a total, but he could not believe the amount was correct. I badgered him to tell me, but he just waved me off, shook his head, and began to tally up again on his now unsheathed calculator. Joe turned to John and then turned to me with a look of absolute amazement, the total verdict, was $33.1 million. With prejudgment interest, the trebeling of civil theft damages and our entitlement to attorney's fees and costs, the total verdict and final judgment would exceed $40 million. This later turned out to not only be the single largest jury verdict in Fisher Rushmer's history, but also one of the single largest jury verdicts in a trade-secret case in Florida's history. It also would have qualified for the top 10 civil jury verdicts of all time in the Orange County Court.

Synderburn was visibly shaken and approached the judge's bench to confirm what he had just heard. He then started to debate whether or not some of his clients were actually convicted of fraud in order to try to seize even some small victory after the fact by limiting the stigma that will now forever be attached with all his clients.

The judge, wanting to put the matter to rest once and for all responded, "I understand what you are saying. Okay." He then turned to the jury and said, "If this is your verdict, we want to make sure we get an affirmative response from each person; say, "that is my verdict' as the court clerk reads your name."

THE CLERK: "Donald Glasser, is that your verdict?"

JUROR GLASSER: "That is my verdict."

THE CLERK: "Elmira Parker McGee, is this your verdict?"

JUROR McGEE: "This is my verdict."

THE CLERK: "Jonathan Grocholski, is this your verdict?"

JUROR GROCHOLSKI: "That is my verdict."

THE CLERK: "Barry Poston, is this your verdict."

JUROR POSTON: "That is my verdict."

THE CLERK: "Clover Wiggins, is this your verdict?"

JUROR WIGGINS: "That is my verdict, yes."

THE CLERK: "Mary Boniface, is this your verdict?"

JUROR BONIFACE: "Yes, that is my verdict."

THE COURT: Let the verdict be recorded. Ladies and gentlemen of the jury, I want to thank you for your service."

John, too refined to let out a yell of victory, just smiled and buttoned his jacket as he strode over to Snyderburn to offer a sportsmanlike handshake. He then thanked the judge and looked at me with his characteristic brow furrowing, followed by a wide-eyed look of pending celebration. I was happy for the verdict, but I had another agenda and lingered in the courtroom for a while to make my agenda known.

First I thanked the jurors as they walked by and left the courtroom.

Then I turned to the judge who was now talking to Snyderburn and bellowed: "Mr. Snyderburn, where are your clients?"

Snyderburn, clearly caught off guard, looked at the judge, then looked at me and said, "I honestly do not know, Mr. Kingstone."

I then looked at the judge and said: "Your Honor, none of this is going to ever matter if they just run off to China."

John was now grasping my arm. He felt that I was crossing the line with the judge. Judicial rules were that I was not allowed to have any direct conversations with him unless I was being questioned by him directly or on the witness stand under oath.

The judge somehow understood the gravity of my concern. Rather than basking in what should have been the thrill of a great victory, instead I was now just now realizing the potential extent of my loss. The whole trial, verdict, and two and a half years of litigation might have been just a waste of time. The Wus were merely a few telephone-bank transfers and one airline flight away from evading all judgments.

Judge Spencer looked back at me and said, "I know." It was the only thing he said to me that day, but somehow, that alone was enough. I just wanted his acknowledgment that after all this, the trial, and even after the verdict, that he understood, that ultimately, it would probably all result in nothing.

Two hundred and fifty miles south of the courtroom, Samson Wu was already in Miami emptying what was left of his U.S. bank accounts. He had already engineered a deal to have Ocean Bank foreclose on all his personal and corporate properties in the U.S., including his Miami warehouses and his mansion on the 14th green of the Doral Country Club. Ocean Bank did so in exchange for settlement of all his outstanding loans. More than 13,000 miles to the East, Thomas Wu was carrying out his brother's instructions to clean out and close all the bank accounts that were disclosed in discovery and at trial. Thomas Wu also transferred all the real estate and corporate assets out of the family members' name to other corporate identities not immediately identifiable or traceable to the family just as his brother had instructed.

John released his grip on my arm. As the Human Computer gathered up his tally sheets, we both had to jog out of the courtroom to keep up with the fast striding Mr. Fisher. Whether it was just decorum or superstition, John Edwin Fisher would not gloat inside the courtroom. But outside the courtroom, was quite another story.

SEVENTY-TWO

"Yes! Yes! Yes! Yes! ...We got those bastards!"
John let out a loud yell. His enthusiasm was overwhelming.

John looked over at me in disappointment; I was not sharing his enthusiasm. For once, the talkative client that he could never seem to shut up was not saying anything. It took John a few minutes to calm down, he knew he had performed brilliantly and whether we collected or not, no one would be able to rob him of the achievement he so deserved.

"So I guess you think you just won a Pyrrhic victory today, don't you?" John said to me while playfully elbowing me in the ribs. "Maybe so, but there will be other battles ahead, we will chase their assets for a year or two, eventually we might get something."

"Eventually" sounded pretty distant to me. I had already paid hundreds of thousands of dollars of fees and expenses to get to trial. I now anticipated that my bill, with up to three lawyers full time for three solid weeks of trial, would grow by at least another $100,000. Someone was going to have to pay that bill and I knew it wouldn't be Wu anytime soon, if ever. I shook John's hand as well as Joe's hand and offered my congratulations to them with the greatest enthusiasm and sincerity that I could muster. They had done a spectacular job; they had a right to celebrate. This was a tremendous legal victory after a long hard battle, even if it might never have been a commercial one.

After the congratulations were over, I excused myself

and Maisa and I went to our car. Maisa knew something was up. I did not say a word to her as we walked across the parking lot to our car.

"Where are we going, Brett?" Maisa asked.

"To try and get some Justice." I replied.

"I thought that's why we were in court." Maisa replied.

"No. That was just the verdict, now we will have to go wake up a few people who are supposed to enforce it."

I told Maisa that we were heading straight to the Orange County Chairman's Office, just a few blocks away from the Courthouse. If my hunch was right, Wu and his crew would be about to board a plane, assuming he hadn't done so already. Perhaps now with the jury verdict in hand, the FBI would indict or at least I could convince the County Chairman, Richard Crotty, to impress upon the Orange County Sheriff to arrest the Wu clan.

We drove quickly to the Orange County Chairman's office. We literally ran up the stairs to the reception area, with verdict in hand. I breathlessly explained to the overwhelmed receptionist what had happened. I doubt she was able to make out more than a few words of what I had said. I then blurted out "George Rodon, George Rodon knows who I am, call him." George Rodon was the right arm of the Orange County Chairman. An impressive, immaculately dressed man with a full head of flowing black and silver hair, he would inspire confidence at every inauguration ceremony and awards dinner that he would attend on behalf of the Chairman.

George had previously met me and Maisa at several of the Top 50 Fastest Growing Company award dinners that Super Vision had been honored earlier. He was also a hot-blooded Latin, a Cuban immigrant; he shared my wife's passion for both life and for justice. If anyone would understand, George Rodon would. George Rodon came out almost immediately, he apologized that he was not joining us with the Chairman himself but the Chairman was away on business. He brought another county administrator, Lex Veach, with him. Lex looked like a man who would make things happen. He was lean and athletic. He did not give speeches or use multi-syllable bureaucratic babble. He listened to the problem and then immediately focused on the result. He moved with force and speed.

I explained to Lex that we had just won a $41.2 million verdict. The reason we were in his office was to ask for help. We believed the Wus were at this very minute preparing to flee the country. In the past, I had called the Orange County Sheriff to take over the case from the FBI after I was informed that the FBI was overwhelmed and could not continue with the case. Now, with a verdict in hand, we had the conclusive "proof" to get the criminal charges pressed and have Caruso and the Wus locked up before they could skip the country.

"Could you help me, Lex?" I pleaded.

Lex Veach picked up the telephone. I was not able to hear the conversation in its entirety, but I did here a few loud "come over here" and "right now...yes right now!" The conversation was brief, and less than 10 minutes later, I had one uniformed sheriff's officer in Lex's office. He was already in contact with the watch commander about following up on the case, but he informed us that there wasn't much he could do now.

"Arrest them!" Maisa yelled.

"It's not that simple," the officer replied. He then launched into a speech on what our civil verdict meant and what it didn't mean. What it did not mean, was that it was not a criminal verdict, indictment or trial. Those things took time and paperwork, but he assured us he would "look into it" and "get back to us." I had heard those same words before from the FBI clerk during my initial call to their Orlando office looking for help.

We are back to square one again, I thought. I told the officer, within earshot of the two key men of the county chairman, that he should report back to the sheriff that if the Wus skip the country with Caruso in tow I will blame them solely for letting them evade justice. Whatever forms needed to be filled out so we might arrest the Wus I would be ready to accomplish anywhere and at any time, as long as it was soon! If my prior calls for justice went unanswered before, perhaps now out of embarrassment, if nothing else, I would at least get some sort of response.

Maisa and I thanked George Rodon and Lex Veach. I then apologized for my display of fury in their esteemed offices. By this time, George's assistant had come out to join us. They all seemed genuinely concerned about our predicament. Lex and George clearly seemed moved by our plight and indicated their frustration at lack of action on our case. The officer was more circumspect. He was sympathetic to our plight, but he had been around long enough to know that it would be less than honest for him to leave us with any false hopes about what may occur in the future. Although extremely frustrated by the officer's response, I still shook his hand before I left, in appreciation of his honesty.

As we walked back down the stairs Maisa turned to me and asked, "So what do you think we accomplished, Brett?"

"Nothing, absolutely nothing."

SEVENTY-THREE

∽

After the Wu family used their vast personal resources to fund legal challenges that resulted in repeated delays to get the case to trial, they used the same tactics again to further delay the institution of the verdict into the final order.

The final order is issued by the trial judge after the jury issues its verdict only when all matters relating to the trial have been resolved. The Wus' crafty legal team, led by Snyderburn, found another loophole that enabled them to delay the issuance of the judge's order, hence the enforcement of the jury verdict.

Snyderburn not only immediately filed notice of appeal of the decision; he filed notice of appeal of the judge's prior order to strike his client's pleadings. Basically, more babble about how his client's rights were unduly denied when the judge sent them to trial without their benefit of pleading a defense to the charges. This was an even more ridiculous, hypocritical ruse, because Snyderburn had confirmed, even prior to the contempt hearing, that his clients would not talk in their own defense at trial since they would all assert their Fifth Amendment privilege.

The tactic succeeded in delaying the final order being signed for almost a year. Meanwhile the Wus relentlessly continued to violate the court's injunction orders with complete impunity. Every effort we made to try to obtain some meaningful sanction or incarceration to stop them was met with some legal roadblock. They actually used our legal system as their accomplice in their attempt to destroy Super Vision. After all the contempt hearings and all the judgments, the Wus still proved to be outside the reach and scope of our laws.

After the Fifth District Court denied the appeal on the contempt order, the judge was able to sign the final judgment order. At that point, there was no sense searching for money now in either the U.S. or in Hong Kong. Not only had the Wus used the delays to wire all their money out of the country and again enlist their bank to render all their tangible properties in the United States untouchable, we also received reports from both Ted and the Hong Kong law firm that the Wus had used the first few weeks after trial to shut down their corporations in Hong Kong and China, close all their known overseas bank accounts, and to transfer title to all their properties under Hong Kong jurisdiction into names of other relatives and friends.

We immediately knew that the collection effort, if there was to be one at all, would require the services of a specialist who would have a level of international experience not found in Fisher Rushmer. John immediately went online to search for a referral from his partners and colleagues in the The Harmonie Group, a legal association, which his firm was a member. Linda Candler's was the first name to pop up on the screen when we searched for an international money chaser.

SEVENTY-FOUR

❧

Linda Candler was a former U.S. Attorney for the Department of Justice. She also served as a prosecutor in the Office of Serious Fraud in London for the British Government. Linda had several stints with private firms as an expert in searching and retrieving overseas bank accounts. Her travels took her often to the Grand Cayman Islands, the Bahamas, Switzerland, and Australia. She had also previously worked under U.S. Attorney Robert Morganthau, the aggressive U.S. attorney with the steely disposition that brought many of the Wall Street master thieves to justice. When Linda was with Morganthau, she assisted him in chasing down the hidden funds of the former savings and loan bank officers who were hit with multimillion-dollar verdicts for their roles in squandering or stealing customer deposits. This was the final outcome of the great savings and loan scandals of the 1980s. Linda achieved a very high percentage rating for recoveries.

When Linda would enter the courtroom or conduct an investigation with opposing counsel, she would frequently be underestimated. This later proved to work in her favor. An attractive woman with long blond hair and an athletic figure, she appeared to some more like a college cheerleader than a hardened, experienced counsel. Just about the time some male attorneys would engage in patronizing behavior, she would do the legal equivalent of kicking the legs of the chair out from under them and then smashing their skulls on the conference room table. She would not only announce that she knew where their client's money was, she would provide proof that the attorneys also knew where their client's money was. She then reminded them that their public denials would lead to perjury charges at least and probably disbarment at best. The lawyers might very well join their clients in jail. The criminal defense lawyer's tune would change very quickly. Linda started getting answers and the U.S. Government started collecting funds.

Linda agreed to take on our case on a contingency fee basis. She would receive ten percent of the amount of recovery, prior to Fisher Rushmer's contingency fee; the remainder would go to Super Vision. Linda told me that she did not want to waste time chasing money where we knew it was not, Hong Kong and the U.S. Wu had long closed all his known accounts since we disclosed them at trial. She wanted to focus on another country: Panama. Our research, and a few of Wu's very helpful and angry former customers and partners, confirmed that large amounts were being transferred to The International Commercial Bank of China branch in Panama City.

At one point, we needed to prove Wu had liquid assets to pay the court ordered $80,000 in legal fees in order for the judge to have a legal basis to incarcerate Wu. The civil law provided you cannot jail someone for not being able to pay; you could only jail someone who you could prove had the money but refused to pay. One of my international sales staff, Paula Vega Ortiz, assisted me in playing sleuth and she came up with the idea to check all of Wu's last known bank accounts in South America.

We knew Wu had prior business dealings in South America. Much more detailed information trickled in from his former customers and agents there. Paula called the banks and spoke to a junior person in either their wire room or the clerical department. She explained in Spanish that she had a check drawn on the account and would not release the shipment of merchandise we were holding until we could be assured the check would clear. The amount would always be over $80,000; usually it was something like $93,750. The bank clerks often proved all too willing to comply with the request in order that their client did not call back later and angrily tell their boss that they had held up his shipment. In several cases we were told the checks would not only clear, but that even for amounts in excess of $200,000 the check would still be honored. Armed with this information we headed to the hearing. This time John stopped us in our tracks rather than Snyderburn.

"The information is only hearsay, Brett damnit!" John growled in disapproval.

"It's not admissible and I am not even sure if what you did was legal." My beaming, self-appreciative smile faded into a frown. Our brilliant sleuthing was now being written off as valueless.

"But John this proves he had the funds in his account," I said.

"It proves nothing that the court will accept. An affidavit from Paula is just your employee's word for it. Only authenticated records from the bank itself will serve as proof," replied John.

"It will be a cold day in hell when these banks in Panama provide us with that," I replied.

John then went on to say that all was not lost. The information could probably be better used later anyway. It would particularly be more valuable if we didn't present it to the court because it would ultimately be presented to Snyderburn. This would guarantee a tip off to the Wus, which would result in those accounts being immediately cleaned out. It was best to save that information when we finally received the judge's order and then to use it for seizures later. Linda asked us to hand over the information that

Paula Vega and I had obtained and immediately determined that Panama was the first place to search and seize.

In order to freeze bank accounts in Panama, Linda said we would need a Panamanian lawyer. John went back on line with the Harmony Group and found Juan Felipe Pitty. Juan Felipe Pitty was young; however, he was experienced and articulate. After my first phone call with him where he laid out his plan to get the judicial seizure order from the Panamanian Supreme Court and later arrange all the necessary bonding requirements to seize funds under that order, I knew we had our man. Juan Felipe, like Linda was impressed with the size of our order and the potential for the recovery. He agreed to a small fee up front with a contingency-based percentage of 10% on the first $1 million and 5% thereafter. If Linda and Juan collected only a fraction of the verdict, it could still mean over a million dollars in fees for both of them.

Ever since the U.S. invaded Panama and removed the funny little guy with red underpants who was running it (now a guest of our government in a federal prison in Miami), we have had several legal and exchange treaties with that country. Panama went from a lawless dictatorship to a democracy in the decade since the invasion by the U.S.

The Panamanian Supreme Court would rule on most requests to pursue assets within its borders from U.S. companies and government agencies. Panama was also world renowned as a "safe haven" for banking and cash deposits. The court often had to struggle between preserving the terms of the treaties with the U.S. and preserving its reputation as a safe banking haven. Panama's banking industry brought billions of dollars to its banking system and thousands of badly needed jobs for its population. Juan explained that key among the criteria that would distinguish a request to seize bank accounts within Panama was the requirement that ongoing criminal trials or investigations had to be proven. This would distinguish the difference between simply a commercial dispute, for which Panama felt someone should have the right of protection of their assets, and a criminal action, whereby someone was not deserving of similar protection under their laws. At least this was the theory and/or last known interpretation on this subject.

We had waited for more than two years for the FBI and the U.S. attorney to act. September 11 was now more than a year behind us and we felt the investigation would pick back up. But although the FBI would visit our trial occasionally, giving us the impression they were going to get authorization to move forward, neither they nor the U.S. Attorney would comment on our case. They also refused to give us the letter we needed to present to the Panamanian government to confirm the existence of the ongoing criminal investigation. We were stalemated.

John had been engaging the now exasperated judge on how to deal with these people who routinely lie in court, violate court orders, and continue their illegal behavior overseas while simultaneously seeking protection under our laws. The judge had an obligation to follow the rules by the book, but even he saw the injustices that were allowed in the process. In one such hearing, the judge suggested, "Well John you can always bring before me an action for Fraud on the Court," John's eyes lit up, he removed the well-chewed cigar from his mouth, turned to me, smiled, and winked. He would not tell me what he was thinking just then in front of the judge, but something told me that he had already developed his game plan and details of execution. Later discussions proved I was right.

SEVENTY-FIVE
৻৶

In the movie, "The Usual Suspects," the most gripping scene is the revelation by one the movie's terrified victims of the horrors that the villain is capable of inflicting. The victim describes how Keyser Soze confronted an armed man who was holding his family hostage and threatened to execute his family if Keyser did not swear to give up his crime organization in favor of a rival clan. Keyser first pointed his gun at the assailant and, seeing that he did not have a clear shot at the man who was hiding behind his wife, then shot his own wife and children in front of the shocked assailant. His last shot he saved for his family's assailant, but he did not wound him fatally. Instead Keyser had him return to his clan with a message. He would now hunt down each and every clan member and their families and kill them all. Keyser later made good on his promise.

What kind of man I thought would be so desperate in his desire for wealth and power that he would sacrifice the lives of his own family in order to protect his criminal enterprise? Such a man must be inhuman. Only the creation of film and fables, I thought. But I learned, there are still such men who would, "eat the flesh of their own children" to survive. Such villains do exist.

To this day, the thing I will never get over about Wu was not what he did to me, but what he was willing to do to his own family. I like to view everyone as a human being, even my enemies. One would think that your enemies could be evil to you, but at least they would show some human emotions with their families. Not so with Wu. He was the personification of evil incarnate. At one point in the trial, it became clear that the Wu Family had violated the court orders on numerous occasions and now were being considered for jail time in response to a contempt of court motion from our side.

The key offense that triggered the judge to consider incarceration for all the key family members was Wu's refusal to pay our court ordered Contempt of Court hearing fees. Wu for some reason disappeared after the first few days of the trial, leaving only his wife and one daughter to attend the hearing on the failure to pay in his absence. The judge instructed the bailiff to not let Susan Wu leave the floor of the courtroom during the lunch break and gave the Wu family just two hours to wire the money or present a bank check for the $80,000 in attorney's fees awarded at the previous hearing. Susan's face went pail and tears began to well in her eyes. Her older daughter, who took time off from her schooling at MIT to stand in support of her, was visibly shaken, if not in shock.

I looked at the sad scene and even felt sorry for them. I then turned to my wife and attorney and said surely Wu would not let his wife rot in jail for $80,000. He would have a check ready as soon as the judge restarts the hearing. Two hours later we were in front of the judge again. There was no check and no response from Wu. He claimed he had no funds. Wu was playing an elaborate game of chicken with the judge, but it was his wife's freedom he was playing with, not his. He basically left his wife standing in the courtroom to collect his punishment.

As the hearing went on, two more bailiffs were called in to stand beside Susan Wu in anticipation of a verdict for imprisonment. Again my attorney's and I commented in amazement, this was even too cruel for even our cruelest imagination of Wu. He was surely proving what his former CFO, David Winkler, later confirmed about the perverse views of some wealthy Chinese, particularly the pampered first-born son. "Women mean nothing in China," said Winkler. "They still practice infanticide there in many parts of the country with female babies. Wu cares for nothing, but himself. He would let his wife and daughters rot in prison for 80 cents let alone $80,000." I thought Winkler's claims were a bit overstated then; however, they were later confirmed by a close friend who had even more experience on the subject.

Years ago, I had arranged to assist a Chinese student to gain admission to Stanford who I met while I was on a business trip in Beijing. His fiancée, Shuye, was assigned to me as a "guide" by the Ministry of Electronics to keep an eye on me and keep me out of trouble during my trip. When Shuye learned that I was a graduate of Stanford she later introduced me to her soon to be husband whose dream was to attend my alma mater. Tiemin Zhao impressed me as a very brilliant and dedicated young man. The admission fee for him was the equivalent of a whole year's salary in China back then and a small price for me to pay to invest in fulfilling someone's dream. I remembered how Morty Davis backed my dream years earlier and decided this would be a good time to return the favor. So I paid the admission fee and wrote a letter of recommendation after getting to know Tiemin better during the trip.

Tiemin scored the highest score on the Test of English as a Foreign Language (TOEFL) in China's history. He also graduated at the top of his class in his university. Tiemin Zhao wound up getting a full scholarship to Stanford and graduated with a Ph.D. in Engineering. After completing his studies, Tiemin remained in the U.S. to participate in a number of founding teams of Silicon Valley start up companies. Unlike Mr. Wu who remained in the U.S. only to steal from it, Tiemin worked night and day to develop several of the new technologies that propelled these companies to public offerings and the rapid creation of new jobs. He soon arranged to fly his entire family and fiancée to California. They all moved into a house in Palo Alto, Calif., just outside the gates of Stanford. Tiemin was proud of his purchase. He had achieved the American dream. I still remember the day I visited during their remodeling. Although plastic tarps and sheets of unfinished dry wall lay everywhere, Shuye and Tiemin gave me a grand tour as if I was being guided through the Louvre.

Years later, Shuye and Tiemin would make me Godfather to their first-born son. It was the highest honor a Chinese family could bestow on a friend. I did not see any chauvinism or pampering in the Zhao household. Shuye and Tiemin raised their son to be honest, dedicated, and hard working. I was very proud of my Godson, Michael.

But Tiemin did warn me during my initial phases of my trial that I was dealing with a very different and dangerous mentality commonly found among those in Asia who have made their riches through theft and depravation. These people believed they were a higher form of life than their employees. They would work their employees in prison camp conditions mercilessly like slaves. Living conditions were horrible in these factories. These rich industrialists would also pollute the environment of the surrounding villages, mercilessly pouring raw sewage and other byproducts of their facilities in the local water supply and spewing unfiltered pollutants from their smokestacks.

These people also felt justified in stealing as long as they were smart enough to get away with it. Often they would act with impunity by bribing local officials with their ill-gotten, financial gains.

"They would eat their own children to stay alive," Tiemin said. I thought that too was a bit harsh and overstated, until I later witnessed what Samson Wu was willing to do to his own wife and children.

At the end of the hearing, the judge concluded that although there was a violation in Wu's failure to pay, unless we could provide proof that he was not financially indigent, he could not use his imprisonment as a remedy for his debt. The case law was clearly on the side of the defendant against locking them up for failure to pay. We would have to be able to come back later with "hard evidence" that he had the financial assets to pay the court ordered costs.

As John correctly indicated earlier, this would mean recent copies of bank accounts and other proof. I thought this was next to impossible since Wu had already shredded his old bank statements so we would not have a paper trail. Wu's new bank statements were someplace only God knows overseas. Wu had again won his game of chicken with the court. His wife collapsed in the arms of her daughter after the judge concluded incarceration was not applicable under case law. For now, Wu was able to slither away unscathed by our legal system, but somehow, I don't think he emerged unscathed with his wife, family, and other co defendants.

SEVENTY-SIX

☙

I still remembered that gleam in John's eyes as Judge Spencer had basically invited him to pursue yet another attempt at incarceration. This time for "Fraud on the Court." To me it was just going to be another effort in futility in which I would receive yet another hefty billing statement. The previous attempts at all the "contempt hearings" had failed to generate one day of incarceration and the rules the court required to provide "proof" of ability to pay were akin to me finding life on a distant planet. Again I thought we were off on another trail to nowhere.

But John's idea to follow up on Judge Spencer's lead turned out to be very valuable. First, John explained that "Fraud on the Court" was a criminal charge, not civil. Voila! We had a verifiable ongoing criminal case that we needed to justify our overseas asset seizures in Panama. Another important result of John's pursuit was that it also led to the turning of another valuable witness to support our efforts to pursue the Wus' bank in South Florida.

Up to now, as eloquently stated by John, holding Wu accountable for his numerous injunction and court violations was like "nailing Jell-O to a wall." So were any attempts to go after those who had assisted him. Several months into the litigation and depositions of the patent lawyers, I approached Willie Gary's staff, Madison McClelland and Linda Weiksnar, with the idea of now launching a suit against the Wus' bank, Ocean Bank of South Florida. They both looked at me pretty much the same as John had when I suggested he litigate the Wus' patent lawyers. They were by now, overwhelmed with their tasks of pursuing both patent law firms. The patent firm's partners were as arrogant as the Wus' and they were determined not to settle. The waves of depositions ordered by their attorneys kept their calendars full. They informed us they simply could not devote any more time to additional prosecutions.

They also counseled me as John did, "Brett, hadn't you had enough yet?"

I hadn't. The same drive that brought me through trial and verdict was propelling me now to pursue some sort of result.

I decided to contact a friend of mine, Marc Ossinsky, who was a partner in the small firm of Ossinsky & Cathcart. I thought Marc was adventurous enough to take a risk.

Marc had previously been afflicted with brain cancer. For a while Marc wasn't sure if he would survive. Marc was a restaurant aficionado. One of the things that Marc told me was that he would like to dine at the Disney famous five star restaurant Victoria and Albert's in Orlando before he died. I told Marc, that better yet, "when you survive this operation and announce your full recovery we will go to Victoria and Albert's together with our wives to celebrate and it will be my treat." Marc survived the operation but the chemotherapy treatments left him bald. Later he grew a small beard and mustache as well as a new lease on life. I told Marc he should get an earring to complete the look, but there was only so far this formerly conservative lawyer would go. I still had fond memories of our dinner at Victoria and Albert's. Marc now pursued both his life and profession with a new passion. I did not think it would be beyond the scope of reason that Marc would take a flyer on my case.

Marc reviewed our case with his partner Chris Cathcart and determined that they would invest some time to review the case. They thought the case looked potentially strong against Ocean Bank, however, they would not be able to file suit against the bank until I uncovered more "proof" of the bank's direct involvement. I was told to go after a third party. Paul's affidavits alone would not be enough. We had to have another eyewitness, preferably from inside the Wu organization who could prove the bank, or the accountants, knew that the bankruptcy filings and wire transfers that were engineered to obstruct or violate the courts injunction. Only this would prove that the bank willingly and knowingly assisted the Wus as co-conspirators and hence could find them liable for some or all of the $41.2 million judgment amount.

Getting such a witness would not be easy. In fact, it would be more like impossible. More undertakings similar to voyages to find life on distant planets entered my mind.

Wu was still paying Caruso's, Winkler's, and almost everyone else's legal bills and, doubtless still, had them all on the payroll. In addition to risking their own legal defense by coming forward, these individuals would probably also be incriminating themselves by helping us. I did not know how I could do this. As it turned out, I did not have to. John's "Fraud on the Court" pursuit did it for me.

SEVENTY-SEVEN

৫৯

The court called yet another hearing on the matter of Samson Wu, Thomas Wu, Susan Wu, David Winkler, and Jack Caruso, to stand trial for Fraud on the Court. His latest delay tactic was to claim indigency. Although Wu could be jailed for lying under oath, the burden of proof of his financial condition fell to us. Samson had previously ducked incarceration for failure to pay his court ordered contempt hearing expenses since we had yet to prove where his assets were. Now Wu's repeated indigency claim would serve as a delay tactic because he knew, probably as instructed by his legal team, that he would need a court appointed lawyer to defend him. This tactic worked again to immediately postpone the hearing. Wu knew that the court would now have to provide yet another extended period of time for his new lawyer to acquaint himself with the case. It also would further support his earlier claims to escape incarceration on the previous charges against him. The necessity for a public defender to take over his case would further support his claim that he had no assets to seize.

Here again was another great travesty of Justice. Here was a man who admitted to spending close to two million dollars in legal fees during the past two years. For years, Wu had openly bragged of his tremendous wealth. Just recently he paid $16,500 for the trial transcript that he used in his appeal. Even our company could not afford to pay for that.

Now he was telling the judge that he was broke and could not afford to hire his own lawyer. In order to make his new claim appear viable, Wu informed his other co-defendants that now they too would have to declare indigency and ask the court to provide them with court-ordered attorneys. He could now no longer pay their legal fees as well. This did not sit well with some of the defendants since they were used to relying on Wu to cover all their bills in this litigation.

The whole situation sat very well with Juan Felipe Pitty, who now had the ongoing criminal case he needed. This allowed him to meet the legal standard required for the Panamanian Supreme Court to issue an ex-parte bank seizure order. Juan Felipe Pitty asked John to fax him the copy of the criminal contempt hearing notice "as soon as the ink had dried on the paper." Juan Felipe literally ran to the Supreme Court with this document in hand. He was advised by the Chief Magistrate of the Court on how he should file his request as well as the requirements the court would impose on the plaintiff's if it were to grant the ex-parte seizure request.

Juan Felipe called me as soon as he returned from the Supreme Court chambers. He gave me the "good news" first. He was led to believe that his request would be granted. Then came "the bad news."

We would be required to post a bond of up to 30% of the total value of the bank assets and/or real property we were to seize. When I inquired about the costs of bonding, I found out that to obtain bonds in Panama from a Panamanian bonding company, you basically have to put up 100% of the cash plus pay a fee of 3–5%. I told Juan Felipe this was the equivalent of robbery. I also did not feel comfortable having several hundred thousand dollars of my company's money tied up in Panama given the uncertainties of the government and the legal system down there. Juan Felipe did not take offense. He simply insisted that is how things are done down there and suggested I try bonding agents on my side of the border.

I contacted our banker, Peter Allport from Wachovia Bank. After finding that most bonding agents would not touch bonds in Panama with a hundred foot pole, I learned that Wachovia had a corresponding relationship with a Panamanian Bank, Tower Bank. Tower would agree to bond for less than a 1% fee if I deposit the full cash value of the bond at Wachovia. I felt a lot more comfortable with our money being on deposit in Wachovia in the U.S. than if it was down in Banana Republicland. I was sure my Board of Directors, whose approval I would need, would agree.

I immediately walked into the office of our current Chief Financial Officer, Dan Regalado. I explained what I wanted to review and request from the Board. Dan told me that our next board meeting was scheduled for the end of the week and he would put it on the agenda. Dan did not really comment on my request, he just agreed that it should be reviewed and approved by the Board. Although Dan did not have much to say on the matter, our Board certainly did.

"You want to do what?!" exclaimed one Board Member.

"Bond several hundred thousand dollars of shareholder's funds where?" incredulously asked another.

"Are you nuts?!" stated yet another.

It was early in the discussion but I could see our older and wiser board members were going to now turn my request into a psychiatric evaluation rather than a review of its merits. I began to feel very stupid for even suggesting this to them, however, the board members sensed it was important to me and did agree to discuss this matter among themselves and Dan alone. I was asked to leave the room while they reviewed the issue.

While waiting in the hallway I was wondering what was going on in there. Perhaps they thought I had totally lost my mind. Perhaps they thought I have become so engrossed in my manic pursuit of the Wus that I have now become blinded to reason, something akin to Captain Ahab who went into the deep in a death grip with Moby Dick, his arch nemesis. It was not more than a half hour later when they called me back. The board explained its position. They have granted me a great deal of latitude in this case and respected my sense of justice, but they felt that this request fell way outside the scope of prudent management of share-holder's funds in a public company. I started to imagine my board members having images of me plunging my harpoon into the belly of Wu the whale as he pulled me into the depths of the dark sea.

Rather than being relieved that the board did not chop my head off at that very moment, I brazenly asked "Well then, how the hell are we going to collect any of the money we have been awarded if we are not willing to post bond for the seizures?"

To that one board member responded "Well Brett, you're an entrepreneur, if you want to be a risk taker, why don't you put up the money and we will allow you to take a percentage of the receipts."

I was dumbstruck at first, but then I understood the bril-liance of the offer, which was also a challenge in disguise. The board did not want to take the risk, but if I was so damn sure this was the right thing, then I should take the risk in exchange for a significant return. They recommended a return of 25% of what was seized, after costs and expenses were deducted, if myself or fellow investors put up 100% of the bond money. If I was not willing to take the challenge myself, then the board had proved its point. They should not even consider engaging in any risk of shareholder's funds that I would otherwise not engage my own. Pretty smart, although I did not think so at that given moment that I found myself in the hot seat. The board was wondering now if my testos-terone level would shut down all neurological activity in my brain. They deliberately remained silent, bating me for a response.

"OK I'll do it then!" I said after a long pause to clear the lump in my throat.

"So moved" said another board member, the rest of the board approved it unanimously, without a beat I was dismissed and they were on to other business.

Oh Shit, I said to myself, *what have I gotten myself into.*

I called Juan Felipe and notified him that I would put up the money. I asked him how much he needed. Juan Felipe said he wanted bonding capacity for at least $3 million. Based on the 30% bonding requirement, this would require at least $1 million in cash. I knew right then I would need partners. The next day I put up $350,000 of my personal savings on deposit with Wachovia Bank. I signed all the necessary bonding documents and the assignment of the bond to Super Vision.

I then had to look for the rest of the money. But after hearing all the bonding agencies and bankers tell me how most banks and bonding agencies in their right minds would not engage in bonding in Panama, I thought it would take a miracle to find someone who would risk their money along mine to collateralize the bond. There was, however, one person who immediately came to mind. A close friend who was a very successful time share entrepreneur. He was one of a handful of billionaires in the state of Florida. His name was David Siegel.

SEVENTY-EIGHT

❦

David Siegel arrived in Orlando 35 years ago after losing his job as a Deputy Sheriff in Dade County for falling asleep on the job. David was holding down several jobs to make ends meet and the lack of sleep just caught up with him. David lived out of his car for the first few months after his arrival. Any money he scraped together he used to buy raw land and old houses that he would develop or rebuild and sell. Soon he started developing condominiums for tourists and then came up with the idea of selling weekly shares of condos to tourists. This way he could effectively sell the same condo 52 times at a reduced rate to the tourists. Many more tourists would also be able to buy these "time shares" than would be able to purchase a second vacation home. David could also make much more money selling it to them this way. His concept resulted in explosive growth for the vacation home business, tapping a huge market that was previously untouched. David literally created the timeshare industry and built Central Florida Investments and Westgate Corporation into timeshare powerhouses. His companies sell hundreds of millions of dollars worth of time share units on an annual basis. David had in the past few years expanded his empire from Orlando, Florida to River Ranch, Florida, Park City, Utah, Gatlinburg, Virginia and Las Vegas, Nevada.

David had always been a personal friend. I met him at a few real estate auctions and liquidation sales. David had a penchant for picking up real estate all over Florida at auctions for cash. Although he was one of the few people who did not need a bank to finance his acquisitions, he was always nondescript in his jogging outfit or blue jeans. People only began to recognize him when his bidder's card was raised and remain raised on almost every item on the auction block.

David was also the kind of person who would never forget a friend. At one recent Thanksgiving dinner, my family joined David's family at his home. David stood up at the spectacular twenty five foot long dining table, filled with family and friends under a large crystal chandelier, to make a toast to one of his old friends that I had never met before. He mentioned that 42 years ago when he was destitute, did not have food in the refrigerator and his wife had to heat his infant's formula bottle with Sterno because the electricity had been shut off; his old friend invited him to his home for a Thanksgiving dinner. David described how it was the "best meal he had in months" and that he made a promise to himself to "someday return the favor." David was now standing before a spectacular meal, catered by his private chef, in his 20,000 square foot mansion on his private island in the most exclusive neighborhood in Orlando, Isleworth. But all David could think of was how happy he was that he could share this dinner with his friend.

David was also involved in several charities that I supported. I respected the fact that he was a self-made man who, despite his great wealth, kept his humility and spent a great deal of his time helping charitable causes. I also appreciated the fact that David and my relationship was based only on our friendship. We did not actively court Westgate as a client; we might have made only one sale to them in the past ten years. For the first five years after our public offering David did not participate in our stock. Although half of Central Florida seemed to work for David, none of my family members relied on him for a job. I never asked him for money and I did not want to. Although I could offer him a respectable return on his investment with the board's approval, I still felt uncomfortable asking my friend for assistance. I discussed this with Maisa, who was a very close friend with David's wife Jacqueline, a striking and statuesque blonde who was a former Ms. Florida. Maisa shared my concern; she also valued her friendship with Jacqueline.

I guess my anger at the Wu Family escaping justice eventually won out over my concerns to mix business with my friendship. I called David's secretary and asked for an appointment. This was something I did not want to ask for over the phone. I met David in his offices in Southwest Orlando, just across the road from Universal Studios. As I entered his office it reminded my of a tropical version of Morty Davis's palatial wood paneled offices in Wall Street. Instead of dark Mahogany on the walls, David had bright pastel paint. The view from the windows was of ponds and palm trees instead of taxis and office towers. Other than that, everything looked almost the same. There was row after row of awards on David's desk and credenza's. The hallways, offices, and conference rooms were covered with photos of David and Jacqueline with current and former presidents, politician's, movie stars, sports legends, and other notables. As I walked into David's office he immediately moved out of his chair behind his desk and sat by my side in the other guest chair opposite his desk.

"So what can I do for you buddy?" David said with a slap on my back and a smile.

"David I am going to ask you for money to bond a seizure of our opponent's assets." I did not want to beat around the bush with David on this subject, I felt uncomfortable asking him in the first place so I decided to get right to the point.

"How much?" David said getting right to the point.

"I think I will need $650,000, I am putting up $350,000 myself." I then explained the whole process in Panama to him, and the results of the meeting of our Board of Directors and the arrangements I have made with Wachovia Bank to wire the money.

"Well how much do you think they got down there?" David asked me.

"I don't know David, our forensic accountant testified that they wired more than $28.5 million out of the country but who the hell knows where it is? It could be in Panama, it could be somewhere else."

"Well tell you what, I won't give you $650, 000," my heart sank for a moment but David continued "but I will give you up to an additional $3 million dollars of bonding capacity which I will arrange through my bank when you need it. If these Wus have socked away that much loot your gonna need a lot more than $650,000 if you find any of it. At least my extra bonding commitment along with your cash will get you to seize up to ten million if you find anything."

I was more dumbstruck then as I was at the board meeting the day before. I did not know what to say to my friend, thank you just did not seem appropriate enough. David saw that I was struggling and stepped in to spare me.

"Brett don't worry about thanks, and I really don't care if I ever see a dime of profit from this, I just want to see these bastards pay for what they did. I am happy to help you as much as I am happy to see these guys burn in hell." With that, David gave me another slap on the back and walked around his desk to get back to business. It was my signal to leave.

As I walked out of the room I said "Thanks David." He just turned to me and winked and then picked up one of the several lines that had been blinking and waiting on hold.

His secretary Jeanie McNeal was kind enough to guide me down the hall. Miracle number one accomplished, I thought; now we need a few more miracles before we are able get approvals and seizure of funds.

But I found that miracles were much harder to come by in Panama. In fact, almost anything is much harder to come by in Panama. If in Mexico most things get put off until "manana" (tomorrow), I learned that further south things get put off until next year.

I notified Juan Felipe of the arrangements and waited for his return call, and waited, then waited some more. After several weeks, David started prodding me for an update and results. I called Juan Felipe who sheepishly told me that all our best laid plans had not gone so well. Juan Felipe explained our misfortune in getting Magistrate Troyano as the judge assigned to our case. According to Juan Felipe Magistrate Troyano was not fond of granting requests to Norte Americanos nor was he fond of piercing the veil of secrecy of Panamanian banks. He wanted to hold an open hearing on the matter with the defendants present; this would guarantee the flight of all funds before you could say even "Hola" at the hearing. Juan Felipe described to me that he was so mad that he "turned red" in Magistrate Troyano's chambers.

Just my luck, I thought, I have found Judge Baker's long lost Latin American twin.

Juan Felipe told me that he had been spending the last few weeks redrafting his appeal to the two other Supreme Court Magistrates and the Chief Magistrate. He was confident the other Magistrates would overturn Troyano's decision due to its violation of the U.S. Panama treaty and Panamanian law. Juan Felipe explained that the law should take precedent over Troyano's personal concerns; however, nothing is ever certain in the Panamanian judicial system.

"How long will this take Juan Felipe?" I asked.

"It's hard to say, these matters tend to take time down here," replied Juan Felipe.

"Take time" was right. After three months since the filing with the Panamanian Supreme Court, and posting all
the bond money required for seizure orders, we had
received only two out of the three necessary Panamanian
Magistrates' approvals necessary to win criminal bank
seizure orders. Our Panamanian attorney had turned red
faced so many times that we started calling him "Panama
Red." Juan Felipe was completely incredulous that the one
remaining Judge refused to sign the orders. At a loss for any
further action he could take, he had threatened to bring
suit against the Panamanian Supreme Court for violating
the U.S./Panamanian treaty and even suggested with me
further actions against Magistrate Troyano for obstruction
of justice. In any case, our efforts to achieve justice in
Panama were to no avail.

At that point I felt we were no closer to Wu's money than
we were to the moon.

SEVENTY-NINE

ᘓᗡ

The first formal court hearing on fraud on the court took place on April 14, 2003. As part of the process to determine if free counsel should be provided to the defendants at taxpayer expense, Judge Spencer required all defendants to fill out a sworn statement listing all their assets. Samson Wu, Susan Wu, Jack Caruso, and David Winkler all filled out the forms, signed the affidavit of indigency and handed them back to the judge. The only person not present at the hearing from the original group of defendants was Thomas Wu. Thomas had to remain in China for "medical reasons." Judge Spencer promptly issued a bench warrant for his arrest for failure to appear in court. John smirked after the warrant was issued and told the bailiff he might as well "file it, because this guy is never coming back to the United States."

The judge accepted all the asset forms and affidavits and took a brief recess while he reviewed the information with the public defender. When he returned, it was announced that Samson Wu, Susan Wu, and Jack Caruso qualified for a public defender, but Winkler did not. He would still have to pay for his own counsel.

Winkler exploded in the courtroom and screamed "what kind of bullshit is this?" He then pointed to Wu and said, "That man is a multi-millionaire, I know, I was his chief operating officer, and he is getting free counsel and I am not!" Winkler's rage was beyond control. Judge Spencer, quite shocked at Winkler's behavior, didn't even bother to stop him. The judge probably sensed that in his rage Winkler might say something of value; anything at this point would be a welcome break in the case.

He went on with his tirade for another few minutes and then declared that he wanted, for the moment, to be his own lawyer and represent himself in court "right here, right now." In order to follow the law, Judge Spencer immediately had to call a hearing to determine if Winkler was competent enough to represent himself. He swore him in and put him on the stand. The judge asked Winkler about his educational background and experience. Winkler, a college graduate and an accountant with 20 years of experience, clearly qualified as a competent professional. Next the judge had to confirm that Winkler was mentally competent. He inquired if he was now under the care of a doctor or was on any medication that might impair his ability or faculties. The judge also inquired into Winkler's past and determined that he had no cause for determining that Winkler was now mentally incompetent or had a history of mental illness. Winkler's only humorous response to the judge's inquiry about his present outbursts was that "he was just plain darn mad." He then turned to John and said "and by the way it was Boston".

"What do you mean Boston?" a very surprised John replied.

"Boston was the answer to your question at my deposition. I knew who was going to win the American League pennant and I was right." said a still angry but very self-confident Winkler.

John now remembering the unanswered question from the deposition three years ago that later caused the jury to roar with laughter. John now turned to the judge with a look of great sincerity and said "He seems quite competent to me Your Honor."

EIGHTY

❧

The judge ruled that David Winkler could represent himself as counsel.

The first act Winkler took on his own behalf as counsel was to immediately call a recess. He pointed at John and Joe and asked for a 10 minute recess so he could now talk to "these guys directly." A visibly surprised Judge Spencer now shrugged his shoulders and looked around the courtroom to see if there was any opposition to Winkler's request. Seeing none, he complied and declared another brief recess. Winkler, John, and Joe walked out into the hallway outside the courtroom. Wu was visibly nervous as they left the room. Winkler then told them that he has completely had it with Wu and was tired of his lies and deceit. He played along up until now and kept his mouth shut, but now Wu had gone too far and he wanted to see this guy "have his balls ripped off and burn in hell." He also told John that he in no way played any part in the numerous contempt of court violations that Wu masterminded. In fact, Winkler was able to provide proof that during the one contempt violation for failure to return the optical bench, he was no longer employed by Wu at the time. Winkler left Wu's employ in 2000; the optical bench was put on a "slow boat from China" in 2002.

John squinted during Winkler's tirade and removed his cigar and pressed his lips hard together. As Winkler continued to spill his bile all over the floor of that courthouse hallway, John would continue to flash sly winks and raised eyebrows at Joe who was by now caught between a state of shock and utter disbelief. Up till now, the young attorney had thought he'd saw it all.

When the tirade finished, John somberly told Winkler that although he welcomed his cooperation he must inform him that they had several conflicts of interest that had to be resolved. One was that even though he has now been declared as his own counsel, he needed to get a formal letter from his previous attorney, Snyderburn, confirming he no longer represented him. This would allow them to continue to talk directly. John also said that although he now believed that Winkler should not be prosecuted for the contempt matter now under review, he had an ethical obligation as the court-appointed special prosecutor to make sure that he dropped this case based on the merits alone. He would not engage in any unethical behavior that might cause anyone to think that he dropped the current contempt case against Winkler as barter for later cooperation. He also wanted Winkler to know that he welcomed his cooperation, but that he had to remind him that at present he represents a client that has a multimillion-dollar judgment against him. John further informed Winkler that he had to proceed with the knowledge that at this point they were still adversaries in the civil case and he would continue to act on his client's behalf to try to collect the judgment.

"Bottom line, David," John said, "if you decide to cooperate with us or not, I now have an ethical responsibility to drop this criminal contempt case against you because I now believe you were not involved. I could not have possibly known about your involvement earlier because you and all your co-defendants were taking the Fifth Amendment. Had I spoken to you earlier about this, I would not have added your name to the list of defendants in the criminal contempt action."

Winkler greatly respected John for his honesty and ethics. After having his belly full of lies and deceitful tactics from Wu and his associates, he appreciated seeing someone in the legal profession who was true to his word and acted on principle. The respect built by the two men during their 15-minute discussion in the hallway would blossom into a trust. This relationship later led Winkler to provide us with information we could not possibly have otherwise obtained. John asked Winkler not to disclose any information to him or speak to him further until he would receive a letter of withdrawal from his past counsel. He further urged Winkler to hire a new counsel to make sure that he would be properly represented in future discussions with him. The three men went into the courtroom and informed the judge that they would continue the criminal contempt prosecution against Samson and Susan Wu and Caruso, but based on evidence provided by Winkler they would most likely sever him from that part of the case. That said, Judge Spencer promptly rescheduled the hearing. Given the turn of events, counsel from both sides were informed that they need to revisit their game plans.

EIGHTY-ONE

Less than a week later, John received the letter of withdrawal from Phil Snyderburn. David Winkler retained Chan Muller to represent him. Chan was a well-known friend of John. John had previously supported Chan in his race to become Orange County Bar Association president. When Chan's son had an untimely death, it was John who stood by his side at the funeral and thereafter until his friend was able to heal from the tragic loss. Chan suggested that we all meet at John's office to hash out the final details in dropping the contempt charges and talk further about how Winkler might be able to assist us in bringing Samson Wu to justice.

We all met in John's conference room on the 15th floor—Chan, Winkler, John, Joe, and I. John first cautioned everyone in the room that he did not want to talk about anything else, but the resolution of the contempt violation. He did not want it called into question later that the contempt charges were dropped as a bargaining chip to gain Winkler's cooperation or future testimony against Wu. After another review of the facts, both John and Chan were confident that the facts alone dictated that there was no reason to have Winkler listed as a defendant in the criminal contempt charge. John then turned to Winkler and said, "David, you can now feel free to walk out of this room and give us nothing in return. I am under an ethical responsibility to drop you from this part of the case."

Winkler did not want to leave. The conversation quickly turned to the $5.4 million judgment against him. Winkler blew up at me telling me that he would sooner die and/or watch hell freeze over before he would pay me a penny. I took great offense at this. Here is a guy who was still arrogant and defiant even after the verdict. I did not need to hear this from Winkler at this time. I basically told him to go screw himself and that I would pursue both him and Wu for collection "till hell freezes over and beyond." The lawyers for both sides were now clearly uncomfortable, this was not the direction they hoped things would be heading and not the reason why they agreed to bring us both together. But Winkler's "fuck you" outbursts were now coming rapid fire and my disgust grew to the point that I just did not want to sit in the same room with him. I really wanted to reach across the table and rip out his throat, but instead, I thought it was better to leave. "Too many witnesses," I thought.

John jogged outside the conference room in his effort to catch up with me before I reached the elevator. I couldn't tell if he was laughing at me or the unbelievable situation he just witnessed. John chuckled a few moments more while he held my arm and said to me that if I would just behave myself and wait in the lobby for awhile he "would try to smooth things over." I told John the only thing I wanted to smooth over was "David's brains spread all over the conference room table." John chuckled again and told me as if he were telling his 9-year-old son, "sit down, shut up, behave yourself," and "I'll be back in a few minutes." I could still hear John chuckling at me as he headed back towards the conference room. I took a seat on the couch in the lobby with my arms folded across my chest and a visible pout on my face like my 4-year-old son would often have when I took a toy away as punishment.

A few minutes became close to an hour. While I was

waiting, I called Chris Cathcart from Ossinsky and Cathcart to tell him not to bother coming to the meeting with Winkler. We had hoped that in addition to his testimony against Wu, Winkler would also be able to incriminate Ocean Bank in assisting Wu. Apparently, I called too late. Just as I hung up with Cathcart's secretary, Chris Cathcart entered the lobby. I explained to Chris that our star witness was now acting more like our star enemy and that I didn't think we would get anything from him. Chris knew that John was trying to turn things around but my description of the situation seemed pretty dire. Chris reluctantly left telling me that he was really hoping for some additional hard independent evidence against the bank.

When John returned to the lobby to retrieve me, I was again scolded on my behavior and warned to "behave." Winkler had a completely different demeanor. He launched into a detailed description of how Wu moved money around the world and where he felt his assets were. Then Winkler jumped to another subject. He became furious again, but this time it was not at me. Apparently, in the half hour or so that I had been absent, Winkler learned from our counsel that we had made several settlement offers to him through his attorney on this case. Winkler was livid and went into a tirade that he never heard that we had made several settlement offers to his prior lawyer, Phil Snyderburn. If accepted, Winkler would have settled out of the case with nothing more than a $75,000 payment. His lawyer had never informed him of these offers.

Winkler was furious at having learned that those two years of misery of being dragged through the courts could have been all avoided. The stress it placed on Winkler's family could have been averted if Snyderburn had simply fulfilled his obligation as counsel to inform him of the settlement offers. It was clear to Winkler that all along Snyderburn was protecting only Wu and not him. Winkler believed he would not have even gone to trial, let alone have a $5 million judgment against him, had Snyderburn informed him of his opportunity to settle. At the time, we thought Winkler was just being stubborn by not settling or that he was still being paid off by Wu not to settle with us or testify against him.

We understood why Wu would never agree to settle, but it did not make sense to us that for as little as $75,000 and some cooperation against Wu, that Winkler would have not jumped at the chance. We now knew the reason was simply that he had never been told by counsel. Snyderburn and his main client knew that if Winkler ever turned testimony against Wu it would be a final nail in his coffin at trial. According to Winkler's description of events, Snyderburn willingly violated the most basic function that is required of a counsel, to inform a client of all settlement offers. If this was correct, Snyderburn would have completely violated his representation and opened himself up to a huge malpractice liability.

This was the first time I didn't see John engage in his usual refusal to consider any action against a fellow member of the bar. John was genuinely shocked at Winkler's accusations. After all the transgressions we witnessed by Snyderburn in the courtroom, here was one thing that John was not willing to forgive or explain. John was clearly moved by Winkler's recounting of the past events and Snyderburn's failure to inform him about any of our settlement offers. He was noticeably silent during the initial talk of malpractice suits, but later concurred that under such extenuating conditions, such action would be appropriate. Joe just rolled his eyes at me through the entire discussion, exhibiting his surprise that his esteemed senior partner was now willing to consider actions that he previously would not consider against a fellow attorney.

Joe finally could not resist temptation; he broke his

silence by leaning over the conference table and whispered in my ear "Dorothy, I think we're not in Kansas anymore…" For Joe , both as a lawyer and as a thespian, this quote from *The Wizard of Oz* would soon take on an even greater meaning. The surreal events taking place before us would later pale in comparison to the even more amazing revelations from Winkler to follow.

EIGHTY-TWO

෯

The malpractice suit was also something
that all parties in the room seized upon to solve Winkler's
current financial problems since he had run into debt with
us and others after he lost his job with Wu. It was made clear
that Winkler could not legally barter or assign any rights or
judgments he would have in any malpractice case against his
former lawyers, but we could agree to hold off on any collection actions against him personally until we saw what
would become of his malpractice suit and recovery. In the
meantime, Winkler would cooperate with us as a goodwill
gesture for our agreement to delay collection actions against
him. It became clear, as discussions progressed, that this
case was yet again taking another turn into the territory of
the absurd. I would now eventually wind up being a witness
testifying on behalf of my former enemy. Snyderburn himself may eventually pay part of the final judgment indirectly
to Super Vision through Winkler.

Winkler's most valuable cooperation was his knowledge
of what countries that Wu hid his funds in and also what
some bankers were willing to do for a fee. Winkler returned
to his outline of Wu's finances and the clandestine methods
by which the Wu family would move money between affili-
ated companies around the world. Much of this was not new
to us because we already had copies from Paul Koren of the
many bank wire transfer letters and internal memos describing these procedures. We also were already undertaking

seizure actions against Wu and his related companies' bank accounts in Panama. We feigned great interest when Winkler touched on this subject, but we did not let on to our prior knowledge or our current actions. We did not want to risk Winkler having another fit, which might lead him back to Wu again, and this time he would have information on our game plan. What I wanted most in that meeting was information to incriminate those I already did not have additional third party evidence against. Number one on my list was Ocean Bank.

My instinct told me that Ocean Bank was neck deep in Wu's plans for the phony bankruptcy, but I had no proof. I saw the Ocean Bank officers hang their arms around Wu's shoulders like in a scene in from a Mafia movie. I still remember vividly their taunting us at the bankruptcy hearing that we, "Wouldn't collect one dime." This was a bit too much familiarity and bravado coming from a banker who was just providing a service. This I figured was also a bit too much cooperation and support from a creditor who was potentially losing several million dollars of its depositors' money on his account.

Winkler said he knew Ocean Bank was guilty in this process, but could not offer any specifics at the time. Winkler was still focused on his obsession to barbecue his former counsel. I kept trying to drag more information on the bank from Winkler. Each time the response was weak and lacked anything I thought would be material or helpful. I left the meeting shaking my head that this whole meeting had been a colossal waste of time.

Winkler followed me into the elevator. Still burning with the excitement of the moment, Winkler still wanted to talk. However, he wanted to talk about something other than what I did. Winkler wanted to talk about his new mission to skewer Snyderburn, and I wanted him to point his sword in another direction at the bank. We walked each other to the parking lot across the street from John's offices. There was a covered pedestrian bridge on the second floor that allowed us to walk across the street to the parking garage. As we left the bridge, Winkler and I turned to each other and shook hands. We did not have much more to say to each other at that point, so we parted and headed to our cars.

It was about 6 p.m. by the time I returned back to my office. Feeling as if I had a completely unproductive afternoon, I wanted to put in a few hours in the evening to play catch up on revenue generating activities. About 6:30 p.m. my cell phone rang and it was Winkler.

Winkler said, "I have the bank; I just realized it; I just made a U-turn off I-4 and I am heading back towards Orlando. Do you want to meet?"

By now any meeting would mean dinner. I told Winkler to meet me at my office and we would go to a restaurant nearby. I immediately called my wife to tell her the news: "You will never believe who I am going to have dinner with tonight."

Maisa by now was not surprised with any of the crazy events from the case; however, she did question my sanity to be even spending another moment with someone who previously had been such a bitter enemy. My instincts told me that Winkler would not have pulled off the road unless he had something important to tell me. Maisa knew not to set a plate for me.

Winkler had never been to our new facility before. The last time he visited was two moves ago. To break the ice, I decided to give Winkler a little tour. Halfway through I could not believe I was now giving a tour to someone who I had spent two years litigating. After the tour, we hopped in my car and drove to my favorite local Italian restaurant, Buca de Beppo, at the Florida Mall. It was a family restaurant with family-sized servings, which people would share.

Perhaps the atmosphere would be more conducive to making Winkler and I feel comfortable together.

As soon as we sat down, Winkler passionately launched into a detailed dissertation of why he "had the bank" by every appendage imaginable. In between the impatient waitress's numerous attempts to extract an order from us, he outlined all the bank covenants that the bank had Wu sign to obtain his loans and how the bank repeatedly allowed Wu to violate every one of them. According to Winkler, this was not only a violation of the bank's own loan covenants, but also a violation of the court injunction order and the rights of all other creditors in the bankruptcy filing.

What was even more shocking was Winkler's recollection of numerous solid gold watches that he witnessed Wu provide to an Ocean Bank executive at no charge and his recollection of a meeting he attended with Wu and several bank officers. At that meeting, Winkler explained how Wu told the bank officers that he wanted to file for bankruptcy; however, there was absolutely no financial reason whatsoever for the bankruptcy filing. Wu did not want the bank to exercise its right to call his loans. He made it clear that the only reason for the bankruptcy filing was to create a diversion to stay Super Vision's impending replevin searches at his facility.

Winkler then recounted that he returned to the office one morning and smelled smoke in the office. He followed the smoke trail with his nose. As the burning smell intensified it led him to the large vault where Marsam Trading housed its gold watches. Winkler entered the vault only to see Caruso and Thomas Wu burning a set of documents. He was later asked by Wu to help him carry other shredded documents to the dumpster the day of my second replevin raid, which I caught on tape.

"Will you put that in writing in a sworn affidavit, David?" I asked eagerly, "Absolutely," was his response. Less than a week later, Winkler kept his word and delivered a detailed multi-page affidavit laying out the bank's willing assistance to Wu. Chris Cathcart now had his important third-party affidavit. I did not delude myself that this effort was going to generate results overnight, but I knew we had a case that would stick, and ultimately, perhaps the bank would cover part of the outstanding judgment.

EIGHTY-THREE

❧

Ever since childhood I was told over and over again by my grandfather, and later my father, about the three biggest lies in America: The first was "of course darling I love you!" The second was "the check is in the mail." And the third was "I am from the government I am here to help you." At first, as a five and six-year-old, I did not understand the meaning of any of the three, although I would laugh along with my grandfather who took great joy in telling this to me. As I grew up and began to take an interest in girls, the first lie started taking on more graphic descriptions. At that point I would chuckle with my father because at least I had a remote idea of the meaning. When I started my first company, the true meaning and importance of the second lie kicked in as I had to constantly hound certain customers for long overdue accounts receivable. This was an education in itself to a naïve young man who up to that time took everyone at their word.

However, it was not until my first experience with the "American justice" system that the third lie came into focus. In my first experience with the justice system I witnessed how the system itself, rather than being used as a method to defend and protect American businesses, was used as a method to destroy them by foreign predators and corrupt lawyers, and corporate executives. My initial contact with the Sheriff's office came at a much lower and more effective level when I turned in the two thugs to Detectives Kelly Boaz and Dave Bareno. Both were street cops who knew how to handle criminals. They were not bureaucrats. Their only concern was to protect the lives of the innocent. They scared the hell out of Simon and Cruz and made it clear what would happen to them if "so much as a single hair on the head of Mike Jacobs or his girlfriend was ever harmed in the future."

But I was not satisfied that just the lower-level pawns were sent to justice, I wanted the higher ups who funded them and benefited from their thefts to be brought to justice. This request, I was told, had to go to the higher ups in the sheriff's department. Days after my meeting with a sheriff's deputy at the county commissioner's office, I had several meetings with rather dour bureaucrats from the sheriff's office. I was told that "we can not prosecute this case due to our concern that the sheriff may get sued for wrongful arrest, we have to protect the sheriff of course." Although my blood was boiling at the repeated concerns for offending the "rights" of these criminals I maintained my composure to try to reason with someone who actually believed in this line of thinking.

"Alright," I said "if you are so concerned with the sheriff's exposure to lawsuits from these criminals, get me in front of the county attorney right now and I will assign $10 million of our $41.2 million judgment to indemnify the sheriff from all claims." I reminded them that years ago, during the infamous shoot out at the Bank of America branch in Los Angeles, a wounded police officer offered to indemnify several other of his fellow police officers by assigning part of his claim to shield his comrades. In an even further insult to justice, the family of the murderous machine gun-toting robbers brought a personal injury suit against the sheriff's office and several officers for allowing one of the two robbers to die after he had just shot more than a dozen people. As I leaned back in my chair and waited for a response I was hopeful that I found a method to insure even the most outrageous of end results. Despite my pleas, I was soon disappointed. "We will take that under advisement and get back to you," said the sheriff's deputy. I have heard this one before; it is bureaucratese for "we'll call to you in the next lifetime." The third lie was becoming all too true.

In subsequent meetings that were arranged due to the constant badgering of fellow prominent friends in the business community, including David Siegel, I was told then by a now even larger group of dour bureaucrats that if I insisted on pressing on with my case I most likely would have to be arrested for violating the rights of the criminal I apprehended earlier and delivered to the jail. Apparently the few hours of questioning Mike Jacob's assailant in my office amounted to "unlawful imprisonment" and the efforts by which I prevented him from immediately leaving our meeting and taking revenge on our staff member and his fiancée was another charge; "assault and battery."

As for the valuable staff member, Paul Koren, who initially informed us about the Wus and was by now making great contributions to our return to growth and profitability, he too "would have to be arrested and imprisoned even if he cooperated with the investigation." When I inquired about all the far more heinous offenders that the newspapers and television have reported receiving immunity deals for much greater crimes and even lesser cooperation then I received from Paul, the response was negligible. Basically, if I was to pursue justice with the sheriff's office it was going to be at the expense of Paul and his family. It was a price too high to pay.

I actually ended the meeting by shaking the hands of all the chiefs, corporals, and deputies and thanked them for not pursuing the investigation. At that point I began to realize how serious they were about locking both Paul and

I up. I did not think I would be able to grow our business from prison and I did not want Paul's incarceration on my conscience. As I walked out of the offices I recall my last thought was "Thanks again for nothing."

As I left the building, I realized that common sense left long before my departure. Criminal's rights to ply their trade are better protected than the victim's rights to defend themselves. There was only one saving grace, a later meeting that was finally arranged by my friend Johnny Jallad. Johnny was a successful entrepreneur and owner of Accredited Insurance. Johnny and I met at one of the many fundraisers for charitable causes that he and his wife, Debbie, would host at their elegant Winter Park home. Johnny was an American of Lebanese descent. He also was a prominent member of the Republican Party and a true patriot. Just after September 11, Johnny volunteered his services to the FBI and the local sheriff's office as an Arabic translator. His work earned him endless commendations from the law-enforcement authorities as well as a special bond of friendship and respect with the Orange County sheriff. During our meeting arranged by Johnny, it was obvious that the sheriff himself, Kevin Beary, was equally frustrated and concerned that the law and sentencing guidelines allowed him few options to pursue. It was clear that the sheriff cared, but it was also clear that, for now, the concerns of the bureaucrats would win out over the passions of the real "lawmen" who yearned for old fashioned justice.

EIGHTY-FOUR

We turned our hopes to the U.S. Attorney's office. After the FBI had started their investigation, I had been informed that Cynthia Hawkins, a well-respected and experienced attorney at the U.S. attorney's office, would preside over the prosecution of my case. After Sept.11, 2001 Hawkin's case load required that my case be passed over to the U.S. attorney in the Tampa office, Donald Hanson, whose case load was lower than the U.S. attorney's in the Orlando Office. I never met Donald Hansen, all my conversations with him were over the phone and limited with the instructions that there was only so much he could tell me related to the criminal investigation. This was the "government's case" not mine. Essentially, I would be granted interviews when appropriate and be questioned when necessary. Donald Hansen was friendly, yet he kept his distance from answering direct questions about the progress of the case and informed me that I would be "notified only afterwards, if and when indictments were to be made."

Later the case was passed back to Roger Handberg at the U.S. Attorney's Office in Orlando. I was finally able to meet Mr. Handberg with our lawyers at Fisher Rushmer's office. He was a young, tall, clean cut, and a well-dressed attorney who looked like he could have been a young congressman or business executive. His youth alone gave me hope. I thought someone who has yet to be jaded by the system would still be idealistic enough to want to provide justice for our cause.

U.S. Attorney Handberg had another FBI Agent, Maureen Perez, in tow who was handling the case after Bill Hajeski retired and Kevin Hogan was transferred to another FBI office to head up the agency's fight against terrorism in Florida. Linda Candler was on the speakerphone listening in at that meeting in Fisher Rushmer's conference room. Agent Perez reminded me of Linda Candler, attractive, intelligent, and driven. She had a reassuring handshake that made me feel like she would follow up the case to some form of resolution. Agent Perez was basically a brunette version of Attorney Candler. I thought the two women would like and respect each other if they ever got an opportunity to meet face-to-face.

Agent Perez engaged in significant follow up later in the case. She initiated the interview between herself, U.S. Attorney Handberg, and David Winkler after Winkler first agreed to provide evidence against Wu. She also sat in on several of the hearings and even during a few days of trial. Her presence alone in the courtroom made the defense uneasy. Although there had yet to be one single indictment or arrest, the fact that the FBI was still showing a visible interest in the case kept the defendants off guard in many aspects of the civil case. Clearly they were more concerned with criminal incarceration than any judgment that would be rendered in a civil proceeding. It was clear to me that the only way we can achieve justice against such lawless adversaries was to jail them. It was the only thing they seemed to fear.

From time to time I would check in on Agent Hogan at his new office and ask for advice. Agent Hogan would answer whenever he was not in the field-planning operations against "the bad guys." Although Agent Hogan was clearly busy, he had not forgot or lost interest in the case. Although the rules of procedure required him not to talk about any specific activity on the case, he counseled me not to get overly optimistic about any action on the part of the

U.S. Attorney. Civil or intellectual property theft, no matter how serious, was just not high up on their list. He has seen many other good cases with just as much merit as mine not prosecuted due to either lack of time, resources, or just lack of interest.

Although he wouldn't say it directly, somehow I had the impression that Agent Hogan was as anxious as me to see that justice would be done in this case. I believed that he wanted to see a criminal conviction of the Wu clan and see that they were made examples of in order to deter future crimes of this nature. But Agent Hogan's constant warnings and cautions not to be too hopeful began to haunt me as time continued to pass. At previous meetings with U.S. Attorney Handberg, both Handberg and my counsel expressed their concern that the statute of limitations on some of the crimes would expire within a few months. January and March 2003 were some of the dates I remembered him pondering aloud in one of the meetings. January and March came and went and still there were no indictments. My heart began to sink as I believed that we would never see any indictments much less prosecutions and sentencing of the Wus for their crimes. After their repeated and blatant failure to comply with all the civil penalties leveled against them, criminal prosecution remained the only hope for any meaningful justice.

After years of frustration with the lack of progress at the U.S. Attorney's office, on the advice of a few friends, I had called the Florida State Attorney's office and spoke with a man named Bill Vose. Several lawyers and people in the business community had told me if there was a way to help, Bill Vose would find it. Bill was a tough prosecutor and former Vietnam veteran who had lost an eye and was severely wounded in the leg during battle. Bill Vose, I was told, had "been around the block a few times," he knew the law and he cared about the results.

Although my phone call came unannounced and I was a

total stranger to Bill, he devoted more than an hour in our initial conversation listening to my plight. "Looks like the shit wagon just overturned on you kid," Bill responded with a loud laugh after I finished my story. I laughed as well thinking that this was the most accurate description that I have heard to date relating to my case. Bill seemed to share my frustration that justice and common sense have long left our "justice system." However, I later learned that he too would be hamstrung by that very same system and would be powerless to help me.

I expressed to Bill that the FBI investigation had been ongoing for more than two years and I was concerned that the U.S. Attorney would not do anything in way of follow up or indictments. Bill told me that the U.S. Attorney rightfully had their hands full with the war on terrorism and terrorism related investigations and prosecutions. He said that although his department does not handle such investigations, he would be happy to refer me to the local statewide prosecutor from the Florida Attorney General's Office who does. The man's name was Rick Bogle.

I met with Rick Bogle the same week. He agreed to meet me within a day or two of my initial call. He did not need to hear much from me on the initial call, apparently Bill had already called ahead to fill him in. In Rick's office I received an education on the local, state, and federal legal system and who is responsible for what offenses and how each department reviews and determines further action on each case. It was the most informative and insightful lesson on the legal system that I have received to date. It was as if I just received a crash course at Stanford Law School crammed into a two-hour meeting. Rick seemed very concerned because, although he would be happy to prosecute the case, he felt that the federal authorities would have much more power and authority to make indictments and prosecute a case that would undoubtedly involve foreign nationals as well as local residents. He also shared his concerns that I would be left again with another hollow victory.

"Brett if I ultimately won a criminal conviction in state court, but did not have the authority to extradite the criminals back to Florida to serve out their sentences it would be just a waste of time and expense," Rick told me. "Your best bet is to get the Fed's to pursue this case. Only they have the authority to work with the justice and state department to extradite foreign nationals." Rick then picked up the telephone receiver and started dialing. I sat patiently and waited for the call to be answered.

Rick looked over at me and smiled as he greeted U.S. Attorney Cynthia Hawkins on the phone and asked her about the case. He mentioned that he had discussed the case with me due to my concern that, if action was not taken soon, the statue of limitations might run out on several of the crimes. I did not hear the responses on the other side, just a few "uh-huh" and "I see" responses from Rick. Rick then said: "We are interested in this case and if by chance you choose not to prosecute this, our office would be happy to consider prosecution." Then more uh-huh's and I sees. Rick then thanked the U.S. Attorney for her time and hung up the phone.

Rick turned to me and said that he was encouraged by his discussion with the U.S. Attorney and she indicated that she liked the case and was going to move forward. Again he could offer any guarantees, but at this stage he felt my case was better off in the hands of the federal authorities. I shook Rick's hand and thanked him for his time. As I left his office I was grateful that he had weighed in on the case to try to motivate the federal authorities to take action. There was a ray of hope and I again began to feel that, after all this time, I may finally receive the justice that had been elusive for so long.

EIGHTY-FIVE

❦

As the matter between Super Vision vs. Allen
Dyer et.al. began to heat up, Allen Dyer's attorney, Ladd Fassett, called a hearing for "Summary Judgment." Summary
judgment is only granted if one of the litigants can provide
clear and convincing evidence that there is no basis for the
lawsuit. If summary judgment is granted, often the losing
party will be also responsible for the other side's legal fees.

We could not figure out what Ladd was up to but we
were very concerned about his cockiness in his belief that he
would get some, if not all his parties, out on summary judgment. We felt we had an excellent case against the Allen
Dyer firm. Our attorneys, Madison and Linda, pointed to
the fact that we had the "smoking gun" in the copies of the
fax memos containing our trade secrets that were faxed to
the Allen Dyer law firm. Furthermore, we had proof that
the Senior Partner, Brian Gilchrist, had misled Judge
Komanski in a previous hearing. Although we knew the presiding judge in this case, Judge Stroker, was not very fond of
cases that involved lawyers suing other lawyers, we believed
that there could be no way that the lawyers could be let off
the hook in summary judgment. We were wrong.

In keeping with my experience that the words, "Equal
Justice Under the Law" should be followed by a disclaimer:
"But Some Are More Equal Than Others," we discovered
that there is actually case law on the books that permits
attorneys to lie in court while engaged in litigation on

behalf of their clients. The law firm itself and one other partner was not removed out in summary judgment because the Willie Gary firm so aptly proved that the filing of patents with the U.S. Patent office could not be considered as "litigation" or advocacy in an adversarial proceeding, which the law required. The senior partner, Gilchrist, however, was able to walk from the case scot-free because it could not be proven that he engaged in any of the patent actions and Gilchrist repeatedly claimed in his prior depositions and testimony that he knew nothing about the prior illegal acts of his clients.

At the hearing before Judge Stroker, Ladd Fassett said Gilchrist could not be held accountable under case law for even lying to a judge. Fassett cited the "Levin" case and thundered in the April 28, 2003 Orange County Court hearing that lawyers are effectively immune from offenses that other individuals would otherwise be held accountable for in a civil suit: "Now the litigation privilege is a privilege that says if you do anything related to a lawsuit, no matter how bad, no matter how malicious, no matter how fraudulent, you can't be sued for it. That's the law in Florida. You can be sent to jail, you can be fined, you can be disbarred, but you can't be sued." Judge Stroker agreed and promptly released Gilchrist as a defendant in the case.

On Sept. 23, 2003, just four days shy of the first anniversary of our civil jury verdict and almost six months after I was told that several of the criminal statute of limitations would soon expire, I was called to a meeting at the U.S. Attorney's Office at the Federal Courthouse in downtown Orlando. Present at the meeting were Assistant First United States Attorney James R. Klindt, Assistant to U.S. Attorney for the Northern District of Florida Paul Perez, U.S. Attorney Roger Handberg, and Joseph Tamborello.

I had met Roger Handberg several times before. This was my first meeting with Klindt, he was a strong and commanding personality. It was clear from the moment I met him that he was in charge. He asked us all to take our seats and then proceeded to tell me in very direct and no uncertain terms of their decision not to prosecute this case.

Although I was very disappointed with his early statement of his decision not to prosecute the case, I was appreciative of his directness and honesty. After the two and a half years of false hopes and run around I received from the federal government in the case, it was refreshing to find someone in the U.S. Attorney's office who at least would bring me some form of closure and direct response.

As Klindt went into detail of the reasons why he would not prosecute this case, which included an extremely over burdened case calendar, he also then started conjuring up the other indictments he would have to make in this case which would have included Paul Koren. "Paul would most likely have to be sentenced to five to 10 years in prison in order for his testimony to be credible to the jury. There can be no free rides in this case." I then responded that Paul had already testified to a jury that was drawn from the same local jury pool and both my attorney and I found the jury to find him very credible and genuinely apologetic for his role in these crimes. "If the only way I can get at Samson Wu in the legal process is to sacrifice Paul and his family, it is just too high a price to pay."

Although I strongly disagreed with the merits of U.S. Attorney Klindt's arguments about the win-ability of this case without the indictment of Paul, I shook his hand and thanked him and Roger Handberg for their time. I left the office feeling relieved that in their turning down my long-awaited hopes for justice at least one of my staff members and his family would be spared. Joe Tamborello, on the other hand, found nothing redeeming about this meeting.

"This sucks," stated Joe as we waited by the elevator.

I looked at Joe and nodded. I was, however, a bit caught

off guard by his blunt and uncharacteristically emotional response. After all the years of legal wrangling and disappointments, it was the first time I ever saw my own attorney, the Human Computer, engage in an emotional outburst. Joe was clearly shaken with disappointment, tears were welling up in his eyes, he turned to me and asked me how I felt.

"Joe, I am so numb with disappointments in my government and this case that I am feeling nothing right now, absolutely nothing."

We walked down the street to the Wall Street Cantina and reviewed our plans to move forward. Although we tried to hide the sorrow of the recent outcome, neither of us did such a good job. I had never seen Joe get to the point of venting his frustrations or falling into despair. His realization that we just might never find justice must have finally caught up with him.

"I did not sign up for this, this is not what I expected after I graduated law school" Joe said in a somber tone. "I decided to practice law because I thought I could make a difference, I thought I could bring justice to my clients. Now I realize that I can't do a damn thing. This is not what I decided to practice law for. This is like swimming in quicksand, it stinks."

By now, Joe had become my friend, but until this lunch at the Cantina, he had never let his guard down in front of me before and exposed his emotions so openly. He was determined and stoic in both his research and representation while in court. I was now witnessing the sight of the terrible toll the justice system takes on the lives of idealistic young lawyers, the very point where their frustration and disappointment finally grinds out the idealism in even the very best of them. If there was another great casualty in our judicial system it is the destruction of hope and idealism of those young souls who had hoped to make a difference. I was witnessing it before me right now.

Neither of us cleaned our plates, we both didn't feel like eating much. At the end of lunch I put my hand on Joe's shoulder: "Joe, you did everything you could to win this case and achieve justice, you did a great job and I thank you for it, the system just screwed us that's all."

"I should have stayed a starving actor, maybe by now I would have made enough money to support my family. I followed my family's advice to go into law but I am thinking now that I want to dust off a few screenplays that I have written, I don't think I have the stomach for this anymore."

Hoping to add some levity to a now very somber meeting, I joked that perhaps I should quit my job too and become a writer as well. I had written a few business books in the past, but perhaps it was time for me to write the "great American novel." After all, "why should I bother inventing or producing anything anymore, every time I either invent or license a great new product or invention, ultimately it is stolen and the government, who is all to happy to tax the profits of the companies manufacturing these inventions, has already proven that they won't lift a finger to protect them."

Not only had I previously lost the flat screen fiber-optic television display system to the Japanese and had just witnessed the unopposed theft of my fiber-optic cable process by the Chinese, but now even our new LED lighting products, which we had filed patents, were being copied in both Hong Kong and China, and a domestic company was now asserting patent ownership of LED processes developed decades earlier by an inventor we had secured licenses with.

I told Joe, "I am not even going to bother suing the overseas counterfeiters of our LED systems this time Joe, it's just a waste of time." I said, "Perhaps I should just give up manufacturing altogether and write a book, maybe one about this case."

We both laughed. As Joe and I left the restaurant, we shook hands goodbye.

Just before leaving, Joe, turned to me and said: "Well Brett, if you write that book, I'll write the screenplay."

In the time most people would take to read this book, dozens of American companies will have been forced out of business and thousands of American jobs will have been lost due to counterfeiting and trade secret theft. The real damage from the real war continues.

EPILOGUE

Martin Caraballo, the young man that saved me from being shipwrecked at sea, died a few years thereafter in a tragic accident. One night, his car drove off one of the dimly lit roads on his family's giant Campo in the Argentine countryside. He hit a large fencepost and was killed instantly. He left behind a 23-year-old wife and a one-year-old daughter. I will never forget my friend or the pain of his loss.

Robert Earl eventually cancelled the licensing agreement with Adiv Macisse and took back the Planet Hollywood Cancun in an epic legal battle that involved courtrooms in Mexico and the United States. Robert immediately thereafter appointed a former Israeli Commando, Guy Friedman, to his personal staff.

At present, I am still chasing the Wus' funds around the world. As of the completion of this book, we finally received approval from the Panamanian Supreme Court to seize the accounts only listed in the individual defendants' names. Most notably absent from their approval were the names of all the corporate bank accounts—which we had previously confirmed that the Wus had stored all their cash and other corporate assets. By the time we got around to seizing all the Wus' personal accounts we found nothing remaining in the banks that would comply with the court order. No doubt they had plenty of time to send the money to other destinations overseas. The convenient delays provided by the Panamanian Supreme Court saw to that.

Even after the U.S. District Court and Panamanian Supreme Court orders were issued, the International Commercial Bank of China branch in Panama simply ignored the court orders and continues to do so to this date. In so doing so they are showing shameless violations of both international law and their trade agreements with the United States.

Our private investigator in Panama City, Brett Mikelson, has confirmed that local officials must have been paid off to destroy ownership records relating to the original owners of properties that the Wus had later transferred to new shell corporations. Some of the Wus accomplices destroyed the paper records, but forgot to destroy the evidence still cataloged on the Internet. This became our only remaining guide to how millions of dollars of property seemed to vanish into thin air when we did our original searches at the Panamanian real-estate records office.

Both the lawyers and bankers have brazenly stood by their claims that they played no role whatsoever in the assistance of the Wus' theft of our technology. The litigation with Allen Dyer, Rothwell Figg, and Ocean Bank continues to this day. Judge Janet Thorpe, who later took over the case from Judge Stroker, echoed her disdain for the proceedings against the lawyers and she ordered Super Vision to pay almost $200,000 in legal fees that Allen Dyer had claimed were required for the defense of Gilchrist. I had to go to my friend Johnny Jallad to bond the judgment to stay Ladd Fassett's threats of "sending over a sheriff to auction off our equipment." Super Vision is currently appealing this verdict. Super Vision has also filed a complaint against Brian Gilchrist and Jeffrey Whittle with the Orlando office of the Florida Bar Association.

The "Fraud on the Court" charge, the only remaining vehicle to incarcerate the Wus for their crimes was delayed for months by the Wus court-appointed and taxpayer funded new counsel. They succeeded in recusing Judge Spencer as judge. They also managed to recuse our attorney, John Edwin Fisher, who was acting as a court-appointed special prosecutor, under an assertion that he was biased in the proceedings. It turns out that the U.S. taxpayers ultimately provided free advice to Wu and his crew that was far better than the previous advice he had paid for. Unlike Judge Baker, Judge Spencer did not try to fight or deny the request. Judge Spencer decided that he had both a legal and moral obligation to recuse himself. The successor judge ruled that John must also recuse himself as well. The court-appointed legal team bought the Wus another round of delays for the criminal hearing, which almost resulted in the removal of all charges.

The new justice, Judge Jay Cohen, requested the Florida State Attorney's Office to take over the case. The request fell to my old friend Bill Vose who, although sympathetic to our cause, refused to provide a state prosecutor for the case due to its "shrinking resources and increasing case load being forced upon us by the legislature." Basically the Wus received an attorney at taxpayer expense to defend their criminal acts, but Super Vision, the victim, could not obtain a state prosecutor to seek justice. The Wus' court-appointed attorneys knew that the prosecutor's office routinely failed to prosecute perjury charges or cases stemming from violations of civil verdicts and therefore anticipated that the prior recusals would result in the dismissal of all charges. Judge Cohen, visibly outraged by this contradiction, demanded that someone should take on this responsibility or our justice system would be "made a mockery."

Bill Vose responded, "The system needs someone to do it, but the people who fund the resources just don't give us the resources to do it." Meanwhile our government continues to spend billions of dollars overseas in questionable foreign-aid programs and billions more on rebuilding the infrastructure of our former enemies, while our own children attend over-crowded schools and we are unable to provide enough federal or state attorneys to protect our own jobs and livelihoods.

The Wus' lawyers did not believe that we would find another private counsel to donate several weeks of their time for this effort. Fortunately, Jerry Linscott, a lawyer with the firm of Baker and Hostettler, later graciously offered to work pro-bono as a special prosecutor to seek justice in the Fraud on the Court trial against the Wus. Had it not been for his personal contribution to act as an unpaid special prosecutor in the case on behalf of the state, Judge Cohen would have been forced to dismiss the charges against the Wus. The Wu strategy would have succeeded.

On New Year's Eve 2003 Judge Jay Cohen sentenced Samson Mong Wu to 10 days in prison for fraud on the Court. Judge Cohen also ordered Wu to pay for the legal fees of his court-appointed counsel. Thomas Wu failed to even show up for the hearing.

The 10 days in jail, although brief, has been the only meaningful justice ever meted out in this case. The significance of this verdict and subsequent actions of Wu were not lost on Caruso.

After serving his sentence, Wu immediately moved back to Panama. He then cut off all support payments to his wife and two daughters that he left behind. Caruso was cut off as well. Sensing he did not need Caruso either, Wu cut off all payments and refused to pay past due salary that he had promised to Caruso. After seeing the evidence of Wu's extensive property and financial holdings in Panama and learning of Brian Gilchrist's and Jeffrey Whittle's repeated denials of having known anything about the transfer of information to them from Super Vision, Caruso decided to stop taking the Fifth Amendment and talk openly. His epiphany came when he had the opportunity to review the Allen Dyer lawyers' own deposition transcripts and hearing testimony before Judges Stroker and Thorpe.

The lawyers in their testimony accused Caruso and Koren of being liars and thieves while denying all knowledge of their illicit acts. Caruso became so enraged that the lawyers from Allen Dyer were continuing to lie, even after their testimony before Judge Komanski, that he volunteered to give testimony in a sworn statement to set the record straight. Caruso finally reached the point that Winkler did at the initial Fraud on the Court criminal trial and decided he had "had enough." Caruso also agreed to provide testimony against Samson and Thomas Wu. The only problem was that at this point there did not seem to be anyone left in government or the judiciary that cared to listen.

In February 2003, I delivered a presentation entitled the *Real War Against America* before several hundred manufacturers at the Manufacturing and Economic Recovery Conference in Chicago, sponsored by *Start* Magazine, Carol Stream, Ill. Also attending this conference was the Undersecretary of Commerce for International Trade, Grant A. Aldonas, as well as several members of the press. As I left the auditorium, there was a group of reporters already recording a heated debate between several manufacturers and the Undersecretary of Commerce. Apparently several manufacturers were outraged about what they just heard and cornered the Undersecretary on the subject. A *Chicago Sun Times* reporter called me over to interview me and very quickly Undersecretary Aldonas provided his assurances that he would "look into the matter" and "do something."

Two weeks later I flew to Washington with Wade West of Media Power, husband of Orlando's Channel 9 News anchorwoman Barbara West. Wade and I made the rounds desperately trying to speak to anyone in government who would see us. We eventually met with Undersecretary Aldonas at his office in Washington, D.C. where he again repeated assurances that he would "look into the matter."

He returned my calls and emails sporadically for a few months until I started to demand concrete action and concrete results.   Months later he stopped responding altogether. In the past two years there has been absolutely no assistance from the U.S. Commerce Department.   In the meantime they continue to sign trade agreements with China which are repeatedly dishonored by the Chinese and unenforced by our government.

To date, the sheriff's office, the Florida State Attorney's Office, the Florida Attorney General and the U.S. Attorney have failed to make one indictment or arrest of the Wus in this matter. Furthermore, there has yet to be a significant landmark test case to support the Trade Secret Act of 1996 or the Intellectual Property Protection Act of 2002 where significant prison sentences have been issued. According to an article published by *USA Today*, and independently confirmed in a study by PriceWaterhouseCoopers, the U.S. has lost more than $59 billion dollars due to international trade-secret theft in 2001 alone and was predicted to lose more than $100 billion in 2003 to these yet unopposed criminal actions. The American Society for Industrial Security has determined that the cost to the U.S. economy from the continued theft of our technology may eventually reach more than $250 billion per year, several times the even worst imaginable annual costs of the war on terror.

According to government statistics, imports have taken $1.2 trillion worth of domestic sales.   Manufacturing employment has plummeted to its lowest level in more than 40 years. Almost 3 million factory jobs have been lost during the past four years. The annual trade deficit in manufactured goods continues to climb to unprecedented heights; more than $450 billion, or $1.2 billion each day.   Our nation's lifeblood is no longer being drained by a trickle.

I have no idea if we will ever collect from any of the defendants or if we will ever be able to bring any of them to justice. The Wus' counterfeiting activities continues to this day, under several new corporations that they have established both in South America and Asia. Although the Wus allowed the bank to repossess their Miami warehouse and Miami mansion at the Doral Country Club as part to their plan to liquidate their U.S. assets, they continue to live in lavish homes in Asia, South America, and Europe, outside the reach of U.S. law.

Joe Tamborello is working on the completion of the screenplay; we still do not know if it will have a happy ending or not.

ACKNOWLEDGMENTS

I have had the good fortune to witness a true renaissance man. He was the original editor for this book, Chauncey Parker III. Chauncey is a Harvard Business School graduate who also had served as a United States Marine. After graduation, Chauncey enrolled in the diplomatic corps. Chauncey Parker's service for the U.S. Marines in World War II did not teach him how to write but it did teach him how to live. The experience inspired him to cherish every day he was allowed to enjoy. Chauncey wrote two books. One was "The Visitor," which became the Warner Brothers movie: "Of Unknown Origin." The other, "In Sheep's Clothing," which forewarned of sexual predators in the church was published about a decade too early. Chauncey is both a man steeped in history and a man ahead of his time. He is also a Professor Emeritus of English at Valencia Community College in Orlando, Florida.

The first full sentence I heard from Chauncey after "Hi" was: "Your writing is just terrible!" He did, however, find promise in my thoughts and ideas. He just felt I needed to learn how to present them better. Chauncey did not just teach me grammar, he taught me how to think. Every meeting with Chauncey was an adventure. He approached this book with enthusiasm. The book became his mission. Somewhere along the way he taught me how to write. I am indebted to his tutelage and thank him for his contribution and friendship.

Peggy Smedley, the editorial director of *Start* Magazine and partner in Specialty Publishing Company, was the first person to publish this story and ultimately this book. Peggy's unending passion and dedication to the American manufacturing industry has met no match. Her dedication to her principles, ethics, and sense of fair play were a constant source of inspiration. For a long time, Peggy's voice was a lone cry in the wilderness while our politicians refused to grapple with this problem. Now journalists and members of Congress are starting to sing about the ills of the decimation of our manufacturing sector in a chorus, largely due to Peggy's constant and insistent warnings.

My wife Maisa provided the same encouragement and support for this book as she did in the events which it chronicles. Whether I was chasing down bad guys in or out of court, or laboring through umpteen edits or redrafts of this manuscript, Maisa would urge me on and provide endless support. "I know you can do it Brett" or "Get off your behind and make it happen" would be her mantra to me during difficult times. Most importantly, her love and devotion was my foundation. From her preparing the unscheduled late-night dinners and teas with Chauncey, to her reviewing the last minute redrafts, she was always there to lend her support. Her greatest gift, however, was the beautiful family she created with me: our daughter Victoria and our son Max.

Although several times throughout this case I lost my faith in the American justice system, I never lost my faith in God. The two greatest gifts that I can provide to anyone who is experiencing serious challenges in their life are:
1. Never give up, always keep trying; and 2. Have faith in God. With persistence and hard work your prayers will be eventually answered.